THE CON AND THE FBI AGENT

THE CON AND THE FBI AGENT

An Unlikely Alliance

David Nadolski

ROWMAN & LITTLEFIELD
Lanham • Boulder • New York • London

Published by Rowman & Littlefield
An imprint of The Rowman & Littlefield Publishing Group, Inc.
4501 Forbes Boulevard, Suite 200, Lanham, Maryland 20706
www.rowman.com

6 Tinworth Street, London SE11 5AL, United Kingdom

Disclaimers: The opinions expressed in this book are those of the author and not that of the FBI. Readers should also be aware that some of the criminal characters in this book use foul language. I tried to get them to clean up their act, but they laughed in my face.

British Library Cataloguing in Publication Information Available

Library of Congress Cataloging-in-Publication Data

Names: Nadolski, David, 1951– author.
Title: The con and the FBI agent : an unlikely alliance / David Nadolski.
Description: Lanham : Rowman & Littlefield, [2021] | Includes bibliographical references and index.
| Summary: "The Con and the FBI Agent is the story of an unlikely alliance between two diametrically opposed people that results in one of the most successful undercover cases in Boston FBI history"— Provided by publisher.
Identifiers: LCCN 2021020652 (print) | LCCN 2021020653 (ebook) | ISBN 9781538159590 (cloth)
| ISBN 9781538159606 (epub)
Subjects: LCSH: Romano, Tony, -2012. | Nadolski, David, 1951- | United States. Federal Bureau of Investigation. | Robbery—Massachusetts—Boston—Case studies. | Undercover operations—Massachusetts—Boston—Case studies. | Informers—Massachusetts—Boston—Case studies.
Classification: LCC HV6661.M42 N33 2021 (print) | LCC HV6661.M42 (ebook) | DDC 364.15/520974461—dc23
LC record available at https://lccn.loc.gov/2021020652
LC ebook record available at https://lccn.loc.gov/2021020653

For Anthony Romano,
may he rest in peace,
and my fellow brothers and sisters of the FBI

Also thanks for all the help:
Dorothy Skelley for excellent editing
and invaluable advice,
Zach Leach, and Maureen Kelly

Most of all for Linda, Elizabeth, Katherine, and Meredith,
who lived this case with me—I love you all!

CONTENTS

PROLOGUE

When it was revealed that Tony Romano was an FBI informant who helped thwart a major heist outside of Boston in 1999, his friends turned on him and his family was confused. To his community, Tony was a "rat." To the FBI, Tony was a hero, of sorts. Heroes come in all forms, not all of them angelic, and Tony was no angel. God knows the man struggled with his demons. But, in this one moment, Tony stepped up, stayed strong, and carried the day. I should know: Tony and I were tied at the hip for two years working on a sting operation that would lead to the prosecution and incarceration of four dangerous criminals poised to launch one of the biggest armed robberies of the twentieth century.

Sometimes people do the right thing for the right reason. And sometimes people do the right thing for the wrong reason. Initially, Tony's reason for becoming an informant was to seek vengeance against a gangster who had turned Tony's ex-wife into a drug mule while he was in prison. He saw an opportunity to work with the FBI as a way for him to bring this guy down. And I saw Tony as an opportunity to help us bring this guy down. Same goal—different motivations. But, over the course of the two-year operation, Tony became fully engaged and committed to the cause. He wanted to create a legacy that reflected a more noble purpose than sticking up gas stations. And my perspective about Tony as just a conduit to justice changed as well. We were forced to trust one another unconditionally. While I took a risk on Tony to pursue the bad guys, Tony risked his life to support the good guys.

I

BAD CHOICES, BAD DAYS

SUFFOLK COUNTY SUPERIOR COURT

Tony Romano was having a rough time on this sultry June day in 1979, and his head was swimming with the grim reality he was facing. Earlier, he and his attorney had been sitting in the courtroom of Superior Court Judge Henry Chimilinski. Tony was being sentenced for a series of armed robberies committed in and around the city of Quincy, Massachusetts. Tony was a drug addict but not a violent criminal, who used a realistic-looking squirt gun for his stickups, which technically constituted armed robbery. Unfortunately, in the eyes of the law and particularly in the view of Henry Chimilinski, he might as well have used a machine gun.

"Young man, you sit before me today for sentencing having pleaded guilty to five armed robberies in the city of Quincy, is that correct?" the judge pried.

"Yes, your honor," whispered Tony, head bowed and looking at his folded hands.

Judge Chimilinski glared at Tony. "Speak up; I can't hear you!" boomed the judge from his elevated bench.

"Yes, your honor," said Tony in a clearer voice, head still bowed. He couldn't bear to look to his left, where his fifty-five-year-old mother, stricken with multiple sclerosis, sat sobbing in her wheelchair. Next to her was his scowling father, contempt and disappointment written all over his face. Tony couldn't bear to look directly at the judge either, who scared the shit out of him.

The judge readied himself for his decision: "Young man, your attorney, Mr. Troy, has made an eloquent appeal on your behalf. He explained how you suffer from the 'disease' of drug addiction and that you are not the type of person who should be sitting before me today. I firmly agree with him. You should not be sitting here today. Your poor mother should not be sitting here today. No one in this whole courtroom should be sitting here today! The problem is we are here, and we are here because of you and the stupid choices you made." He didn't wait for a response. "Isn't that true?" he bellowed from the bench.

Tony gulped, managed to lift his head a few inches, and whispered, "Yes, sir."

"Okay, get on your feet, Mr. Romano." With that command, Tony and his lawyer stood to face the judge.

"Mr. Romano, I think you know where we are headed with this. I am not inclined to excuse your criminal behavior because you cannot manage to get through a day without sticking a needle in your arm. I'm going to give you the opportunity to clean yourself up once and for all. I'm going to remove you from the temptation of the streets and introduce you to a new environment where your life on drugs will become a distant memory. Mr. Romano, you are hereby sentenced to twelve to fifteen years at MCI [Massachusetts Correctional Institute] in Walpole."

With that Judge Chimilinski banged his gavel, lifted his considerable bulk from his chair, and walked from the courtroom. The court officer called out, "All rise; court is adjourned."

As soon as the judge was out of the courtroom, Tony's knees buckled, and he landed back in his chair. He felt as though he was going to pass out. *Twelve to fifteen, Holy God,* thought Tony. He looked to his lawyer, who was impassively packing papers into his briefcase. Troy looked back at Tony sympathetically and put his hand on his shoulder.

"Sorry, kid, tough break" was all he could say.

With that, Troy beat a hasty retreat from the courtroom. Tony felt the manacles close onto his wrists and turned to face his mother. The look of anguish on her face was more than he could bear, and he started to sob along with her.

Down in the holding cell beneath the courtroom, Tony reflected upon the words of the judge. He was right, of course: there was no one to blame except himself—still he wondered how he went from a fat and happy middle-school kid to a skinny, full-blown heroin addict driven to stick up convenience stores for his next fix.

He knew where it all started. His teenage weight problem had been solved with methamphetamines, or "speed." He had figured out how to "doctor shop" for the pills and began overprescribing himself. They worked great initially, and for the first time in his life, he was dropping the weight and getting the attention of the girls.

Tony's dad had owned an automotive-repair shop called A to Z, located in the tough Roxbury section of Boston. Tony had worked in the garage on weekends and learned the trade from his dad and the other mechanics. He became quite skilled at repairing cars to the point that in tenth grade he told his dad he was quitting school to work full time. Surprisingly, his dad didn't try to talk him out of it.

Drugs were rampant in Roxbury, and Tony's taste for speed eventually spread to a taste for cocaine. The disco craze was in full swing at the time, and Boston was awash in coke. The dealers had the money, nice cars, apartments, and, of course, the chicks. Soon the allure of the stinking, greasy auto-repair shop wore off and was replaced with a desire to get high all day and go clubbing at night. Of course, drugs weren't cheap, so Tony moved in with a drug dealer friend and joined his business as a runner.

One night, he delivered an ounce of cocaine and liquid morphine to a new customer. Tony didn't know "Harry," but he appeared to be a burned-out hippie. The minute Tony got to his rundown apartment, Harry answered the door with "Like, yeah, man, glad you got here; I don't dig waitin' when I'm crashing like this!"

"So you got the money?" asked Tony.

"Yeah, sure, but I need to try the shit first," Harry said.

Tony reluctantly agreed to allow Harry to test the product. Suddenly, a purple velvet Crown Royal bag appeared in his hand, and Harry emptied the contents on the table: two slightly bent and discolored teaspoons and two syringes.

Tony looked at the equipment and asked, "What are you doing?"

"I'm trying it," Harry said.

"Like that?" asked Tony.

"Yeah, man; you don't have to watch if you don't want to," replied Harry.

Tony was intrigued, so he answered, "No problem; go ahead, man."

The old hippie put a little cocaine in one of the spoons, sucked up some water in a syringe, and squirted it into the spoon. He then mixed it around with the plunger of the syringe, dropped a piece of cigarette filter in the spoon, and sucked the liquid into the syringe. He flicked the syringe like a doctor, squirted a little out and put it down. Harry then took the second syringe and sucked some of the liquid morphine directly into it and repeated the doctor routine again. He extended his left forearm and stuck the cocaine needle right into the vein between his forearm and bicep.

Tony watched with fascination as the guy drew blood into the syringe and slowly pushed the plunger in. Harry simply closed his eyes and said, "Hmmmmmm."

Next, he removed the needle; immediately picked up the second one, loaded with morphine; and repeated the process. After taking the second one out, Harry covered his arm with a paper towel to stop the bleeding. He took a deep breath, smiled a lazy smile, and said, "Good shit! I'll get the money."

Tony had just witnessed his first "speed-ball." Less than an hour later, he would try it on himself and be happy with the results. Before long, Tony figured out that a cocaine and heroin mix was a cheaper combination but just as potent. From that point on, Tony was officially hooked.

It didn't take long before heroin was no longer a pleasure cruise, getting high and letting the world pass by. Instead, the drug had become Tony's primary focus in life, and by January of 1979, he couldn't make enough money selling to support his own habit. By this time, he had borrowed or stolen from all of his friends and family and was left with one of two options: somehow get off this drug or make enough money to support his growing habit. Tony knew he couldn't turn his back on the needle, so he decided to start pulling holdups. *What the hell?* he figured. *If no one is going to give me the money, I'm going to have to start taking it.*

That said, he knew he didn't have the stones to actually stick a real gun in someone's face, but he could do it with a plastic toy. He found a nice-looking squirt gun, semiautomatic, which he painted to look convincingly real. Just like the cowboy train robbers he had watched on TV, he covered his face with a bandana and started hitting gas stations, convenience stores, and any business where he didn't expect to be challenged. The take was usually small and only enough for a few hours' worth of drugs, so he'd be out again later the same day. Tony preferred the suburban towns around Boston because the store owners were more likely to give up without a fight, which was true for the most part.

By June of 1979, Tony's drug addiction had reached an all-time high and he was desperate for money. On June 21, he found himself in the Dorchester area of Boston, where he looked up Billy Lynch, an old friend. Billy had a car, and Tony needed a driver for the score he had planned. This robbery was going to be at a major market and deli where he knew he would find a considerable amount of cash. Tony conned Billy into driving him to the deli in his 1969 Rambler station wagon. He didn't tell Billy what he had in mind, and he really didn't think a Rambler station wagon was a suitable getaway car either, but beggars can't be choosers.

"Billy, pull over here. I gotta get a soda from this deli. Want anything?" asked Tony.

"No, Tony; just make it quick, will ya? I gotta get to work," said Billy.

Tony walked in and looked the place over. One cash register was manned by a heavyset, middle-aged man behind the counter. His nametag read "Rocco." Tony grabbed a Coke and stood off to the side until the place emptied out. When it looked clear, he covered his face, pulled out his squirt gun, quickly approached the counter—gun extended, and pointed directly at Rocco.

"This is a holdup! Gimme all the cash, now!" screamed Tony. Rocco staggered back a step or two and looked totally shocked.

"Move it, old man, or I'll blow your fucking head off!" Tony screamed.

That's when Rocco did something unexpected. Instead of opening the cash register, he reached beneath it and pulled a real .44-caliber magnum revolver and cocked the hammer as he began leveling it on Tony.

"Holy shit!" screamed a panicked Tony, who dropped his squirt gun and dove for the door just as an enormous roar erupted behind him. Instantly, several glass jars exploded on a shelf next to his head!

"Holy shit, holy shit, holy shit!" Tony covered his head with his hands and blasted through the front door. He saw the Rambler about a half a block away, still parked at the curb. "Thank you, Jesus!" he said to himself. Tony reached the car at a dead sprint, skidded to a stop and yanked the driver's-side door open, shoved Billy into the passenger seat, and climbed behind the wheel.

Tony, panicked and wildly looking in all directions, floored the accelerator and peeled off down Dorchester Avenue, desperately looking for any sign of the cops. Tony looked over at Billy, who was scrunched up against the passenger door—mouth wide open, arms wrapped around his legs, pulling them into his chest. He looked more like a ball than a human being.

"What the *fuck* did you do?" he screamed at Tony.

Tony was unable to answer just yet as he was maneuvering as best he could for the expressway that would get him away from Dorchester and into the suburbs south of the city as fast as possible. Unfortunately, while he did make it to the expressway, he had a Boston Police Department car on his rear bumper.

To make matters worse, the cruiser was soon joined by two motorcycle cops who pulled onto either side of the Rambler and motioned for Tony to pull over. Billy was screaming for Tony to pull over, but instead he floored it and took the first exit for his hometown of Quincy. By this point, two more police departments had joined the chase, and a few minutes later, Tony finally lost control and smashed the Rambler, right in front of Quincy City Hall.

The next thing Tony remembered was being face down on the pavement with his hands behind his back, looking over at Billy who was in the same position. Billy was bleeding from his nose and lip and had a nasty cut on his forehead, not to mention a look of pure hatred on his face.

"I'm sorry, Billy" was as all Tony could manage to whisper.

2

LIKE FATHER, LIKE SON

DANANG, REPUBLIC OF SOUTH VIETNAM

While Tony was serving his twelve to fifteen at "convict" college, I was in training to become an FBI Agent—my lifelong dream. Like most folks in law enforcement, my first steps began with a tour of duty.

"Yo, Nads, what are you going to do back in the world after thirteen months of this shit? Your mind's too messed up to do anything useful," Richie called out.

My name is Dave Nadolski; therefore, my natural nickname is "Nads." Private First Class (PFC) Richie Delgado didn't pull any punches; he told things like he saw them. In fact, everyone in my unit was like that, which was the refreshing thing about being in the Army in Vietnam: no chicken shit. The guys you served with got real personal, real quick, and the friendships (or hatreds) were out there for everyone to see. It was genuine, and I liked that.

"Well, jackass, at least I won't have to see your ugly face first thing every morning. So no matter what else happens, I'm ahead of the game," I said.

"Dude, what you going to do for work, be a stickup man in 'Deeee-troit'?" Richie asked.

I laughed. "No, I'm not going to be a stickup man. I'm not an LA hoodlum like you. In fact, I've been giving this a lot of thought, and I'm going to try to become a cop like my old man."

"Your old man's a cop?" Richie asked, amazed. "What kind of cop?"

In fact, my dad was a narcotics detective on the Detroit Police Department. He would not approve of Richie, so I didn't plan to talk about him when I finally got home. I didn't plan to talk about much of anything that went on over there, actually.

"My dad's a narc on the Detroit PD," I replied.

"A narc! Oh my God, I don't ever want to meet that guy, no way!" Richie said.

Richie had that right; he wouldn't want to meet my old man. Norbert was a good cop, a good husband, a good dad, a devout Catholic, and definitely somebody you didn't want to screw with. He went to work with brass knuckles in the pants pocket of his suit. He was old-fashioned in a lot of ways and pretty much adhered to a "the ends justify the means" philosophy in life. In other words, he got the job done without a lot of fuss or hand-wringing. Consequently, he had a lot of arrests and a book full of commendations from the police commissioner.

We had a handyman named Willie around the house from time to time. He didn't live in our neighborhood, and all I knew about Willie was he worked with my dad. That was strange to me because he sure didn't look anything like the other guys that worked with Dad. This guy looked like a criminal. My dad always said not to bother Willie when he was painting the house or pouring cement steps, but I wanted to hang around and watch the guy at least. He was really nice and polite, and he spoke very highly of my dad. After I grew up and Willie was no longer in the picture, I found out that he was my dad's top drug informant. He provided the intelligence and made the buys. Dad took care of him as best he could and paid him to do some odd jobs around our house. I thought to myself, *How many other people have drug informants hanging around the house? That's cool!*

Dad was my role model, and I admired and respected the work that he did. He was the first in his family to become a police officer, and eventually I was the second. I grew up playing cops and robbers. My favorite toy was a Dick Tracy snub-nosed cap gun with a plastic shoulder holster and silver detective badge. *Just like Dad's*, I thought. I also had a pedal-powered police car just like Dad's, sort of.

I graduated from high school in 1969, and that summer I was not inclined to head straight to college. I had been an indifferent high school student, and I wanted to go into the Army. My three brothers were serving or had served in the Army, Marines, or Air Force. Rick was serving in the Army and was stationed in Korea. Jerry had been a Marine Corps officer and led his Marines in the bloody battle for Hue City. Mark served four years in the Air Force as a medic. I really wanted in on this action, but my problem at the time was my age. I was only seventeen years old when I graduated from high school and therefore needed my parents' permission to join the military. Rick told me that I should volunteer for the draft. A little-known fact at the time was that anyone could register for the draft and go directly into the service for a two-year commitment. All other enlistees had to sign up for at least three years. The biggest difference was, as a draftee, I would have no choice of military assignment or even a guaranteed branch of service. In other words, my ass truly belonged to Uncle Sam.

Believe it or not, my mom was okay with this idea, but my dad was not. Jerry had just gotten back from Vietnam and Rick was still away in Korea, and Dad wasn't nuts about his seventeen-year-old kid going into the service. I told them that the Army was basically a social program that took young high school grads, such as myself, and taught them a useful trade, so as not to be a burden on society. They bought the story, and reluctantly Dad signed off and happily I signed up.

On September 5, 1969, Dad dropped me off at the draft board office in Roseville, Michigan. He shook my hand, gave me a hug, and really looked worried. I assured him that everything was going to be okay, then loaded onto a bus with thirty other guys reporting for duty. The next stop was Fort Wayne, an active-duty Army processing center south of Detroit. Once there, my fellow draftees and I went through a final physical examination and filled out some paperwork; then I took my oath of allegiance along with everyone else.

I reported to Army basic training at Fort Knox, Kentucky. During the first week of basic training, draftees were given a battery of tests to determine their eventual military occupational specialty. I volunteered to test for helicopter pilot training; helicopter pilots were cool. Candidates were sent to Alabama to learn to fly and eventually promoted to the rank of warrant officer. Best of all, chicks dig pilots!

The testing consisted of a full day of spatial recognition problems designed to simulate a helicopter flying sideways and upside down and diving toward the ground. I surprised myself by doing well on the tests and made it to the next phase of the program. I was told to report to a particular auditorium at a specified time for a briefing with all the other pilot candidates. At the appointed time, I was filing into the auditorium with the other guys. I happened to notice a particularly mean-looking first sergeant eyeballing everyone who entered the building. As I was about to enter, I was grabbed by the back of my shirt and pulled out of line. I quickly turned to look into the angry face of the first sergeant. He put his hands on his hips and bent down and hissed, "Where the hell do you think you're going, pissant?"

I said, "I'm reporting as ordered for the helicopter pilot briefing, First Sergeant."

He then asked me, "How old are you?"

I said, "I'm seventeen, First Sergeant."

He barked back, "Get out of my auditorium and go back to the Boy Scouts!"

So much for my career as a helicopter pilot. I was sure I'd never get chicks now. Eventually, all good things must come to an end, and it was no different for Basic Training. During the last week, we received our orders for Advanced Individual Training (AIT). I drew the Communications School at Fort Gordon, Georgia, where I spent the next eight weeks basking in the southern sun and sipping ice-cold soft drinks. Well, not quite, but it was better than Basic Training.

After completing all my communications training, I received orders to report to Fort Myers, Virginia, for what I was told would be a special assignment. Upon arriving at Fort Myers, I was instructed to report the next day to the Pentagon, where I was greeted by an NCO (noncommissioned officer) who said, "Welcome to the office of the Assistant Chief of Staff for Intelligence."

Okay, so now what? I asked myself.

I joined a group of about six other bewildered soldiers. We were shown a big wall map with pins in it. Some pins were in Alaska, some were spread around Europe, and a bunch of pins were stuck in Vietnam. The NCO asked, "How many married guys?"

After two guys raised their hands, he continued, "Well, as you can see, we have pins in the map behind me. They represent openings. You two married guys are being assigned to use your communications training to support intelligence gathering in Alaska and Europe. The rest of you are off to Vietnam to do pretty much the same thing with one small difference: they shoot at you over there, ha, ha! Ahem . . . well . . . welcome aboard. See the receptionist for your official orders. You're dismissed."

So much for the social program.

When I first arrived in Vietnam, we landed in Saigon. It had been a surreal twenty-four-hour flight. We were crammed onto a commercial airliner with pretty female flight attendants. They had all been really chatty and friendly until we entered Vietnam airspace, after which they suddenly became quiet and concerned. I looked out the window and saw a moonscape. We were flying over a shell-cratered landscape and a desolate jungle countryside, interspersed with corrugated steel shacks here and there. I was sure I could smell and even taste rank smoke from burning shit entering the plane. The plane made a direct approach and wasted no time smacking down on the runway at Tan San Nhut Airbase in Saigon. I found out later that this was a typical landing, designed to make the plane harder to hit with rocket fire. After enduring a typical Army "hurry up and wait," the door of the plane finally opened, and we were overwhelmed with the most God-awful blast of hot, wet air that I had ever felt. We climbed down the stairs to the tarmac, blinked into the searing sun, and looked over at a group of grinning, tanned veterans wearing faded jungle fatigues and filthy boots covered with the red clay that I would eventually know so well. They were waiting to take the plane back to civilization. One of them looked at us and yelled, "Good luck, suckers!" The rest of them laughed and howled like they had heard the funniest joke of their lives.

All in all, Vietnam wasn't so bad. In fact, I liked it so much I stayed an extra month. The way that things worked at the time, a soldier with less than four months left on his enlistment would be automatically discharged upon returning to Oakland Army Depot in Oakland, California. I had to stay an extra month to qualify, but I was happy to do so. Above all else, I wanted to avoid being a lame-duck soldier sitting around some crappy stateside post for the last four months of my enlistment. I saw those guys when I was in basic training. Everybody looked at them funny. I would have "re-upped" for another Vietnam tour just to avoid that. Luckily, I didn't have to because, in May of 1971, I got my orders to head back home and out of the Army.

Now I was the veteran, and it was my turn. I was back in Saigon, heading in the opposite direction this time. As the new batch of pasty white meat in clean, crisp jungle fatigues climbed down the stairs from the plane, I yelled, "Good luck, suckers!" I climbed into that Freedom Bird and didn't look back. Better them than me.

3

THE FBI ACADEMY

FBI ACADEMY, QUANTICO, VIRGINIA

The Yellow Brick Road is a long road, but it's not yellow or actually made of bricks. It winds through the scrub brush and pine tree terrain of northern Virginia on the campus of the FBI Academy. It is the official torture track of FBI new agent training. I believe the name Yellow Brick Road was somebody's attempt at humor. The academy is located within the sprawling US Marine Corps officers training base known as MCB Quantico.

This day was the final endurance run for our class, and I occupied my usual spot in the pack: dead last. Graduation for Class 83-3 was scheduled for the next day, and this was the final hurdle that every candidate needed to complete in order to stand proudly on the auditorium stage before our gathered families and receive the credentials and badge of a Special Agent of the Federal Bureau of Investigation. Unfortunately for me, the fairly routine six-mile run felt like six hundred miles. During my whole three and a half months of training, I had battled chronic Achilles tendon injuries and shin splints. The typical treatment for these injuries is rest, but that wasn't possible. In order to graduate, a candidate had to complete all requirements within the prescribed period of time. Failure in any aspect of the training resulted in a candidate being called out of class and immediately dismissed from the Bureau. That sucks if, like I did, you have a family to support. I had a strong incentive to prevail no matter what it took.

As I slowly put one painful foot in front of the other, I looked down the lonely ribbon of blacktop ahead. Heat was reflecting up in waves and causing the landscape to shimmer and blur. High above, a soaring red-tailed hawk carved lazy eights in the air and seemed to be looking down at me and screeching. I'm sure he was saying, *Better you than me, pal!* To take my mind off my present situation, I began to think about the events that led me to be on the lonely Yellow Brick Road on this hot spring day.

Prior to my college graduation from Wayne State University in Detroit with a bachelor's of science in criminal justice, I landed a job on the Sterling Heights Police Department. Shortly after that, I landed a job as husband to the lovely Linda Hamilton. I first met Linda while working part-time for Sears. This was just a few months after I had been discharged from the Army. I took a job in the security department as a store detective, discreetly patrolling in search of shoplifters (and good-looking babes). One day, a fellow security officer gave me a hot tip.

"Nads, did you see the new chick working in the luggage department?" asked Denny Bosso.

"There's no new chick in the luggage department, just old Betty," I laughed.

"Wrong, my friend. Allow me to introduce you," he replied.

As I rounded the corner and started for the luggage department, I was suddenly thunderstruck. I was looking at the most beautiful blonde I had ever seen, and if my eyes weren't deceiving me, she was wearing a Sears name tag.

Denny walked me into the department and said, "Linda, I'd like you to meet a friend of mine, Dave Nadolski. Dave works in security with me."

Linda looked at me, put on an amused smile, and said, "Well, Denny, if he's a friend of yours, I'd better steer clear of him. Thanks for the warning."

I wasn't sure if she was joking or not, but at least she had an accurate read on Denny. One thing that wasn't so funny was the large diamond on her left ring finger.

"Linda, it's a real pleasure to meet you, and I hope you will not make the mistake of assuming I have anything in common with Dennis Bosso," I said.

She laughed and we chatted awhile, and eventually Linda gave me a nice smile and a wave as I reluctantly walked away and she got back to doing her job. I liked everything about her except her taste in jewelry, but that was just a speed bump I was determined to overcome.

Eventually I did overcome that speed bump, but I wasn't responsible for breaking up her engagement. As it turned out, that relationship was already on the rocks and ended with no help from me. Our lives went down different paths for a while, but eventually we began to date and before long we married. Linda came from a great family. Her dad was a much-beloved doctor in family practice. Linda's mom was a wonderful, generous woman and doting mother and grandmother for her own three kids and three grandkids as well.

We married in April of 1977, just a month after I started working for Sterling Heights PD. Linda was not happy living in an apartment and immediately started looking for a house to buy—the first of many as it turned out. She found a handyman special in a nice neighborhood only a half-mile from the police department. She wasn't afraid to tackle make-overs, so we followed our realtor's advice and bought the second-dumpiest house on the street. Unfortunately, the dumpiest house was next door. Our place was a four-bedroom colonial style with a living room, dining room, and family room, plus a full basement. We paid $31,000 and had to get my dad to cosign the loan. Linda got straight to work, painting, wallpapering, gardening, and remodeling. She was in her natural element; I, on the other hand, was becoming the reluctant Mr. Black & Decker, learning home repairs by the Braille method.

As Linda was busy adding value to our home, I was working as a uniform patrolman on the 3:00 p.m.–11:00 p.m. shift at Sterling Heights PD. I liked the afternoon shift as it was generally the most active. We made the most arrests and took the vast majority of calls, and as a result, I learned my trade while working with fellow cops who, like me, enjoyed that faster pace. I worked with a lot of Vietnam veterans and immediately felt the comfortable camaraderie of being with cops who shared a common past. Life was good.

Several high-profile cases solved with the assistance of evidence I had collected from crime scenes finally brought me the attention I was looking for. One day, I was called into the office of the captain of detectives.

Captain Nalepa was short, wide, and muscular. He looked you straight in the eye. He dressed in nice suits; had a neat, businesslike office; and exuded command presence. Numerous awards and commendations hung on his walls, and pictures of him and his wife and daughters adorned his large desk.

"Sit down, Dave. You've been on the department for four years now, and I've seen your name on a lot of the reports coming across my desk. I appreciate your attention to detail and see you have a fundamental understanding of what it takes to build a solid case for court. Are you happy to stay in uniform as a crime scene tech or would you like to be considered for an opening in the detective bureau?" he asked.

Are you fucking kidding me? I thought to myself.

I broke into a wide grin. This was the call to the bullpen that I'd been waiting for!

"Captain," I said, "I'd crawl through a mile of broken glass to get a shot at the detective bureau, and if this is some kind of joke, I'm diving out your window right now!"

Captain Nalepa let out a hearty laugh and said, "No joke, kid; stay in your seat. I'm tired of replacing my window!" He stood up and extended his meaty hand. "Welcome aboard, detective."

The detective bureau, or "DB" as everyone referred to it, was really my cup of tea. Detectives were assigned to day shifts and afternoon shifts and generally had weekends off. Of course, we were subject to being called in during the middle of the night or on weekends if a major crime occurred, and this happened quite a bit.

I was assigned my caseload and given my own cubicle and a new high-tech communication device known as a "pager." I drove an unmarked car and essentially worked alone, except for when I needed another detective or when the squad came together to work a major crime.

I learned how to conduct surveillance as a detective. Surveillance driving was very demanding and required an ever-changing landscape of chase vehicles. The closest car would have to remain at least three cars back from the subject vehicle, and the next surveillance car in line would take over when the subject turned a corner or pulled into a parking lot. Getting caught at traffic lights usually meant one or more cars had to blow the red light when it was safe to do so, causing panic for unsuspecting motorists. Surveillance driving was a skill set that would serve me well later in my law enforcement career.

I really enjoyed building cases and quickly learned that the fastest way to infiltrate a criminal organization was through the use of a reliable informant. Law enforcement officers obviously cannot move freely within the criminal underworld. We've all heard about major undercover operations, but while they do exist, they are few and far between. We relied upon criminal informants to keep us supplied with intelligence.

The Hollywood image of a typical criminal informant is a skinny, drug-addicted, sniveling lowlife who delivers "golden" information for a $20 bill. He looks from side to side, stashes the bill into his shirt, and whispers into the cop's ear. Of course, the audience looks at him and immediately thinks, "Lousy lowlife rat!"

The reality is that informants come in all shapes and sizes and have different motivators. Some are motivated by money, some by revenge, some by simply remaining out of jail themselves, and surprisingly some are motivated by having someone to talk to. The one thing that all informants have in common is access to a criminal world that is outside the reach of law enforcement and unattainable without their help.

Developing informants is a delicate business; I learned that the hard way. Sterling Heights was once again at the mercy of a gang of daytime burglars. They were working a large section of our city and were managing to stay one step ahead of us. We knew it was a larger, organized group because they would strike different neighborhoods at the same time, often entering through basement windows or simply kicking in the front door. If someone was unfortunate enough to be at home, they were quickly subdued and tied up.

Eventually, due to a lucky tip from a vigilant neighbor, we were able to catch a pair in the act. We had them at the station and kept them separated from one another. I took one suspect, a kid in his early twenties, from his cell and into an interview room. I started talking to him about the burglaries, and he immediately copped an attitude. He was extremely disrespectful and belligerent, and I was about to return him to his cell when he asked me, "Where am I, anyway?"

I told him that he was in an interview room in the detective bureau of Sterling Heights PD.

He suddenly brightened up and said, "Detective bureau? Are you a detective?"

I said, "Yeah, of course. Who did you think I was?"

"I thought you were some kind of rent-a-cop!" he replied.

Apparently, he thought detectives were cool because he immediately extended his hand for me to shake, and that's when I made my mistake. I was still pissed at him, and instead of taking advantage of this rare opportunity, I just glared at him and kept my arms folded. I needed to let him know who the boss was. The smile immediately left his face as he retracted his hand and turned to look at the wall.

"Put me back in my cell. I want a lawyer," he said.

Man, I really blew this one and immediately knew that my dad would have handled this in an entirely different way. I had this guy ready to talk; all I needed to do was swallow my pride and show some respect in return. I could have talked to him, listened to him, and possibly obtained the information I needed to roll up the rest of the gang. All I had to do was treat him as a fellow human being, but no, instead I put up a wall. That lesson stuck with me, and I learned from it. Never again would I be so stupid.

At around this time in my police career, a fellow officer applied to the FBI. I had a vague notion of the Bureau, based primarily on television, but I had never worked with an FBI agent and had never even met one in person. I was intrigued and found out that to become an FBI agent, a candidate was required, at a minimum, to have a bachelor's degree. I was good for that. Furthermore, the applicant must pass a stringent background investigation—check. The applicant was required to have three years of professional work experience and be willing to move out of state—check. As far as I could tell, I was good to go.

After a couple years of waiting, due to a federal hiring freeze, I finally took and passed the written exam and oral interview for the Special Agent position. I received my official appointment letter on January 15, 1983, and was ordered to report to FBI Headquarters, Washington, D.C., on February 5 for swearing in. That same day, I would begin the three and half months of new agents training in Quantico, Virginia.

Sitting in my hotel room the night before the swearing-in ceremony, I reflected upon what I had done. Obviously, it was an accomplishment, starting out as one of a group of five thousand applicants and ending up as one of thirty selected for new agents class. I was proud of that but very apprehensive as well. As a police detective, I considered myself a big fish in a small pond. Now I was most certainly a small fish in a big pond. What right did I have to be here? Did I make the correct decision? I'd never spent a night away from Linda or our one-year-old daughter, Elizabeth, and now I was going to be away for three and a half months.

How difficult was training going to be and what if I couldn't cut it? My job at Sterling Heights PD was gone. I had taken a significant cut in pay to become an agent, and assuming I made it through new agents training, I would be transferred to some other part of the country. I would have to sell my house with no help from the government. I puked in the toilet.

The next day, I was led into a large conference room at FBI Headquarters. I'm not sure what I expected the building to look like, but it was fairly drab and sterile. The exterior was poured concrete. The interior walls were pale green, and the floors were cheap linoleum. The conference room itself had a little more class, as the walls were paneled at least.

My fellow classmates were gathered, and we introduced ourselves to one another. I was impressed with the diversity of the women and men who were gathered there. Everyone was a professional of some sort. We had a number of lawyers; some were criminal defense attorneys, a couple practiced civil law, and others had been prosecutors. We had business owners, accountants, former military, former FBI support employees, and some former law enforcement. I was thirty years old and could tell I was one of the oldest in the group. As apprehensive as I was the night before, I now realized that most of these folks had never fired a gun, made an arrest, or grappled with a suspect. Hell, I was ahead of the game.

The academy consisted of a series of brick multistory buildings, all interconnected by glass corridors, sort of like a gerbil habitat. It was possible to traverse the whole complex without going outside. In fact, if you didn't have firearms training, you could pass a whole week without going outside. It was kind of odd, but eventually we got used to it.

The next day, we reported at 8:30 a.m. to the classroom that would become our home for the next three and a half months. It had lecture hall–style seating with rows of long tables and seats starting low at the front of the room and rising with the highest row in the back of the room. A large blackboard covered the wall at the front of the class. Each seat had a name tag and was our assigned seat going forward. Seats were arranged in alphabetical order. Classroom attire was dress slacks, dress shirt, and tie for the men and dress skirts and blouses for the women. We had twenty-four men and six women in the class.

A man in his late forties, with dark hair and a moustache and wearing a cheap-looking gray suit, was standing at the front of the class, facing the students. "Good morning, Class 83-3. My name is Special Agent Jerry Pino. I am your class counselor and will be with you for the duration of your stay with us, however long that may be."

Encouraging, I thought.

Each class had a counselor who, in real life, was a street agent recruited to shepherd a class through the academy. Jerry was based out of Pittsburgh but was going through a divorce. He needed a place to crash for a few months, so he volunteered to be a class counselor. He did not have teaching responsibility for the most part but did accompany the class during their training and was the after-hours go-to guy. He essentially babysat us.

Jerry explained the three phases of training we would be subject to. First, there were classes in various law enforcement subjects with periodic tests, all of which must be passed with an 80 percent or higher. Failure to pass a test would result in immediate dismissal from the academy. Second was firearms training, which involved pistol, shotgun, and rifle instruction and eventual qualification with each. Failure to qualify with any weapons or a significant safety violation would result in dismissal from the academy. Finally, physical fitness and defensive tactics training would be conducted, and failure to attain minimum physical fitness requirements or failure to demonstrate proficiency in defensive tactics would result in dismissal from the academy.

After that cheery pep talk, we were ready to hit the ground running (or maybe start spending a lot of time in the boardroom, which was a bar located above the academy cafeteria). As time went on for us, we did fall into a routine. The training was not as difficult as it was made to sound, but they were serious about maintaining standards, and some folks did disappear for one reason or another. I found most of the curriculum to be easier than I expected, but I was having significant problems maintaining the minimum standards in physical training. I was fine with the upper body—pull-ups, push-ups, sit-ups, and so on. My problem was the endless running we did, which left me nursing chronic leg injuries. I'd never been much of a runner; in fact, I hated running and thought anyone who did it for sport needed their head examined. Consequently, I was still on the bubble the day before graduation.

Now, as I plugged toward the final half-mile marker on the Yellow Brick Road, I began to feel a little more confident. I broke into a big grin when it sunk in that, somehow, I was finally going to make it, but it wasn't until I made the final turn toward the finish line and saw my whole class lined up on both sides of the road that I knew for sure.

Two of my classmates yelled out, "There's Nads! He's going to make it!" Bob Yonkers ran to greet me and run next to me. "Yo, Nads, move your lumbering ass." I'll never forget the loud chorus of voices screaming in unison as I crossed the finish line, "Go, Nads! Go, Nads! Go, Nads!" Unfortunately, that nickname stuck.

4

LIFE ON THE INSIDE

MCI WALPOLE

Tony blinked as he stepped from the back of the dark sheriff's van into the bright sunlight of the prison yard. The area was empty except for his fellow passengers and the guards.

"Single file, ladies; head for the gray door ahead," barked the stocky deputy.

Tony's hands were manacled to a chain around his waist, and his ankles were also restrained, requiring him to shuffle along. He walked in a line with four other prisoners. The tall, skinny black guy in front of him was saying, "Oh, shit" over and over, and based on the smell coming from his way, it seemed like he really meant it.

The group passed through one large security door into a sally port. The door closed behind them, and after a few moments, the door in front of them buzzed and made a loud *thunk*. That door slid open, and the group shuffled into a brightly lit hallway. Three corrections officers were waiting.

"Step forward, one at a time, men," commanded one of the officers. His name tag read "Dallas."

The black guy went first, and all three officers started coughing and laughing.

"Oh, man, this dude shit his pants! Jimbo, your turn," said Officer Dallas. Jimbo led the man into another room off of the hallway.

"Okay, the rest of you guys, let's go," another guard instructed. "Step forward one at a time."

As each man stepped forward, the restraints were removed from their hands and feet. Once that was done, Dallas yelled, "Okay, everyone in single file now; follow me. We got to meet the reception committee."

The group followed Officer Dallas about fifty feet down to the end of the hallway to another large metal door. *Buzz. Thunk.* The door automatically slid open. Tony and the rest of the group stepped into a brightly lit, cavernous room. Along both sides of the walls were three tiers of cells. The doors were open, and prisoners, dressed in blue jeans and shirts, were standing on the catwalks in front of the cells.

The catwalks had metal grating from floor to ceiling. The prisoners were up against the grating, fingers protruding out of the holes. One particularly muscular Hispanic guy, with tattoos covering his arms and neck, shouted down from the second tier, "Hey, skinny, little white boy, I got my eye on you, sweetheart! You and me gonna be close friends real soon, baby! Ha, Ha, come to Daddy, pretty boy; I'll treat you good! See you in a few days!"

With that the whole place erupted into catcalls, banging on grating, and men grabbing their crotches and howling. Tony thought he was going to shit his pants.

After receiving prison uniforms consisting of those same blue jeans and shirts, white underwear, socks, and tennis shoes, Tony and the rest of the men were assigned to the "new man section" for the first few days. This was an area consisting of four individual two-man cells, each with a single toilet bowl (minus the seat), a sink bolted to the wall, and two bunks bolted to the floor. This new man section was where fresh prisoners were kept under observation to see how they held up.

After a dinner of soupy mystery meat in the segregated chow hall, the men were ushered back to their cells. At 9:00 p.m. sharp, the cell doors slammed shut and the lights went out. After adjusting his eyes to a dim light coming from somewhere down the hall, Tony was able to just make out his new roommate—Darnell, the black guy who had shit his pants.

Darnell was moaning, "Can't do this again, man; just can't fucking do this again!" He covered his face with his skinny left arm and sobbed like a baby.

That's when Tony, recalling the words from Dorothy in *The Wizard of Oz*, whispered to himself, "Toto, we're not in Kansas anymore."

The next day, after a hearty breakfast of green stuff and yellow stuff, Tony was directed to the office of Jim Bender. Tony entered the eight-by-eight room, which was completely filled by three freestanding gray metal file cabinets, a gray metal desk, and one metal folding chair on the floor facing the desk. Bender—a short, skinny, balding man in his midthirties with oversized glasses; a Kmart white, short-sleeved dress shirt; and a cheap, blue clip-on bowtie—was sitting behind the desk, absorbed in the paperwork in front of him.

The man looked up and with a tired smile said, "Have a seat, Tony. My name is Jim Bender. I'm going to be your case worker while you are assigned to this institution. I'll get into what that means in a bit, but first off, tell me, how did you sleep last night?"

Tony was surprised by the question but eager to answer. This was the first normal-looking guy he'd seen since shuffling in with the other new prisoners the day before.

"I didn't sleep at all, Mr. Bender. For one thing, the other guy in my cell kept crying, but I doubt I'd have slept even if he wasn't there," Tony admitted.

"Well, that's to be expected, but don't worry; life will develop into a routine here. I like to talk to the new guys, and I see from your record that this is your first prison experience. Just like on the outside, you have some control over how difficult a time you'll have in here. You've got no black marks against your record; you're starting clean," Bender explained. "As you might imagine, the correction officers call all the shots in this place. If you don't like what you are being told, just suck it up and don't complain, understand?"

"Yes, sir, don't complain," repeated Tony.

"Another piece of solid advice: pick your friends wisely. Don't hang with the hoods unless you enjoy being a boy toy. They may seem like friendly guys at first, but you'll never be one of them, just someone they can use for . . . whatever they want," Bender continued.

Tony pondered this and remembered the menacing Mexican from yesterday. He had already figured out that he would need to stay clear of that guy but wasn't quite sure how to do it.

"Tony, prison is a community within a community. This community has very different rules than the community you came from, and you will need to adapt. I can't tell you exactly how to do that, as every man needs to figure that out for himself. All I can say is that you should try to keep your nose clean and do not get involved in any criminal activity while you're here. If you get mixed up in stuff, you will inevitably piss someone off and something bad will result, guaranteed," Bender warned. "I'm going to review your file and administer some tests over the next few days, which will help us decide what services we can offer you and what kind of work you are best suited for," he added.

"Mr. Bender, I don't know what information you have about me already, but I can assure you I am coming into this with the best of intentions. You may have heard this a million times, but I'm not a criminal, swear to God!" Tony proclaimed. "I'm a drug addict, and any program you can get me into to help me change that would really be appreciated. As far as skills go, I grew up in my old man's auto repair shop and I can fix anything with four wheels. I was a dumbass teenager and quit school before I graduated, so I'd love to get my GED," Tony continued earnestly.

Bender was fairly impressed with this kid as he seemed to have a strategy at least.

"Well, I admire your determination, Tony. That's a good first step. You'll have plenty of time to work on your goals because, since you were sentenced to twelve to fifteen years, you will have to do eight years before you can see a parole board. That's the law as it currently stands," Bender summarized.

Back in his cell that evening, Tony was stretched out on his cot, watching a cockroach scurry hurriedly across the ceiling. He was thinking about doing eight years in this stinking, goddamn shithole and about the advice Bender had given him. He was just twenty-two years old and was wondering how to navigate this minefield without blowing his legs off, when suddenly the answer slid through an opening in his cell door.

Tony sat up suddenly and looked down where a brown paper grocery bag lay on the floor. He looked at it for a full minute before Darnell said, "Pick it up, motherfucker, or I will! I know that special delivery ain't for me. That was a guard that pushed it through the hole. Man, you somehow got friends in high places!"

Tony cautiously lifted his right leg off the bunk and placed his foot on the floor. He continued to stare at the bag and wondered if this was some kind of test or, worse yet, a setup. He knew he would eventually have to at least look into the bag, so he continued to swing both legs out of the bed and moved cautiously toward it. No noise, no smell, just a crumpled paper bag with something inside of it. Finally, Tony reached down and picked up the mysterious delivery. It felt somewhat heavy, and he could tell it contained several items.

Shit, here goes nothing, thought Tony, as he opened the package. A look of total astonishment came across his face as he poured the contents onto his bunk. A carton of Kool cigarettes, his favorite brand; several matchbooks; two magazines—*Penthouse* and *Time*; seven candy bars; and a folded note. He was amazed and very baffled. As he started to open the note, he was struck by a sickening thought: what if this stuff came from the Mexican? If that was the case, he had decided to shove it all back through the hole in his door and hide under the covers, perhaps forever.

Luckily, that wasn't the case. The note looked like it was scrawled by a sixth grader. It simply read: *I'll see you when you come upstairs. Meet me in the yard, Mello.*

"Well, I'll be damned," whispered Tony to himself.

The next few days consisted of "new man training" by the corrections officers and administrative staff, including the case workers, and a few words from the Catholic chaplain.

"Father Bill" actually seemed kind of interested in Tony and his fellow new blood. He gave a rather upbeat pep talk to the men, dealing with making the best use of prison time to reflect upon the old habits and behavior that caused them to be in the audience that day. He threw in a heavy dose of individual responsibility, then wrapped up with making Mom proud by eventually turning their lives around. Tony judged it a seven on a scale of zero to ten. Not bad.

During a smoke break, Darnell was telling everyone who would listen about Tony's mysterious care package from Mello. Tony decided this was a good opportunity to let it be known that he was in close with one of the prison's most notorious and respected inmates.

"Yeah, me and Mello go way back; he practically raised me," Tony lied. "I used to call him Uncle Mello, and the fact is he thinks of me as a nephew as well. Here, boys, why don't you all have a cigarette on me? There's plenty more where these came from."

"I know Mello from my last bit here. He's a solid con and somebody you don't want to fuck with," remarked Darnell.

"A damn good man to have in your corner. You are one lucky prick, Tony," added another "new man" named Bill.

Mello was in fact considered a "solid" con—a convict who never snitches, will stand up in a fight, and will kill someone if need be. Really, Mello was all that and more. He was connected to the Mafia guys in Boston. He was a fringe mobster who knew all the "made" men. He worked deals with them and was respected by them, but he was not one of them and preferred it that way. In prison, Mello had status due to his relationship with the Mafia alone, but on top of that, he was very personable, got regular visits, and had money. All these attributes gain a con respect on the inside.

Tony was eating it up. Let the word spread far and wide that Tony Romano was under the protection of Carmello Merlino.

Tony had first met Mello about fifteen years earlier. Tony was seven years old at the time and hanging out at A to Z with his dad. Mello was one of the regulars who met in the back of the garage to conduct business. The back room was a meeting spot for bookies, loan sharks, and shady hoodlums of all types. Mello hung out there a lot, at least when he wasn't in prison for bank robbery, extortion, assault, and other crimes.

Mello had grown up with Tony's dad. They shared common views on life, but while Mello was a criminal by nature, Tony's dad was a straight shooter. He enjoyed the company of these colorful characters and even gave them a place to meet, but he didn't join in with them when they went to "work." He had a family and a business and wasn't inclined to screw up either one.

Tony was attracted to Mello like a bee to honey. Mello carried himself with swagger and had the respect of others; he was considered a "stand-up guy" by the rest of the A to Z crowd. Tony listened to Mello when the back-room stories and liquor would flow. He was the pied piper, and Tony was just one of his many little followers.

Four days after arriving in Walpole, Tony was transferred to 7 Block, where the new guys were all assigned. Tony felt much better knowing that Mello was around, even though they had yet to connect. He slept better at night, and the nervousness started to drain out of him. The future wasn't so uncertain anymore.

Three days after arriving on 7 Block, Tony got his first chance to join the regular population for exercise in the yard. The yard was a huge open area consisting of a walking track, weight-lifting area, basketball courts, and picnic tables scattered randomly around the landscape. The area was walled on three sides and had two rows of ten-foot steel fencing topped with looped razor wire. The fifteen feet of space between the two fence lines was considered "no man's land"; no man lucky enough to get over the first fence would ever make it to the second. Each corner of the yard was dominated by a watchtower, where armed guards were positioned. Every tower had a commanding view of the entire yard and a clear field of fire.

Tony blinked in the bright sunlight as he and three other 7 Block members entered the yard for the first time. There were a couple hundred guys milling around in groups—smoking, playing basketball, walking the track, or lifting weights. As Tony scanned the crowd, he finally spotted Mello holding court at one of the picnic tables. He was gesturing with his arms and obviously telling a story. There was a chorus of laughter from the men gathered around Mello. Tony looked at the scene, and while Mello was obviously older and heavier and had less hair, it was like being back in his father's garage with Mello and his cronies. Tony couldn't help but think, *It's déjà vu all over again.*

Finally, Mello spotted Tony and barked, "Get over here, you scrawny little prick!"

Tony wanted to run and hug Mello but kept his cool and walked slowly toward the group, who had all turned to size him up. Mello instead had a huge grin on his face. As Tony got within reach, Mello made a big show of pulling him to his side and giving him a bear hug.

"Guys, this here is Tony Romano. I've known this little jerk-off his whole life. His old man and me go way back. Tony is new to this clubhouse and has a lot to learn, so don't be offended if he makes a few mistakes. You guys all remember your first time here," Mello lectured.

Tony was relieved to see the faces were fairly benign. Nobody was scowling at him.

"Hi, Mello. Thanks for the care package. You've already made me some friends here with that," Tony responded.

"Don't worry, kid; life in here ain't all bad. Look, let's take a walk around the track and catch up," Mello said warmly.

Mello put his arm around Tony's shoulder and started toward the weight-lifting area. To his horror, Tony saw the tattooed Mexican spotting for another guy who was lifting a huge amount of iron. The Mexican had a concerned look on his face and was eyeballing Mello and Tony as they approached. Mello stopped a few feet from the Mexican and, pointing directly at him, said, "Chico, get your ass over here!"

Chico immediately left the guy on the bench struggling with the over-loaded bar. He trotted over, put a smile on his face, and stuck his hand out to Mello. Mello ignored it.

"Chico, this here is Tony Romano, and he's a friend," Mello said as stared at Chico.

Chico immediately grabbed Tony's hand and shook it vigorously. "Yo, glad to meet you, Tony. Hey, sorry about that little show I put on when you first got here. I didn't know you were a pal of Mello's, and I like to joke with the new guys. Are we cool?" he asked in earnest.

Tony was thunderstruck. He had been dreading the day he ran into Chico and certainly never envisioned it would go this way.

"Sure, we're cool," replied Tony.

With that, Mello and Tony turned away and continued on toward the track. After getting out of Chico's earshot, Mello said, "I heard what that fucker said to you the day you got here, and I wasn't happy. He's in for the first time as well and has only been here for six months. There's a lot of loudmouth assholes in this joint, but you won't be hearing from that one anymore. More of those fucking street scum are ending up here, and they're starting to give the prison a bad name."

Tony wondered about that twisted logic.

Once they reached the track running next to the perimeter wall, Mello started in with his briefing on prison life: "Look, I know your case work-er, Jim Bender. Jim is a good guy and means well. I'm sure he told you to keep away from the troublemakers and keep your nose clean. I'm not saying that's bad advice, but it's not the way life really works here. Your first priority is getting out alive, and sometimes that requires breaking the rules. Let me show you."

Mello made a slow turn and made sure nobody was nearby. He put his left foot up on the seat of a bench and made as if he was tying his shoe. Instead, he quickly raised his pant leg three inches to reveal the butt end of something concealed in his sock. He finished "tying his shoe" and started walking again.

"Was that what I think it was under your sock?" asked Tony cautious-ly.

"Well, that depends on what you think you saw. If you think you saw a wooden-handled shiv with a four-inch blade, you're right. And if I got caught with that, I'd be in the hole for a week, but I'd rather be alive in the hole than dead in a hole outside these walls, if you catch my drift,"

Mello explained rather poignantly. "My point is, following all the rules means putting yourself at a disadvantage in here, and you never want to do that," he warned.

Tony thought about that advice but wasn't sure what Mello was driving at.

"Listen, kid, you gotta play all the angles in here, starting with the Screws. You see that guard standing fifty feet away from us?" he asked.

Tony looked around and saw a uniformed correctional officer keeping an eye on the activity in the yard. He wasn't looking at Mello and Tony but rather had his back to them.

"That's Officer Miller. He delivered your care package the other night. Miller's on my payroll, and right now he's watching my back. He knows I'm carrying this knife; in fact, he gave to me," Mello revealed.

For the second time in a span of maybe ten minutes, Tony was utterly stunned. He stopped walking and looked directly at Mello. "What the fuck? Are you shitting me?" he exclaimed.

Mello laughed. "Don't look so shocked, kid. The man makes a crappy salary and has a wife and three kids. One of the kids is disabled, so his wife can't work. I've got something he could use, which is cash. I need a guy in his position, and he needs a guy in my position, so it works out well for both of us," he explained. "Anyway, all he really does is help me stay alive and turn a blind eye to some of my money-making ventures."

"What do you mean by money-making ventures?" asked Tony.

"Believe me, there are guys in here with plenty of money but nothing to buy. They like their drugs and don't want to do five to ten without them," he replied. "I've got a way to get the shit in here. Of course, it's risky and I charge a lot, but everything is set up so that I don't see any money and I don't touch any drugs," Mello bragged. "It's foolproof and very profitable."

Tony could hardly believe what he was hearing. Mello was running a drug operation in prison. He was carrying a weapon and had a guard watching his back. Tony suddenly realized that he had a lot to learn about this place, and more importantly, he was very thankful to have Mello in his corner.

"Romano, get your skinny ass over here," barked the guard as Tony was leaving the chow hall. "I've got your new work assignment; follow me."

Tony followed the guard out of the main building and into the yard. The morning was bright and seasonably cool for an early-autumn New England day.

"So do you like working in the fresh air, kid?" asked the guard.

"Yes, sir," Tony answered truthfully. He couldn't believe his luck. This must be Mello's doing, he thought.

The guard led Tony down the hill to the industrial building. They entered the massive structure, jammed with machinery and clanging with the sound of metal on metal. Inmates were busy operating various machines, and the general din was ear-splitting. The guard walked Tony up to an overweight, middle-aged colleague, who was munching on a bag of potato chips.

"Hey, Larry, here's your new guy," said the first guard.

Larry looked over at Tony. "Uh-huh" was all he cared to respond.

The first guard grinned down at Tony. "I know you like to work outside in the fresh air and warm sunshine, and someday I'm sure you will, but until then you're making license plates in this shithole."

Both guards had a good laugh at that one. Tony sighed quietly.

Larry motioned Tony to follow him and began his run-through of the job: "Today you're going to get familiar with the press machine, and I'm having you work with Latrell Johnson. He isn't the brightest bulb, but after losing two fingertips, he finally got the hang of the machine." Larry laughed again. "Come on, your station is right past gift wrap. Good luck, kid," the guard said walking away, laughing at his own joke.

Goddamn, they really do make license plates in prison, thought Tony. What he'd seen in the movies would now be his reality.

Luckily, Tony was no stranger to machinery and, not long after starting his job, was promoted to the more detailed job of applying the luminescent paint to the raised numbers and letters. He managed to avoid losing any appendages in the process and eventually got the hang of manufacturing license plates. It actually appealed to his artistic side.

Inmates are also assigned work details outside of their normal everyday job, and Mello got Tony assigned to a job that he needed him for: Tony became the visiting room cleaner. This job entailed emptying cigarette butt cans, rearranging tables and chairs, sweeping, mopping, and waxing the floor, and, most importantly, locating and smuggling in hidden drugs for Mello.

The drugs were always disguised in a piece of trash left behind by a visitor. Tony would simply pick it up with all the other waste products and put them into his rolling barrel. He never knew which trash items in particular contained the drugs, so he had to make sure he cleaned up everything. Once back inside the secure area, he would head to the trash compactor. This was the tricky part because there were cameras everywhere. Instead of dumping the whole barrel into the compactor, Tony would reach in and grab several discarded items and toss them in. While leaning inside the barrel, he would locate the drug package and quickly stuff it into his shirt. After a couple more barrel dives, he would pick up the barrel and dump the remaining trash into the compactor and move along with the drugs safe and secure on his person.

Tony didn't actually need to worry about being that sneaky, as the guard overseeing this process was none other than Officer Miller, Mello's buddy. Miller would give Tony a discreet nod as he left the trash area, and Tony would head back into the main prison where he would meet another of Mello's associates in the latrine for the handoff.

The drug of choice in Walpole was Talwins or "Ts." Ts were pain-reliever pills that could be crushed and injected for a heroin-type of high. For his work, Tony earned a small cut of the product. *Maybe prison won't be completely dreary after all*, he thought.

5

DOING MY OWN TIME

FBI, DETROIT DIVISION

In 1983, it was Bureau policy that new agents returned to their home office for six months before transferring to a second office for the next one-and-a-half years. In my case, that first office was in Detroit. The field office was located downtown. It was 7:00 a.m. on May 25, 1983, and I had arrived on the twenty-fifth floor of the McNamara Federal Building. I flashed my newly minted FBI badge and credentials at the young receptionist behind the bulletproof Plexiglas.

"Hi, my name is Dave Nadolski and I'm reporting in," I announced enthusiastically.

"Good morning, agent. We've been expecting you. Welcome to the Detroit Division," she replied with a smile. "Have a seat and I'll get someone from Squad 6 to escort you in."

I took a seat and looked around. I remembered the lobby from my interview. Unsurprisingly, it was the nicest room in the office. There was a huge, blue "Federal Bureau of Investigation—Detroit Division" sign on the wall. There were nice, red-leather-upholstered armchairs with matching dark-wood corner tables, and the room had expensive, deep-blue carpeting. There was a display case with various awards and trophies along with a black and white photo of what I recognized as khaki-clad agents, all firing their revolvers using the classic, two-handed "wedge" shooting stance. I didn't notice any ear protection on those guys—old timers were hardcore.

A door suddenly opened to my left, and a tall, blond man, about thirty-five years old, wearing a gray suit, white button-down dress shirt, and red tie, stepped into the room. He extended his hand and said, "Hi, Dave. My name is Doug Martin. I'm your training agent."

Doug had a half-grin on his face, like he knew something funny that I didn't. "Follow me and I'll take you to the squad area. The supervisor wants to meet you," he announced.

We walked through the open door and started down a long hall. As nice as the lobby was decorated, this hallway was purely industrial grade. The walls were a light green, and the floor was brown linoleum. There were no pictures or decorations of any kind. Lights were florescent bulbs attached to fixtures on the ceiling and covered with opaque plastic. My bunker in Vietnam had a cozier feel.

I followed Doug down the hall until it emptied into a very large open room that occupied a corner of the building. Two interior walls were the same green drywall, while the other two walls were glass and overlooked the Detroit River and Windsor, Ontario, beyond. Not a bad view at all.

There were at least fifty desks in the room, arranged in groups of four. Two sat side by side, facing the other two desks. They were all a gun-metal gray. Most were occupied by men and a few women who were writing and talking on the phone, and a couple agents even had their feet up and were reading the newspaper. Cigarette smoke hung in the air. All the desks were littered with brown covered files, which I would later learn were individual case files.

Doug stopped and explained the layout: "Dave, this first group of desks belongs to the Bank Robbery Task Force squad. The supervisor has an office over in that corner." He pointed, indicating the glass wall over-looking the Detroit River nearest to where we were standing. "The rest of the desks belong to our squad, the Theft from Interstate Shipment or 'Truck Squad.'"

The FBI has jurisdiction over crimes committed interstate, or over state lines. The reasoning is rather than have several state police agencies working on the same group of criminals, the federal government can, as a single law enforcement entity, cover all criminal activity that crosses state lines.

The Truck Squad was developed to investigate thefts from interstate shipments. These were mainly comprised of tractor-trailer hijackings or thefts from interstate trucks, interstate car theft rings, and any other criminal activity involving wheels crossing state lines. At the time, I didn't know jack shit about trucks other than my slow driving habits usually pissed them off.

"Dave, this is Judy Lyons, our squad secretary," Doug went on.

"Glad to meet you, Judy," I said as I shook Judy's rather meaty hand. "So you're the gatekeeper for the boss, huh?" I joked.

"That's right! It's my job to keep the undesirables out of his office, which pretty much means three-quarters of Squad 6!" Judy and Doug shared a hearty laugh over that one.

Doug turned to another young woman sitting at the desk next to Judy. "Dave, meet Kassondra White. She's our rotor clerk."

I knew from new agents training that a rotor clerk was the person who controlled the squad case files. Agents didn't maintain their own filing cabinets for case files. It was Bureau policy that all case files would be maintained in one central location under the control of a squad rotor clerk. The title "rotor clerk" derived from the shape of the filing cabinet the files were kept in. It was round and large and spun in a circle. Files were maintained numerically and further subdivided by violation code. When an agent wanted a file, it had to be checked out, like in a library, and returned to the clerk before quitting time. At that time, the rotor clerk locked all the files away in the rotating cabinet. Agents were not allowed to keep files in their desks or remove them from the office. J. Edgar Hoover himself was very proud of this inventive system, and as strange as it may sound, it did a good job of keeping track of sensitive FBI materials.

Doug finally brought me in to meet my first Bureau supervisor, Bob Kosinski, a large, affable man. Bob rose from his cluttered desk and extended his hand. His suit jacket was thrown over a chair, and his white dress shirt was unbuttoned at the collar. He looked like he'd been at work all night. Behind him was a table with case files stacked in piles. His desk faced the door, and behind and to his left were glass walls affording a nice view of Canada and lake freighter traffic on the Detroit River. Far downriver, the stacks of the venerable Ford Rouge auto-assembly plant were visible on this clear day, and I thought I could see the large American flag from Ft. Wayne, where I was sworn into the US Army many years before.

"Good to meet you, Dave. I was hoping we'd get some help from the new agents assigned to the Detroit Division. I understand you're a former Sterling Heights police officer; is that right?" Bob asked.

"That's right, Mr. Kosinski. I was with Sterling Heights PD for six years before joining the Bureau," I said.

"Hey, first off call me Bob. We don't stand on formality here."

"Okay, Bob," I replied.

"I like former cops on my squad, Dave, and I've got several. You guys have already made arrests, conducted interviews, and hopefully know how to relate to people," Bob explained. "This is first and foremost a people business. Everyone thinks that the FBI uses the latest techno gadgets to solve crimes. What a load of crap! Cases are made by talking to people, establishing relationships, and getting information. Welcome aboard."

I could tell I was going to like Bob.

I spent the first few days getting the lay of the land, meeting my fellow squad mates, and reading the cases I was assigned. They were all theft from interstate shipment cases, which required me to call the complainant (the person whose goods were stolen from the truck) to determine exactly what details he had regarding the theft. Usually there was a preliminary report from the police department where the theft had occurred. That document often had a lot of helpful details. Next, I needed to contact the truck driver (who was inevitably out on the road and virtually unreachable) to determine if what he originally told the cops was accurate.

Oftentimes, it was at this point in the investigation that the story changed somewhat. It was usually the driver who "accidentally" left the trailer unlocked or parked it in a bad part of town while he got a cup of coffee. More often than not, the driver was behind the theft because he was somehow screwed over by the freight company and felt this was the simplest way to get what was owed him.

The most difficult part of my job early on was getting access to my desk phone. Doug and I sat side by side (literally) and shared one desk phone. Doug loved talking on the phone and spent a big part of every day doing just that. In order to do my work, I had to find someone's unoccupied desk and borrow the phone. Needless to say, it wasn't long before Doug started to get under my skin.

The next challenge was finding a car to go out and conduct interviews. There were more agents on the squad than available cars. I'd start with

Doug to see if his car was available. It should have been because he was always on the phone, but usually for one reason or other, his car was unavailable. So, in order to do my job, I had to scrounge up a car somehow, gas it up, clean the coffee cups out of it, and hope it didn't break down on the road. And God forbid if it wasn't returned exactly on time.

Luckily for me, most of my squad mates were generous with their cars or found ingenious ways to acquire more than one. Jack McDonough, a likable hot shit, was running an undercover case where agents were buying stolen auto parts. Jack was assigned a red Corvette to tool around in and wore some nice gold jewelry in order to enhance his undercover role. The Corvette had once belonged to a drug dealer in California and was now property of the US government.

"Here, Dave, take the 'Vette. I won't need it for a couple days" was the best thing I had heard in my first two weeks on the job. I felt like Magnum PI, at least for a few days.

After a couple of weeks on the job, I came home late on Friday night, as usual.

"You look like you could use a drink, sailor," Linda said, as I staggered in the door.

"Damn right. Make it a double," I responded, after throwing my briefcase on the kitchen table and slumping into a chair. My suit coat was off, tie askew, dress shirt unbuttoned, and I was worn out. Linda mixed me a vodka and tonic and sat down next to me.

"Want to talk about it?" she asked.

After gulping the first one, I said, "Do it again, barkeep," and Linda complied. I didn't really feel like talking about it, but I knew that wasn't a possibility. Linda has an eerie sixth sense when it comes to reading my mind, so if she wanted to talk, we talked.

"Listen, these first two weeks have been eye-opening," I began. "I'm not too sure I did the right thing here. I used to have a great job that I loved with the police department. I had a private cubicle with my own phone, had a city car that I brought home, lived five minutes from the station, put in an eight-hour shift, and got paid for every cent of overtime. I worked a variety of good cases, including occasional homicides, and made a lot of arrests. Now that I'm a hot-shot FBI agent, I work in a gigantic fishbowl of an office investigating meaningless crap, don't have a pager, seldom have a phone, and have no car assigned to me. I leave the house at 5:30 a.m., drive twenty-five miles into the city, pay to park my personal car, and finally crawl home at 7:00 p.m. But at least I'm doing it for half the money I used to make! I guess the joke is on me," I complained.

I buried my head in my arms. "Oh, and did I mention they're going to uproot us and make us sell our house in less than six months so that we can move to some other strange place? Do me a favor: hide my gun."

"Okay, Sparky, listen up!" barked Linda. "You're better than this. You knew most, if not all, of this when you signed up. You've only been on the job for two weeks, for God's sakes, and your head is still spinning! You're the new guy, and this is the toughest it's going to get for you. As time goes on, you'll figure things out and adjust accordingly. You always do. Sure, you're not making much money now, but that will change over time. We both agreed to this, and maybe you thought everything was going to go smooth as silk, but at least I expected a bumpy road for some time anyway. You may find this hard to believe, but I'm looking forward to moving somewhere new. This is an adventure, and you, me, Liz, and the cat are in this together!" Linda said, wrapping up her vehement speech.

Linda had hit the nail on the head. My main concern was involving my family in something that was primarily my dream. I could see that what I did had an impact on my family, but Linda's reassuring words instantly put me in a better mood. I could see this career was going to be difficult enough without having a resentful spouse. I knew at that moment that I was very lucky to have Linda as my life partner. Little did I know then how much I would need her even more in the future.

I knew going into the FBI that Detroit would be my first office. The only thing I knew about the identity of my second office was that it would be a "medium-sized" office. Medium-sized offices consisted of relatively smaller cities, such as Memphis, Little Rock, Albany, New Orleans, or Indianapolis, for example. There were many medium-sized offices, and the Bureau gave us no hint as to which office a new agent may end up with. After one-and-a-half years, new agents would be transferred from the medium-sized office to a "large" office. There were ten large offices, including New York, Los Angeles, Cleveland, Washington, Boston, Miami, and Detroit in fact. The whole reasoning behind this system was that agents would first learn their trade in a comfortable, local setting; then hone it in the smaller offices; then be reassigned to a large office with some experience under their belts.

Orders can be expected after three months in the home office, so it was no surprise when, in mid-August, I was called into the office of my assistant special agent in charge, Mike Byrnes. As I stepped into the office, I noticed my supervisor, Bob, and Mike standing side by side.

Mike said, "Dave, I've got an envelope for you from headquarters, and if I had to guess, I'd say it's your transfer orders." He handed me a plain, white #10 envelope inscribed, "For the Personal Attention of Special Agent David T. Nadolski," along with a letter opener. "You don't mind opening it here do you, Dave? Bob and I have a friendly wager going."

"No problem, Mike." This was only a major moment in my life, but I guess their friendly wager was important too. I carefully slit the top of the envelope and removed the single sheet of paper and silently read: *Special Agent Nadolski, upon receipt of this notice you may make immediate preparations for a house-hunting trip to your next duty station, Atlanta, Georgia. You will be expected to report for duty, in Atlanta, no later than September 15, 1983.*

I folded the paper and held it in my hand. My immediate reaction was that this was a great assignment, and feeling a weight lift off my shoulders, I decided to play along with the wager.

"Mike, what was your guess?" I asked.

Mike said, "North of the Mason-Dixon line."

"Sorry." I handed him the paper. "You lost." He snatched it and quickly scanned it.

"Goddamn it, this is the third time in a row I lost!" Mike complained.

Bob put his arm around my shoulder and said, "Good job, Dave. Let's go."

Linda was thrilled with the news and so was I. We could have landed in some really dumpy place but instead drew one of the most desirable offices in the Bureau. Luckily, our house in Sterling Heights had been on the market for the last few months, and we had just accepted an offer of $38,000. Interest rates had come down since we purchased our home, so we were eligible to look for a more expensive house in Atlanta.

With only four days to locate and buy a house, we had to move quickly. Linda and I were struck by the beauty of the area, the new subdivisions with young families, and the overall friendliness of the folks living there. After viewing at least twenty houses, we settled on a new house in a subdivision that was three-quarters built out. It boasted a large community pool, tennis courts, and a pond. Our house was a three-bedroom colonial with a basement and drive-under garage. It had a spacious great room with a gas fireplace, a formal dining room, and a kitchen with a breakfast area. The kitchen led to a large deck overlooking our private backyard. The house had floor-to-ceiling windows and central air. Best of all, it had a wonderful wraparound front porch. We were happy to be in Georgia. The Nadolski family had died and gone to heaven!

FBI, ATLANTA DIVISION

On September 15, 1983, I reported to the Atlanta Division, and I was comforted to discover that I was in familiar surroundings. Our squad area was another large, open area crammed with gray metal desks, but at least this time around I had my own phone. Agents were still allowed to smoke, but luckily only a couple had the habit and they tried hard to keep it under control.

I had been assigned to the Foreign Counterintelligence/Civil Rights Squad. Our mission was split between the two programs. I was assigned to conduct Foreign Counterintelligence (FCI) investigations primarily, which was new territory for me. The FCI program was designed to discover, monitor, and catch foreign spies in the act of espionage against the United States. At the time, we were targeting the military and civilian intelligence services of the USSR, China, and the Eastern Bloc Communist governments, plus the Cuban intelligence service. The largest FCI programs were in the FBI offices located in New York; Washington, D.C.; Los Angeles; and San Francisco, with New York and Washington, D.C., carrying the brunt of the load.

Spies traditionally work out of embassies, or in the case of New York, the United Nations. Spies have cover positions in the embassy or UN Mission, which gives them diplomatic immunity. Armed with immunity, they are free to pursue their actual objective, which is recruiting people to provide them sensitive information. This can be classified military documents, civilian trade secrets, or other sensitive information to which they are not legally entitled. If caught spying, the intelligence officer is briefly arrested but quickly released and deported from the country. Typically, this is followed by one of our overseas CIA officers being arrested, sometimes beat up, and deported as well.

Catching a spy is extremely difficult. We know who they are, but they are very cautious about being followed. The spy is most vulnerable when he attempts to recruit someone who has access to sensitive material. If that person becomes suspicious and calls the FBI to report this contact, we allow the contacted person to continue meeting with the foreign spy before moving in when the time is right. That doesn't happen very often.

Atlanta did not have a large FCI program. We had a large Russian émigré community and Chinese nationals to keep track of. Additionally, we were tasked with monitoring known spies traveling from New York and Washington to the Atlanta area. Before I could work on anything FCI related, I had to go back to Quantico for two weeks of intensive training in this program.

My supervisor in Atlanta was Theo Scott, aka "Scotty"—one of the nicest guys I've ever met and a true gentleman. Scotty was among the first African American agents hired by the FBI and was born and raised in Atlanta.

Scotty assigned Special Agent Wayne Johnson, a Georgia good ol' boy and fellow Vietnam veteran, to be my mentor. Wayne, who had been a Marine Corps officer, seemed taken aback when I introduced myself. He looked at me and said, "Are you related to a Marine officer by the name of Jerry Nadolski?"

"My brother Jerry was a Marine lieutenant and served in Vietnam," I answered.

"Damn, boy, I know your brother! He relieved me when he reported in-country in 1966!"

Thanks to my brother, I could do no wrong in Wayne's eyes. Wayne was part of the Marine Corps Mafia that existed in the FBI. Marine officers, particularly Vietnam vets, were recruited by the Bureau, and many rose to high management positions.

Shortly after returning from my FCI training at the FBI academy, I was called into Scotty's office along with the rest of the squad for a special briefing.

"Ladies and gentlemen, we have been handed an assignment from the New York Office. Three Russian 'diplomats,' aka known spies, will be flying down here to spend five days in the area. Their purpose is supposedly as cultural liaisons, but these guys are no doubt here to meet up with an asset they must have recruited. Our job is to relentlessly follow them and disrupt the meeting from ever taking place," Scotty addressed the group.

I learned from FCI training that any travel by foreign intelligence officers is for the purpose of conducting some type of spy activity. They do not have the budget for frivolous travel, so any travel is a huge red flag.

We were not going to be able to conduct effective covert surveillance; therefore we planned to "bumper lock" these guys and let them know they were being watched. Our squad, assisted by the Atlanta surveillance squad, planned to conduct 24/7 close coverage of the group.

On the day of their arrival, agents from the New York Division followed the Russians from their residence in Manhattan to JFK Airport and observed them board a United Airlines flight for Atlanta. Having been previously provided pictures of the men, we were waiting at the Atlanta airport and observed them deplane, retrieve their luggage, rent a van, and head to a modest hotel outside downtown Atlanta.

We determined what rooms they were assigned: two in one room, two in another room, and one (presumably the boss) entered a third room by himself. They knew who we were, and we made sure they saw us. After a few days of shadowing these guys to the same cheesy Chinese restaurant and babysitting them everywhere they went, I had an idea of how to speed things up a bit.

While in FCI training at Quantico, we learned that flipping an intelligence officer was the prime objective. Convincing a spy to join our team is as good as it gets in the intelligence game. During this assignment, I was paired with another new agent who had attended the same training I did. Agent Dharia Lewis was a former Minnesota state trooper. Cops are not necessarily known for subtlety, so she was game for my idea.

"Listen, Dharia, I'm sick of babysitting these jackasses. Let's do something unexpected. Why don't you and I see if the Russian boss will talk to us? Maybe we can make a friend," I suggested.

"Well, it would be a real coup, that's for sure. But what if it doesn't go well?" she replied.

"Anything is better than what we are doing. I'm sure everything will go fine," I assured her.

So, with a plan in place, we marched up to the room and knocked on the door of the boss, Ivan. He opened up, and we showed him our credentials.

"Ivan, I'm Agent Nadolski, and this is Agent Lewis. You know us, right?"

Ivan looked shocked. His mouth dropped open.

"We were hoping you'd like to have a chat with us. Mind if we come in?" I asked.

Ivan overcame his shock and quickly looked up and down the hallway.

"Are you crazy? I am fucking DIPLOMAT! I will file complaint with your embassy!" With that, he slammed the door in our faces.

Dharia and I looked at one another. *Oh, shit*, we both thought.

After I confessed to Scotty what we had done, he turned as pale as me, which is saying something. He looked at the both of us, removed a handkerchief, and wiped his brow.

"Please tell me that you are bullshitting me! Do you know what kind of trouble you're in?" bellowed Scotty.

Clearly, I did not, but I wasn't going to tell him that.

"I am really, really sorry. It was all my fault, Scotty," I said.

"Jesus Christ! This could bite us in the ass big time! Okay, I'm going to sit on this and see what happens next. Stay in the office! DO NOT get within one hundred miles of those Russians!" he ordered.

As it turned out, the Russians returned to New York and complained to their superiors that they were harassed mercilessly by the Atlanta agents. The New York office intercepted this intelligence about the Atlanta trip, and the FCI boss from the New York office actually sent a teletype to Scotty congratulating our team for a job well done. Scotty's blood pressure returned to normal, and I was out of the doghouse.

Shortly after moving into our new house, Linda and I were kept awake by a loud party at the house across the street. We hadn't yet met our new neighbors, but it was apparent they were party animals. All night long I was hearing loud music and one particularly booming voice coming from their backyard. It seemed like every few minutes we'd hear, "HAR, HAR, HAR, HO, HO, HO!" It would be quiet for a while, then all of a sudden: "HAR, HAR, HAR, HO, HO, HO!"

"Linda, it's freaking 2:00 a.m., and that moron is keeping the whole neighborhood awake, for God's sakes! Think I should call the cops?" I asked.

"No, don't call the cops; that wouldn't be a particularly good way to meet the neighbors. He'll pass out eventually," Linda advised.

Well, the party did break up at 2:30 a.m., and thankfully, the lights went out and Linda and I finally got to sleep. The next morning, I saw the homeowner out front raking the dirt in front of his house. Getting grass to grow was a common problem in the red-Georgia-clay soil.

"Linda, I'm going to go over and introduce myself. I'm sure he just had a loudmouth at the party and couldn't figure out how to get rid of the guy," I said hopefully.

"Sounds good to me," Linda said.

So I walked across the street to meet my new neighbor. I could see he was my age, and he waved as I approached his property.

As I drew next to him, I extended my hand and said, "Hi, I'm Dave Nadolski. Quite a party you had last night. I'm glad you finally got rid of that loudmouth because I was getting ready to call the cops."

My neighbor leaned on his rake and looked at me.

"I'm Fred Parcells, and I'm really sorry about the loudmouth," he squeaked in a very hoarse voice, "but I'm glad you didn't call the cops because the loudmouth was me."

I'm glad I didn't call the cops as well because that awkward meeting was the beginning of a friendship that is still strong to this day. Fred, Nancy, and their two boys, Fred Jr. and Spencer, have become extended family to us. We ended up on their back deck roaring and hooting on a number of Friday nights, as did most of the neighborhood. Fred was a Vietnam veteran and Army officer, and while our paths took us to different parts of the country, we always stayed in touch. We visit as much as possible and always attend the big celebrations in one another's lives. True friends are very rare and need to be cherished.

While I was fairly underwhelmed by the FCI work I was doing in Atlanta, things were going well otherwise. So much so in fact that Linda became pregnant again. Everything proceeded normally until about five months into the pregnancy. Linda was feeling poorly, so she made a doctor's appointment for the next day.

That day I came home early from work and took her to see her doctor. Dr. Reynolds was a short, round, single lady of about forty years of age. She was a native of Marietta and set up her OB practice there. I was waiting in the reception area for about fifteen minutes when the medical assistant came out.

"Mr. Nadolski, Dr. Reynolds would like to see you. Come this way please," she directed.

I entered the exam room to find Linda crying and the doctor with a very concerned look on her face.

"Mr. Nadolski, we have a serious situation here, and I need to get her into the hospital right now," Dr. Reynolds quickly explained.

Dr. Reynolds helped me take Linda out to my Bureau car and get her into the backseat, where the doctor ordered her to lay down as best she could.

"Get going, Mr. Nadolski. I'll see you at the hospital."

With that, I whipped out of the doctor's parking lot and over to Kennesaw Hospital. We arrived at the emergency entrance and were met by a couple of attendants with a stretcher.

I watched as they wheeled Linda into the hospital and had a sick feeling in the pit of my stomach. I joined Linda and the doctor who had just completed a more thorough exam. She explained the situation: "I do not know if we have a healthy baby. This condition could be nature's way of eliminating a fetus with serious health problems. You two need to talk and decide if we should let nature take its course or fight to save the baby. Fighting to save the baby will mean Linda will have to be hospitalized and completely bedridden for the rest of her pregnancy."

With that news, the doctor left us alone. Linda and I looked at one another for a long time. We didn't want to speak the words that needed to be said.

"What do you think, honey?" I finally asked.

Linda started crying again and held her left hand over her eyes while squeezing my right hand with hers.

"I'm not the one laying on this stretcher or the one who has to make this work; you are. I'll support whatever decision you make," I said.

"Dave, I don't know what to do, but I'm thinking we need to give this baby a fighting chance. I don't want to quit," Linda said.

"Well, what if it means you have to spend the next four months in the hospital, literally flat on your back worrying that the baby has severe birth defects?" I asked.

"Dave, I really believe the baby is okay and this is a problem with my body, not hers. I want to try to save this pregnancy," Linda said earnestly.

I have never loved Linda more than at that moment.

The next morning, I returned to the hospital as soon as I could get Liz back over to the Parcells' house. I walked in to see Linda was still on the stretcher. Doctor Reynolds, who had spent the whole night in the hospital, was beside her, and they both had smiles on their faces.

"Good news, Dave," said the doctor. "Linda is doing much better this morning; the best possible outcome occurred overnight. I'm going to need to sew a few stitches to help the baby remain where it belongs. This is not a guaranteed fix by any means, but the baby seems to be doing well."

I broke out into a wide grin and Linda laughed. We hugged and I said, "I knew you could do it, honey!"

As it turned out, Linda did not have to remain in the hospital for the rest of her pregnancy. She was allowed to return home under strict orders that she not move from her bed except to use the bathroom. We had a second-story bedroom that I outfitted with a television, small refrigerator, and microwave. Linda had to remain flat on her back. Nancy Parcells was Linda's constant companion and helper. She stayed with Linda every day. We also had help from my mother and Linda's sister-in-law, Nancy, who both traveled to Atlanta to help out for a couple weeks. For my part, I switched my work schedule to cover the day shift at home and worked in the office during the evening, when things were a little less hectic at home. Scotty understood my position and didn't expect too much from me during this time. That was a big load off my mind.

Near the end of Linda's pregnancy, I was due to receive my next transfer to a large office. It was almost certain to be New York, better known as "Hell on Earth." The thing about New York was that it was extremely difficult to find an affordable place to live on an agent's salary. Most agents had to move seventy miles away in order to find affordable housing. Agents were living in New Jersey, Connecticut, and Pennsylvania and had to carpool with four or five others to drive into the city. The average commute was upward of two hours one-way. Add that to a nine-hour workday and you've got a melancholy situation.

I was working with two other second-office agents who were up for transfer. The first one received his orders for New York on a Monday and promptly walked into the SAC's (Special-Agent-in-Charge) office and quit the Bureau. The second agent received his orders on a Wednesday and waited until Friday to quit. I was next in line.

I was called into the SAC's office. "Dave, I've got your transfer orders here. No surprise, you're going to New York. So are you quitting too?" the SAC asked.

"I don't think so, boss. I've got one kid, another on the way, and no other job to go to. I'll take my chances," I said.

The SAC grinned and held out his hand. "Thanks, the Atlanta Division was starting to get a bad reputation," he said.

I broke the news to Linda, who figured we had more important things to worry about since she was about to give birth. It was with a huge sigh of relief that a completely healthy Katherine Laurel Nadolski was born on January 7, 1985. With our minds finally at ease, we were ready to face the next Bureau adventure.

A couple weeks after Linda gave birth, we once again imposed on Linda's sister-in-law, Nancy, to cover for us while we took our New York house-hunting trip. Linda and I decided to look for houses in New Jersey and Connecticut. New Jersey was my choice since it was the closest commute to Manhattan and loaded with New York agents. Connecticut was Linda's choice. Guess who won out.

Our Connecticut real-estate agent was a very professional guy by the name of Ken Martin. Ken explained that with our budget we would never get any closer to New York than Stratford, which was eighty-five miles from the FBI office in Manhattan. Our first outing with Ken was on a blustery, rainy day in February. Tree limbs were crashing down onto the street—great start. We looked at a few dreary places that we couldn't afford before heading back to Ken's office.

"Let's take another look at the listing book to see if we can get something in your budget," said Ken.

Linda had already beat Ken to the punch and was leafing through the book. She located what appeared to be a sizable house located on a pond in Stratford. It was within our budget.

"Ken, what's the story with this house and why didn't you show this to us before?" Linda asked.

Ken looked at her and said, "Well, Linda, I'm reluctant to show you this place because the people there are scary as hell and it's a dump."

"Well, set it up. Dumpy houses are our specialty," Linda said.

As luck would have it, Ken was able to get a showing for later in the day. As we drove down the street, we observed nice houses on the block, but that changed dramatically when we reached our destination. The house was a two-story, cedar-shingled colonial and in sad shape. The house had brown paint that was flaking off, the shrubs and grass were wrecked, the garage doors were sagging, and the roof and gutters were obviously in bad condition.

"Ken, what's that smell?" I asked as we exited the car in the driveway. "The house," he replied.

I looked over at Linda, and to my horror, she was smiling and nodding.

Ken rang the doorbell, and immediately a very large and vicious German shepherd hit the front door barking, snarling, and foaming at the mouth. A woman on the inside screamed, "KILLER, NO!"

As she opened the door with one hand, the other wrapped around Killer's thick leather collar, she casually greets us with "Oh, hi, let me lock up the dog."

Ken turned around and mouthed, "I warned you."

A few minutes later, the lady returned to the front door and invited us in. As we entered, the smell got worse. I looked down at what appeared to have been carpeting at one time. It, like the walls, was dingy brown and had been worn through to the underlying hardwood in a path extending from the kitchen to the living room. As we entered the living room, I noticed three adult males wearing motorcycle jackets and shirts displaying Harley Davidson insignia. They were all flopped on the couch, watching TV. Did I mention it was a weekday?

"Hi, guys, sorry for the short notice, but we would like to look at the house," Ken announced.

No answer.

I looked at Linda, who cheerily proclaimed, "Oh look, hardwood flooring under the carpet!"

We quickly walked through the living room to a door that led to a side porch. I peered out and observed that the flagstone floor had collapsed, and the screens were all torn up and laying in the side yard. *Must be Killer's room*, I thought.

Next, we ventured into the kitchen. No surprise, it was a total gut job. We climbed a set of stairs to the second floor where the bathroom and bedrooms were located. As I neared the top stair, I half-expected to see Kathy Bates round the corner with an ax leveled at my head. Luckily, that didn't happen. In fact, the upstairs rooms were in fairly nice shape except for the master bedroom, which was painted black and had swords and firearms adorning the walls. Not our decorating taste. I'd seen enough, so we thanked the nice lady and got back to the car. Once inside, Ken and I started laughing out loud.

When I finally caught my breath, I said to Ken, "Oh my god, you were right! What a freaking dump!"

Ken replied, "Don't blame me! I tried to steer you away from it!"

Linda interrupted, "Let's make a full-price offer. I don't want to lose it."

I looked at her skeptically. "Sweetie, I think you've already lost it. I'm talking about your mind!"

"That's the problem with you guys; you have no vision, no artistic sense," replied Linda. "This place is a diamond in the rough. The problems are cosmetic. The house is located at the end of the street on a beautiful pond. It has hardwood under that ugly carpet. The kitchen just needs new cabinets and flooring. The exterior needs painting, and you'll have to do something with the garage doors and fix the side porch. The rest of it is okay."

She continued, "I'll paint the inside and do the wallpapering. By the way, did you notice something when we were in the kitchen? Despite the fact that the wind is blowing forty miles per hour out here, you couldn't hear a thing. The windows are good! Get me back to the office, Ken. We're writing an offer!" Linda ordered.

FBI, NEW YORK DIVISION

The New York Field Office (NYO) was, and still is, the largest FBI office. It's located on Broadway in lower Manhattan. In 1985, it consisted of two whole divisions, staffed by a thousand agents and support employees. One division was devoted entirely to FCI work, and the other division was devoted to the investigation of criminal violations such as organized crime, white-collar crime, violent crime, public corruption, drugs, and fugitives. There were task forces consisting of FBI agents, other federal agents, New York City cops, and state cops. The office was a beehive of activity and bursting at the seams with agents.

I was assigned to the Cuban squad of the FCI Division. During this era of Cold War tension, one half of the FCI Division was devoted exclusively to monitoring the Russian intelligence services. The other half covered the intelligence services of the other Communist Bloc countries, such as

East Germany, Poland, Bulgaria, Lithuania, Cuba, China, and North Korea. All of these countries had representative "missions" to the United
Nations, which conducted legitimate UN business, but they also had intelligence officers assigned as diplomats to the missions. Our job was to
catch the intelligence officers in the act of spying.

It's fair to say that the Bloc country intelligence services were considered the little brothers of the Russian intelligence services. The Russians
fielded two teams, the KGB and the GRU. Both were highly trained and
very good at their jobs. The KGB went after civilian intelligence, and the
GRU focused on military intelligence. The smaller Bloc countries had
single intelligence services, and most of those received their training from
the Russians.

The Cuban intelligence service was closely modeled after the Russian
KGB. They, like the KGB, were staffed by highly competent people.
Unlike the Russians, the Cubans were primarily concerned with self-
preservation. Fidel Castro had managed to beat back one invasion of his
country by the US during the Bay of Pigs disaster but was worried about
another. He had good reason to worry because there were Cuban émigré
groups in the US just itching to launch another attack to reclaim Cuba or
at least kill Castro.

The thing was, despite being an effective and intelligent adversary, the
Cuban intelligence service held no interest for a former cop from Michigan. In other words, I really couldn't give a shit about them. I tried to
care, but all I wanted to do was get over to a criminal squad. Unfortunately, so did everyone else who was stuck doing FCI work. As a result, there
was a rule that anyone assigned to FCI work had to put in at least two
years before even requesting a transfer somewhere else, so I settled in to
do my time.

After about a year and a half on the Cuban squad, I heard the Special
Operations Division was expanding. Special Operations consisted of ten
squads of surveillance agents assigned to support the Criminal and FCI
divisions. I was desperate to get off the Cuban squad, so I went to see
James Kallstrom, chief of Special Operations. Jim was an NYO legend.
He was a Marine Corps officer and Vietnam combat veteran.

As I entered, I introduced myself. "Jim, my name is Dave Nadolski,
and like you, I'm a Vietnam veteran. Before joining the Bureau, I was a
police detective in Sterling Heights, Michigan. I have extensive experience conducting moving surveillances, and the word is you are looking

for additional agents on SO. I'm very interested in transferring to Special Ops."

Jim looked at me and said, "Have a seat, Dave. You have an interesting background. Where are you assigned now?"

"I'm on the Cuban squad," I replied.

"How long have you been in New York?" he asked.

"A year and a half, Jim," I hesitantly replied.

"Damn it, I wish you had said two years. It's tough to get guys out of FCI with less time than that. They've got this ridiculous rule. As much as I'd like to get you on one of my squads supporting the Organized Crime program or Bank Robbery Task Force, I don't have any openings on those squads right now. Tell you what, though: I'm starting two new squads to support FCI operations, and since you are already in FCI, I'd like you to consider a spot on one of these two new squads. I can make that happen right now," Jim said.

A bird in hand is worth two in the bush. I had done my homework on Jim Kallstrom, and the one thing I learned was not to reject any offer he made, even if it wasn't exactly what you had in mind. If I did reject him, I'd spend the rest of my life on the Cuban squad—or worse. I stood, smiled, and offered my hand.

"Jim, I'd be honored to serve on one of your new squads. Thank you for the opportunity!" I said.

A week later, I was off the Cuban squad and on the newly formed Special Operations Squad #11. This squad was created because of some high-profile disasters in which American military men with access to highly classified information had simply walked into Soviet embassies and offered to trade their information for cash.

It was a great break getting out of the office and finally working on the streets. Additionally, I was assigned my own surveillance car, which I could take home. Our squad worked ten-hour shifts, covering days and evenings with some overlap in between, and most important of all, we commuted in and out of Manhattan during nonpeak hours. I finally had my own car, worked a varied schedule, and seldom, if ever, went into the office.

For administrative purposes, we maintained two small residential apartments in the area, one of which was the office of our supervisor, Frank Heaney. Like most of the supervisors, Frank started out with Jim Kallstrom on the Organized Crime squad. When Jim started the Special

Operations Division, he handpicked his supervisors from his squad mates. Jim valued loyalty. He offered it and expected it in return.

Frank didn't take life too seriously. He left the running of the squad to his team leaders. Hector Rivera was our team leader. He was easygoing but expected his team members to give 100 percent to the mission. If, for example, we suddenly found ourselves starting out on a surveillance ten minutes before the normal end of shift, he expected his teammates to do whatever it took, for as long as it took, to identify the subject before calling it quits. During one surveillance, that didn't happen until we finally put the subject into a house in Philadelphia. Long day. Another time we had to follow a guy eighty miles to Bridgeport, Connecticut. Another long day.

Meanwhile, back at the ranch, Linda was itching to put our house on the market. By this time, we had repainted the inside and outside, repaired the side porch and garage doors, and totally gutted and remodeled the kitchen. We had removed the funky carpeting and updated the electrical. The only thing we couldn't improve was our next-door neighbors, Billy and his mother.

Billy was a total juvenile delinquent who lived in his grandma's house with his mother. Mother liked to drink a bit and basically ignored Billy. Billy had a group of likewise delinquent friends who took up residence in the basement and garage, where they played loud music, screamed and yelled, and smoked a lot of dope.

Billy's uncle was a Stratford cop, and on more than one occasion, I had to help him round up Billy's friends and put them against the wall of the garage for pat downs and transfer to the police station. This place was not the restful haven I was seeking, so I was all for finding a quieter place to live.

One day Linda says to me, "Dave, Ken Martin is showing us a house in Trumbull today."

"Oh, really?" I replied suspiciously. "How is it we can afford a place in Trumbull?"

"Oh, don't worry, hon. This house is a real bargain!" she assured me.

"Hmmm, you've got something up your sleeve," I responded.

Trumbull, Connecticut, was a big step up from Stratford, even though the towns bordered one another. While all the houses in Stratford were blue-collar homes built on small lots during the first half of the decade,

Trumbull houses were newer, built on one-acre lots, and were much more upscale.

The next day, we met Ken at a large, white, two-story Greek revival–style house on busy Daniels Farm Road in Trumbull. As I exited the car, I noticed a concrete silo in the backyard, the only remnants from the days when this property was a farm. The garage looked fairly run-down, had a dirt floor, and didn't have a door. The house itself was sad looking, old, and covered in asbestos siding.

Linda was beaming. "This is better than I expected. Let's go inside!"

As we approached the house, I noticed the bulkhead doors on the side of the house were open. I could hear someone down in the cellar. We walked closer and peered into the dark interior.

"Hello? Mr. Nadzam? I'm here to show the house," yelled Ken.

I stepped past Ken and started down the stone stairs. After two steps, I stepped in water up to my ankle. "Whoa, little water problem, Mr. Nadzam?" I enquired.

Mike Nadzam emerged from the gloom wearing rubber waders. "Yeah, 'bout three feet and rising. Guess I could use a sump pump. Let's go inside."

We walked through a dingy back porch into the kitchen. "You don't find original features like this anymore," he proudly announced.

He was certainly right about that. The floor was covered with fifty-year-old green linoleum, and a decrepit kitchen table with peeling yellow paint sat in the middle of the room. The appliances had to have been from the 1940s, at best, and the cabinets were falling off the wall.

I'd seen enough and was about to thank Mike for his time when Linda said, "Okay, let's check out the upstairs bedrooms." With that, she started up the stairs.

"Watch the railing!" called Mike. "It's a little wobbly." I took his advice and slowly followed Linda, keeping my body close to the wall.

The upstairs consisted of five small bedrooms. The floors were sloped, the walls were cracked and bulging in spots, and the ceilings were in bad shape. There were two ancient bathrooms. Like the downstairs windows, the upstairs windows were big and let in a lot of light. Unfortunately, the light illuminated a gigantic potential construction project.

Back outside, I took Linda aside. "Please don't tell me you want to take this on," I pleaded.

Linda said, "It's got good bones, and it's on a fantastic corner lot. I already priced out what it would cost to replace all the walls and ceilings on the first floor. We can do the rest, believe me!"

Already priced it out? What the hell has she been doing while I've been at work?

"Well, I've always wanted an indoor swimming pool in my basement," I glumly replied.

Since Ken was going to represent us on the purchase of the Trumbull place, he was okay with us listing our house as a "for sale by owner." In fact, he provided us with advice and contract paperwork in the event we landed a buyer.

As it turned out, we were offering our house during a time of low housing inventory; it was a seller's market. We decided to list the Stratford house for $75,000 over what we bought it for a year earlier, and we figured holding an open house was the way to go. We advertised the open house for 11:00 a.m. to 3:00 p.m. on the next Sunday.

Linda had the house decorated perfectly but couldn't stand to be there when people walked through. She took the girls to her sister's house and left me to deal with the potential customers. At 10:00 a.m., there was a knock at the door. I opened it to a nice-looking middle-aged lady who introduced herself as Sarah.

"I know we're early, but we are very interested in this area and this house in particular. I grew up down the street and have really admired the work you've done on this house over the past year."

"Hi, Sarah, I'm Dave. Come on in and take as much time as you want. If you have any questions, I'll be available," I said.

With that, Sarah and her companion swept in and started inspecting every square inch. I heard "ooohhhs" and "aaahhhs" every few minutes. After about a half hour, Sarah approached me and said, "Dave, I know what I like and I like this house. I love this neighborhood as well. I want to make a full-price offer right now."

To say I was shocked by the offer coming in before the start of the showing would be an understatement. I was equally shocked by the number of interested buyers that poured through the doors starting at 11:00 a.m. When all was said and done, I had spoken to three potential buyers who made offers that day. I called Linda to report in.

"How'd it go?" she asked. "Did anyone show up?"

"Actually, we did have some interest. In fact, the last bid was for $10,000 over asking price," I answered.

"Stop screwing with me, damn it. I'm serious! What really happened?" Linda demanded.

"Linda, I AM serious. We have a bidding war!"

"Oh my God, Trumbull here we come!"

For the next five years, I continued to work on the surveillance squad and Linda set about rehabbing the "farm." She researched the history of the house and determined it was built in 1830. We were rescued early during our renovation by Stanley Kowalski, a retired carpenter, WWII combat veteran of the Pacific campaign, and guardian angel. Stanley was a dead ringer for Clarence from *It's a Wonderful Life*. Swear to God, he looked just like him. He was chomping on an apple and wearing a blue stocking cap, despite the fact that it was spring. He stood about five feet, five inches; was hunched over and missing a bunch of teeth; and dressed like a homeless person.

"Here I am. What do you want?" Stanley asked.

Linda showed him the garage. "Looks like you need doors; you don't have any, ya know," declared Stanley.

"Right, that's why you're here, remember?" I responded.

"That's a big job, I work slowly, and I'm old in case you didn't notice," Stanley replied.

By this time Linda was looking for someone to jump out and declare, "You're on *Candid Camera*!" "Okay, Stanley, I get it. Do you want the job or what?"

"Don't worry, little lady; I'll handle it. Just don't expect miracles, okay? I'm hungry; think you can fix me lunch?" Stanley asked brazenly.

I guess most people would have kicked the troll off their property, but Linda just made him lunch instead. That was lucky because that was the first day of a five-year collaboration that eventually resulted in the complete transformation of the dump we bought. I worked under the direction of master carpenter Stanley Kowalski and learned more from him than just about anyone else in my entire life. Admittedly, he was rough around the edges, but we loved the old goat and he practically became a grandpa to Liz and Kate. He taught me how to build. He gave me an old Sears table saw that I still use. In many ways, Stanley was a renaissance man. He had ideas and opinions about everything. He was an inventor, a thinker, and the most politically incorrect human being on the planet. I don't think he wandered more than ten miles from his home in Bridgeport, Connecticut, except to fight in WWII. He was a lifelong bachelor too, which amazed Linda.

"Stanley, why didn't you ever get married?" Linda asked one day.

"Well, I had a girlfriend once who I thought was going to be my wife, but she left Bridgeport and that was that," explained Stanley.

"Where did she go, California?" asked Linda.

"Nope, she moved to Waterbury," Stanley said.

"Stanley, you can get to Waterbury in a half hour," noted Linda.

"Not me," responded Stanley.

Maybe it's better that Stanley never married. He would have required a very special mate.

New York was my third duty station with the FBI and could have been my last if that was my desire. I had fulfilled all the mandatory transfers, so any additional transfers would be my choice. Agents can request a transfer to any particular office by getting on a list for their "office of preference." In my case, I chose the Boston Division for my office of preference. Linda and I didn't have any particular connection to Boston, but we had vacationed in Massachusetts and other New York agents who grew up in Boston described the city as a paradise and the office as a fantastic place to work. Boston is a very livable city, and the office has a lot of interesting work for agents. Linda liked New England; therefore, Boston seemed a likely choice. The problem was Boston was popular and had a long list of agents waiting for a transfer there. Many had more time on the job than I did, so my chances of getting a transfer were pretty slim. By this time in our lives, Linda was ready for another move. The house was as fixed up as it could be and would probably sell quickly.

During our stay in Connecticut, we spent a lot of time in a very quaint and special town located twenty miles further inland from Trumbull. Newtown was nestled in the hills and had the special small-town atmosphere and welcoming feel that we were looking for. While living there would add considerably to my commute, I was angling for a transfer to the New Rochelle, New York, resident agency, which is a satellite office located east of New York City and within commuting distance of our proposed new home.

Linda and I decided to build a new house this time. We located a four-acre parcel in a secluded section of the town just down the street from where our kids would go to school at Sandy Hook Elementary School.

We put the Trumbull house on the market and met with a builder. Timing would be crucial, but we were sure we could pull this off, so we offered $100,000 for the building lot. Our offer was accepted, and we found a buyer for the Trumbull property when, all of a sudden, the plan started to unravel. First, the transfer to New Rochelle fell through, but at the same time, I received another call from FBI headquarters—they wanted to know if I was still interested in a transfer to Boston. I called back and asked for more details. I was number twenty-three on the transfer list, so I couldn't understand why they were calling me. I was told that Boston was adding two more squads to cover the recent rise in bank failures caused by rampant financial institution fraud, and they needed twenty-five agents in Boston as soon as possible. I had twenty-four hours to decide and get back to them before they moved on down the list. We were scheduled to close on the Newtown property the very next day. We had put down $10,000, which was nonrefundable.

"Linda, what do you think? Should we take the financial hit and go for the Boston transfer?" I asked.

We thought about it and talked it over and ultimately decided to take the transfer. I called my lawyer. "Bill, we can't close on the Newtown property tomorrow; I'm being transferred to Boston," I said.

"Dave, you realize that you are walking away from the $10,000 down payment?" he asked.

"Yeah, Linda and I decided that Boston is a better decision in the long run," I said.

"Okay, I'll call the owner's lawyer and cancel the deal. Let me make a suggestion. The land is owned by a nephew of Aristotle Onassis, and if you write him a personal note explaining that you were suddenly transferred, he may reconsider the nonrefundable down payment. It's worth a shot."

"Good idea, Bill. I'll give it a try," I said.

So I did write to Aristotle Onassis's nephew and explained my situation. I received a note from his lawyer that half of my down payment was being refunded. I sent a second note expressing our sincere gratitude for his show of generosity. This transfer was a lifesaver in another way because my buyer had backed out of the Trumbull deal. Without the Boston transfer, I would have been stuck with a $100,000 building lot and an unsold house, but the transfer made me eligible for an FBI buyout for the Trumbull house.

When an agent is transferred, a company hired by the federal government will step in to buy the house if the agent is unable to sell it. The agent receives less than what he or she could get on the open market, but it's a sure deal. This provides real peace of mind because unsold houses, as a result of FBI transfers, were a serious problem for agents, some of whom actually had to declare bankruptcy. Well, we were finally putting New York in our rearview mirror, and I was happy as a pig in slop.

6

TUNNEL VISION

MCI NORFOLK

Tony was beginning to learn the ropes. The most direct prison path starts with a stint in a maximum-security prison or a medium-security prison, which leads to a minimum-security facility, then work release in a halfway house back in the community. Tony's sights were definitely set on doing well and eventually getting out, but the next step was surviving Norfolk, a medium-security prison where Tony was transferred from Walpole after six months. MCI Norfolk was physically located a short distance from Walpole, but as a place to do time, it was as different from Walpole as you could find. Norfolk had programs, school, vocational training, and campus-style housing. The guards wore street clothes instead of uniforms. The place was still surrounded by walls, wire, and gun towers; after all, it wasn't summer camp.

While eating in the chow hall on his first day in Norfolk, someone slid up behind Tony, put a strong grip on his shoulder, and hissed in his ear, "Watch your back, asshole, or somebody will jam a blade into it!"

Tony's first reaction was to bolt, but since that's not the way it's played in prison, he slowly lowered his fork and turned to face whoever it was.

"You cocksucker!" exclaimed Tony. He was looking into the beaming grin of Kevin Gildea. Kevin was a burglar by trade and fellow Quincy, Massachusetts, homeboy.

"I heard they sprung you from Walpole. It's nice to see a friendly face," commented Kevin.

"Hey, likewise, Kevin. Still drawing pictures of naked women?"

"Sure, bro. Wanna buy one?" asked Kevin.

Kevin was an interesting character, and Tony was glad to see him. He was a very gifted artist who specialized in pencil sketches, paintings, portraits, blueprints, and schematics. Kevin physically resembled the mad professor from *Back to the Future* and had an IQ to match, but his short-comings included drugs, prostitutes, and gambling, which led to problems with lock picking and breaking into houses and businesses. Kevin was very lazy, and real jobs bored him to death. The "big score" was all he really cared about, and his relentless pursuit of that goal would one day result in an unlikely alliance between Tony and the FBI.

"Dude, I'm working in the sign shop. Come visit me up there when you get a chance," said Kevin.

"Sure. As soon as I have some freedom to move around, I'll look you up," said Tony.

Tony started hanging around with Kevin. Tony knew Kevin to be a master manipulator, but it was easy to let your guard down around a seemingly friendly person when you were in an environment surrounded by the potential of sudden death.

"Dude, that's close but not quite right. Hold the pick loosely in your right hand and close your eyes. No distractions, just feel for the pin. It's subtle, but it's there," said Kevin.

Before he knew it, they were practicing lock picking. Kevin taught Tony how to make a serviceable lock pick and how to use it.

"Bingo!" exclaimed Tony after his fifth try. The shackle popped open with a rewarding thunk sound.

"Man, I'm going to make an honest burglar out of you yet," exclaimed Kevin.

Kevin and Tony spent hours practicing on all sorts of locks: door locks, cabinet locks, desk locks. It was fun being able to get into doors that the guards needed keys for.

"Tony, I want to let you in on something I've been thinking about," whispered Kevin after the two had been hanging out together for a few months.

"Yeah, what?" asked Tony.

"Well, I've been checking out this prison, and there's a series of underground tunnels. In fact, the kitchen is located underground. The tunnels are no big secret, but there are some secondary tunnels leading from the main tunnel that I want to explore," Kevin announced.

"Why?" asked Tony.

"Because one of them heads right to the wall," Kevin responded.

"And how would you know that?" questioned Tony.

"Have you ever been in the yard and noticed that the snow is melted in a straight line from the main administration building to the wall?" asked Kevin.

"No, I haven't actually," remarked Tony.

"It's supposed to snow tonight. Meet me in the yard tomorrow during break, and I'll show you what I'm talking about," Kevin said.

Sure enough, while standing in the freezing yard the next day, Kevin pointed out his find.

"Look, Tony; what do you see over there?" Kevin nodded to the right.

Tony saw a bare line in the snow heading under the wall and out to the powerhouse beyond the wall.

"And look over there," said Kevin nodding to his left where Tony observed another straight line of bare ground heading from the administration building to the wall between two watch towers.

"Well, I'll be damned!" exclaimed Tony. "Can you put your ear on a railroad track and hear a train coming as well?"

Kevin laughed and slapped Tony's shoulder. "Man, I gotta get into those tunnels, and you're coming with me," he said.

Tony wasn't about to add more time on by trying some whacked-out escape plan, but he did agree to a little tunnel exploration with Kevin. Just getting caught in the tunnels would have earned them attempted escape charges, but boredom got the better of Tony. The next day they located the secondary tunnel running toward the powerhouse. This tunnel was off the main tunnel near the kitchen and was locked, but the door was out of view of any eyes, staff, or inmates.

"Keep an eye out, dude," whispered Kevin as he removed his lock pick from his sock.

He was through the lock like a hot knife through butter, and they were inside. The tunnel was a "pipe chaser" that transported steam from the powerhouse to the main prison. The tunnel had incandescent bulbs with little cages hanging by their cord, and the pipes in the tunnel were long and numerous.

"Oh man, look at this pipe; it's huge!" exclaimed Kevin. "This mother must need a huge opening through the wall. Let's go!"

Kevin took off running. They traveled about sixty yards, which should have put them under the wall. Sure enough, the wall was there, and the pipe went through it all right. Unfortunately, there was only about an inch of clearance around the pipe.

"Shit, a mouse wouldn't fit through that hole," complained Kevin.

"Roger that. Let's get the fuck out of here," said Tony.

Back in the sign shop, they discussed the situation.

"Kevin, we were lucky to get out of that tunnel without being caught. You had that fucking pick in your shoe to pick the lock at the end of the tunnel. That's enough to get us busted," Tony warned.

"We made it out okay, didn't we? There were no cameras or microphones or motion detectors down there. We could have camped out. I've got to get a look at the second tunnel. I have no idea where it goes, but I need to get down there and see for myself," remarked Kevin.

The entrance to the second tunnel was located about thirty yards away from the entrance to the first one, so a few days later Kevin and Tony found themselves picking the lock leading into it.

"Jesus Christ, hurry up, Kevin!" exclaimed Tony. Kevin was having a harder time with this lock. It was older and possibly rusted on the inside.

"Shit, I don't get it. It should just give easily," said Kevin as he feverishly worked the pick. Tony was ready to leave the lunatic behind when the lock suddenly gave way and the door creaked open.

"Come on, let's go!" hissed Kevin. They were inside and had the door closed behind them in seconds. This tunnel was darker and wetter and didn't have any steam pipes. In fact, it was unclear why this tunnel even existed.

"Goddamn it, look at that!" whined Kevin. They had gone about forty yards when they encountered what appeared to be a cave-in. Most likely, it was deliberately filled in because the rock and dirt extended another twenty feet to the wall.

"End of the line, Kevin. There's no getting beyond this stone pile," said Tony.

"I'm not so sure," commented Kevin, examining the wall with his flashlight. "I think we can dig through."

Shit, thought Tony, *this guy is nuts!*

Back in the sign shop, Kevin and Tony debated the wisdom of going back.

"Tony, stick with me on this. I know we can dig a hole through the wall and be out on the other side," Kevin argued.

"Man, that's just crazy. I know you like doing nutty things like breaking into occupied houses, but this is just not my bag. Even if we got out, how long do you think we'd stay free?" asked Tony anxiously. "I am officially out of this harebrained scheme. If you want to do it, fine, but this is not going to work, and I'm not about to add time to my sentence!"

Tony was officially out of the escape plan and was staying away from Kevin to avoid any connection with him should, as Tony expected, Kevin get into trouble over his latest obsession.

While Kevin was hatching his escape plan, Tony focused on the newest problem in his life. In order to keep them from screwing with him, Tony had been buying drugs from Tyrone Flowers and Willie Johnson, a couple of the guys in his housing unit. He reasoned, correctly, that they wouldn't burn a good customer. The operation was simple. Tyrone got the drugs in through a guard or from a visit. He sold the drugs to an inmate. The inmate got his people on the outside to send payment to an address provided by Tyrone. So long as the money was delivered, everyone was happy. The problem was inmates were hurt or killed due to a late check, bad check, or simply no check. Tony was calling everyone he knew, with off-the-wall stories for why he needed them to send money to these people. Eventually, his funding dried up, and Tony found himself in debt to Tyrone and Willie. Figuring he had only one way to avoid a beating or stabbing, he decided to cooperate with the prison officials and put Tyrone and Willie out of business.

Prisons have an elite unit of correctional officers known as IPS (Inner Perimeter Security), who conduct investigations within the prison walls. They investigate inmate crime and conduct internal affairs investigations of crooked guards. Tony secretly contacted IPS officer Randall Forester and arranged a clandestine meeting in a private interview room away from the general population.

"So, Tony, what's up?" asked Officer Forester. "Did somebody steal your Jell-O?"

Forester was a no-nonsense eighteen-year veteran of the correction system and had seen it all and done it all.

"Not quite, boss; I hate Jell-O. I want to talk to you about an established drug ring operating in my housing unit," replied Tony. This got the interest of Officer Forester.

"Who, exactly, and how does it work?" asked Forester.

"Flowers and Johnson are bringing in a lot of Ts. They have a pretty sophisticated operation," explained Tony.

"Actually, Tony, we are aware of these guys but have never been able to get close enough to do anything about it. Are you willing to help us out?" asked Forester.

"I am, boss. I can let you know the next time a load comes in and you can catch them dirty, but I need your promise of something in return," replied Tony.

"What's that?" asked Forester warily.

"These fuckers are going to kill me pretty soon, so I need them out of my hair once and for all, and then I also need a transfer to a minimum-security prison. They got friends who will eventually put this all together and come for me, even if Flowers and Johnson are taken out," Tony said.

"When's the next shipment, Tony?" asked Forester.

"Pretty soon. Do we have a deal or what?" replied Tony.

Forester stared at Tony for a full twenty seconds and appeared to be pondering the request.

"I don't run this place, Tony, but I'll talk to the warden this afternoon. Meet me back here tomorrow, same time. I'll have an answer for you then."

That night, Tony had a tough time sleeping. He lay on his back, wired and staring at the ceiling. He listened to the snores of twenty inmates and the distant footfalls of the housing guard making his rounds. He realized that he had crossed a big line and was playing a very dangerous game. His life was now in the hands of Officer Forester, who could save him or throw him to the wolves. One way or the other, this time next week he would be either dead or in a better place. The thing that disturbed him most was the realization that dead might be a better place.

The next day Tony opened the door to the interview room and found Officer Forester waiting for him. He had a wide smile as he said, "Sit down, Tony. I've got some good news for you."

Tony felt the stress start to drain from his body as he slowly lowered himself into the metal chair. "Really, boss? I haven't heard any good news in a long time," remarked Tony.

"Well, your ship has finally docked. The warden is very interested in stopping Flowers and Johnson. We feel this could be a huge bust, and I am authorized to tell you he's accepted your offer. After this thing goes down, you'll be transferred to a camp. Easy living for the rest of your sentence. How's that sound?" asked Officer Forester.

Tony couldn't believe this was happening. It was like winning the lottery! A minimum-security camp? Unreal.

"Thanks, boss. You don't know how relieved I am to hear that!" exclaimed an excited Tony. "Don't worry; this thing will go down like clockwork, and you'll get these guys dirty as hell."

Forester had a wide grin as he stood to shake Tony's hand. "Just what I wanted to hear!"

Because Tony was buying drugs and living in the same housing unit as Tyrone Flowers and Willie Johnson, he was in a perfect position to set them up. A week after his meeting with IPS officer Randall Forester, the drugs were coming in. Tony had gotten word to Forester and arranged for a signal to indicate when the drugs were in Flowers's possession.

At 3:00 p.m., Flowers walked quickly into his room. He had just come from a meeting with a visitor who had passed him a load of pills. When Tony was sure that Flowers was counting and dividing his load, he stepped out of the housing unit and zipped up his jacket. While Tony didn't see the officers, he was sure they were watching, and by zipping his jacket, he had given the signal that the drugs were inside.

Suddenly all hell broke loose. A dozen IPS officers stormed the building and charged into Flowers's room. He and Johnson had nowhere to go and didn't have time to flush the dope. They were caught red-handed. Tony watched from a distance as the cuffed dealers were led away. A little while later, Tony returned to the unit.

"What's this I hear about Flowers and Johnson getting busted?" he asked another inmate. "I was looking forward to my delivery. I can't believe this shit!" Tony kicked a wastebasket down the hall in a show of frustration at losing his dope. Secretly he was having a difficult time managing to keep a straight face.

Unfortunately for Tony, his elation was short lived. Suspicion that he was the informer quickly spread, fueled by an unlikely source. Kevin

Gildea had screwed up and got caught exploring the tunnels beneath the prison, and the day after the drug bust, he was charged with attempted escape. He quickly let it be known that Tony informed on him. That wasn't even close to the truth, but it didn't really matter because most people were beginning to believe it.

Tony made a beeline for Officer Forester. "Boss, I came through for you and got you the dope peddlers. Trouble is I'm being fingered for setting up Flowers and Johnson. You've got to get me transferred like you promised! I won't live long otherwise," complained Tony.

"Tony, relax. I can't just snap my fingers and get you transferred, and I can't control what the guys think. Maybe your best bet at this point is PC," Forester said.

PC, or "protective custody," is an isolation area within the prison where pedophiles and informants are locked up in individual cells. "Boss, if I go into PC, I might as well write 'TONY IS A RAT' on the cafeteria wall!" Tony complained.

"Tony, that's the best I can do for you now. This will all blow over and you can rejoin the general population, you'll see," Forester said.

"Mr. Forester, what about my deal? Can't you talk to the warden? I stuck my neck out and you're going to let it get chopped off!" Tony asserted.

Forester wasn't used to an inmate talking to him this way.

"Listen, you little prick, I don't need your bullshit! Take PC or take your chances in general population; I don't give a fuck one way or the other. Now get out of my office!" shouted Forester.

Tony was pissed, but he wasn't crazy, so he went from Forester's office directly to his counselor and pleaded, "Mr. Bennet, I've got a real credibility problem in general population and I need PC now."

That night Tony was in an isolation cell staring at the cracked concrete ceiling and hoping it would just fall in on him and end his troubles. He felt like a fool for trusting Forester and vowed that if he lived through this, he'd never trust another cop again. But the person he was really pissed at was Kevin Gildea. He was the guy responsible for Tony's current situation. *Watch your ass, Gildea. Payback is a bitch,* thought Tony as he finally drifted off.

7

THE PROMISED LAND

FBI, BOSTON DIVISION, 1991

The sale of the Trumbull house went fairly smoothly, thanks to the FBI's buyout program. It was 1991, and we were in the midst of a slight economic recession, which was having an impact on property values; they were tumbling through the floor. We quickly accepted a buyout for $20,000 less than the private cash purchase we had arranged before that buyer mysteriously backed out. At least we still came out ahead and were heading to Massachusetts knowing what we could afford at the other end. We were granted a house-hunting trip, and after viewing houses north and west of Boston with several realtors, we started working with Margie Mitchell, a RE/MAX realtor covering the northwest suburbs of Boston.

Margie introduced us to her ex-boyfriend, Bob, who was a carpenter. We looked at a few places Bob had built and agreed to hire him for our build. Next, we located four acres of wooded property in a proposed subdivision in Groton, Massachusetts, that had gone under during the housing slump. The lots had been repossessed by the bank, and not a single house had been built. The land was beautiful, rolling farmland with views of the hills in western Massachusetts.

Groton was upscale and home to two very prestigious prep schools, the Groton School and Lawrence Academy. The downtown was located on one main street and contained the quintessential elements of old New England—historic churches, houses, and a rambling eighteenth-century hotel known as the Groton Inn. The town cemetery had gravestones dating back to the Revolutionary War.

We loved the feel of Groton and decided to put in an offer on the four-acre wooded parcel. The bank was asking $100,000, but we offered $80,000 and they quickly accepted. We later learned that no offers had been put in on any of the lots they were stuck holding. This particular lot was elevated and had a lot of trees, many of which would need to be cleared for the house and backyard.

Linda had a building plan for a stately, four-bedroom, colonial-style house and negotiated the build with Bob. We settled on a price and obtained a building loan, and Bob got to work with his crew of three.

With domestic life under control, I was able to concentrate on beginning my professional career in Boston. I was assigned to the Public Corruption squad. As the name implies, we investigated corrupt public officials. The office was located in the JFK Federal Building, physically located next to Boston City Hall in an area called City Hall Plaza. Our squad space was the typical setup: a huge room with desks jammed next to one another and no privacy, but at least it was painted institutional gray. It was nice to be back in the office again.

I partnered up with a young agent by the name of Stu Robinson. He and I were assigned to the same Bureau car. Since Stu was single and lived in an apartment close to the office, I was free to take the car home. Stu could have been an ax murderer, but I would have loved him nonetheless, all because he walked to work. In truth, Stu was an excellent agent. He was young, only twenty-six years old, having joined the Bureau right out of law school. He was six feet tall, athletic, and well-built. He had an engaging personality and no trouble finding a date. Stu was a native of Chicago and had the congenial personality and familiar sense of humor of a fellow Midwesterner.

Since Stu and I were assigned the same Bureau car, we paired up for cases as well. Unlike police detectives, FBI agents do not have partners formally assigned to them. We were assigned our own caseload and would team up with other agents as needed. If, for example, a search warrant was being executed or a subject was being arrested, the whole squad would come together to assist. The case agent would work up the arrest plan or search warrant, brief the squad on individual assignments, then call the shots at the scene.

Jimmy Siracusa and Angelo Rinchuso were a couple of squad mates who were joined at the hip. Jimmy was a Boston native with a keen nose for crime and the tenacity—and temperament—of a bulldog. He loved working public corruption cases and was great at informant development. He looked a lot like Columbo and employed the same techniques. Jimmy was five feet, eight inches and rumpled, balding, and a little overweight. Basically, he looked like a guy waiting for a bus.

Angelo was another Chicago transplant. He had been a Chicago Police homicide detective before joining the Bureau. Unlike quiet, unassuming Jimmy, Angelo was a bull in a china shop and a practical joker. He'd glue your phone, desk pad, and pens to your desktop as a prank. He'd sneak into your Bureau car and flip on the emergency lights and siren so when you started it in the garage, it would explode with flashing beacons and screaming siren sounds. At firearms training, Angelo liked to wear his black Chicago Homicide sweatshirt with a picture of a handgun pointing at the viewer. The phrase below the gun read: "Chicago Homicide, Our Day Begins When Your Day Ends."

Jimmy's method of operation would be to "stop in" to have a conversation with a low-level corrupt public official, who, upon seeing his FBI credentials, would no doubt think, *Are you shitting me? Who is this guy really?* A half-hour later, this same guy would be sweating, stammering, and trying to remember how many lies he'd told. Jimmy, still wearing his Columbo raincoat, had the guy twisted in knots. At this point, Jimmy would just close his notebook, look the guy in the face, and say, "So you know and I know everything you just told me is pure horseshit."

He'd look over at Angelo who was eyeballing the suspect like a drill sergeant. Jimmy would then say, "We can work this out one of two ways: we've got enough on you to go to the US attorney, which would be a real shame because you're just a bag man. As much as we'd really hate to do that, however, we'll settle for half a loaf if that's all we can get."

At this point, Angelo has pulled his chair a little closer to the suspect and is looking very grim, but he's actually enjoying this immensely. Jimmy continues, "What we really want to do is get to your boss, and we could use some help. The choice is yours, of course, but you need to tell us now because once we leave this room, all bets are off."

The suspect knows the roof has just caved in on him, but he wants to survive. Hell, he figures, all he did was pick up the bribe money and deliver it to the mayor. Why should he spend years in prison for that greedy prick?

"Okay, I'll wear a wire," he says out loud.

With that said, Jimmy sits back and glances over at Angelo, who's nodding his head. "Yahtzee."

This was the way business was conducted on the Public Corruption squad, and as such, we chalked up a lot of convictions and made a big impact in the Boston area. While we were riding high, we had no way of knowing about the lit powder keg the Boston Division was sitting on.

My first supervisor on the Public Corruption squad was a small, skinny man by the name of John Morris. John had previously supervised the Organized Crime squad. I was disappointed in the way John looked and acted; he was not my picture of a macho, streetwise FBI veteran. He looked more like a meek bookkeeper.

I didn't know it at the time, but I could have made the biggest public corruption bust of my life by simply getting up from my desk, going into John's office, and putting the handcuffs on him because John was on the take. While supervisor of the Organized Crime squad, John began taking money from notorious Boston gangster and FBI informant James "Whitey" Bulger.

John, after seeing the writing on the wall, made a full confession of accepting bribes from Whitey, who was the informant of Special Agent John Connelly. John Connelly was a decorated FBI agent working on the Organized Crime squad, and Whitey, considered a leader of the Irish mob, was providing Connelly information on the Italian organized crime family in Boston. While the formal relationship between Connelly and Whitey was one of agent and informant, the lines became blurred, and there were serious questions about who was running the partnership. So much so in fact that Connelly was convicted of federal racketeering and sentenced to ten years in prison because of his relationship with Whitey. Whitey, who was charged for his ongoing criminal activity, escaped capture and spent sixteen years as a fugitive. He was eventually captured by the FBI in California and returned to Boston. On August 12, 2013, he was found guilty of thirty-one counts, including racketeering charges and eleven murders, and sentenced to two life terms. He was murdered in prison on October 30, 2018, two days after being transferred to the federal prison at Hazelton, West Virginia. He was beaten to death with a padlock in a sock. He was eighty-nine years old and in a wheelchair. Needless to say, Whitey had a lot of enemies due to the life he had led.

After a few years on the Public Corruption squad, I went in to see ASAC (Assistant Special-Agent-in-Charge) Mike Ward, who was in charge of the squad I was yearning to join. C-6 was the Boston squad handling the VCMO cases, which stands for Violent Crime, Major Offenders. In other words, they investigated all the fun stuff I joined the Bureau for in the first place. They handled all the bank robberies, armored car robberies, kidnappings, extortion cases, art thefts, homicides, and so on that were covered by federal jurisdiction. If it was a case you'd kill for, it was handled by squad C-6.

I went after ASAC Ward like a bad case of poison ivy. I stopped in, wrote him memos, accosted him on the street, and generally became a pain in the ass. I worked him like I worked Jim Kallstrom in New York, only a lot harder. I pleaded to his sense of fair play, reminded him that I did my time in New York like a good soldier, pointed out that my police background was a perfect fit, and declared that I had generally crawled through enough shit to earn a break.

"All right, God dammit, I give up! The next opening on C-6 is yours. Now stop coming in my office," Ward complained.

I left Ward's office with a huge grin on my face. All I had to do now was murder someone on C-6. Luckily it didn't come to that. In fact, an audit revealed C-6 was down two slots, so I slid in unopposed.

C-6 consisted of fifteen agents and six police officers. The police officers were from the Massachusetts State Police, Boston Police Department, and Cambridge Police Department. The cops had desk space on our squad and were primarily responsible for working the numerous bank robberies that came into the Boston Division. The FBI agents were assigned bank robberies as well but were also responsible for the other violations that fell under federal jurisdiction. We worked together as a team known as the Bank Robbery Task Force.

Everyone was expected to develop informants to keep track of the criminal gangs who were committing bank heists and armored car robberies. One agent was assigned as the Bank Robbery Coordinator for our squad. While I was on C-6, that job was held by Special Agent Margaret Cronin. Peg was the only female agent on our squad and was a very quiet, diligent, and meticulous agent. She was a Boston native and started her law enforcement career in the Massachusetts Department of Corrections and eventually earned an appointment to the FBI. Peg supervised the bank robbery investigations and as coordinator developed much of the intelligence on the gang members who were committing the bank and armored car robberies. Peg had a special knack for developing informants within criminal gangs. She knew how to relate to people and by using her nonthreatening, mild-mannered method of talking would gain the trust of some of the worst criminals. Peg was a real-life version of Special Agent Adam Frawley of *The Town*, the Ben Affleck movie about a violent gang of bank robbers from the Charlestown section of Boston. In the movie, the cops and FBI eventually confront the gang in a deadly street battle. The movie was pretty close to the truth in fact.

During March and April of 1996, we were experiencing a larger-than-normal number of armed and unarmed bank robberies in the towns north of Boston. We were unable to observe any particular similarities as some were committed by a single male passing a note and others by a male and female couple using firearms and announcing a bank takeover, and it didn't appear as if the same people were involved. The only similarity was the fact that everyone was disguised in some way and the robberies were north of Boston.

On April 8, 1996, the new squad supervisor, John Trahon, called a mandatory squad meeting. John and Peg were at the front of the room, and after everyone was assembled, John made an announcement.

"You all know that we have been getting our butts kicked north of Boston. Peg has developed an informant who is involved with these robberies. Until now, we were unaware that there was one particular group responsible for all these jobs, but as it turns out that is exactly what is going on. Peg has learned they plan to strike tomorrow, so we are putting on a full-court press and plan to catch them in the act. Peg will fill you all in on the details," explained John.

"Thanks, John," responded Peg. "I had a meeting with a disgruntled member of the North Shore gang today. He needed a friend. I found out that four members are planning to rob a small bank located in a strip mall on Alewife Parkway in Cambridge tomorrow. My source identified the four participants as three men and one woman. These folks have been involved in armed and unarmed bank robberies before, so we can't take any chances. We must assume they will be armed and dangerous. I know where they will be meeting up first thing in the morning. If they follow their normal pattern, they will at some point steal a car to use in the robbery. They will either have with them or will purchase disguises. After stealing the car, two of the suspects will use the stolen car for the robbery. One of the two will drive, and the other will actually enter the bank. The remaining two will be in a 'clean' car and will meet the two robbers after the holdup. All four will get into the clean car for their escape."

Peg continued her instruction: "We need to have discreet surveillance on this group at all times, which, as you know, means two specialized surveillance squads will be following the group on the ground and from the air as well. All of you guys will be following behind the surveillance teams monitoring their every move. Once the suspects get into the vicinity of the bank, I'll call on one of you to go into the bank. That agent will hold the door shut, thus preventing the robbers from entering the bank. The rest of you will surround, subdue, and arrest the suspects as they approach the bank. All of you need to be in your cars and on the radio at 7:00 a.m. tomorrow. Make sure the radios are coded and scrambled. We can't be communicating in the clear just in case they have police scanners. Any questions?" Peg asked.

There were no questions as this was a fairly routine takedown operation, but I did have a personal issue I needed to discuss with Peg.

"Peg, can I talk to you for a minute please?" I asked.

"Sure, Dave. What's up?" replied Peg.

"Well, I've got a problem with tomorrow. I'm committed to address a large group of high school students at 10:00 a.m. I agreed to give my speech on careers in the FBI, and the school resource officer would look like a real ass if I didn't show up. If you think you'll need me, I'll get him to reschedule, but it seems like this is going to be a real Cecil B. DeMille operation with more people than you actually need," I said.

"Don't worry about it, Dave. I've got more than enough people, and I understand not wanting to go back on your commitment to the school. Actually, there's a good chance that things will still be playing out by the time you finish up, so just join in when you're available," Peg said.

"Thanks, Peg. I appreciate your consideration. I'll limit the questions and get back here as soon as possible," I said.

Throughout the morning, I was worried about missing the big takedown, but I was thankful there were no hard feelings over it. At around 11:00 a.m., I jumped back into my car and headed directly back to Boston. The day was cloudless and warm for early spring in New England. I knew visibility would be perfect for the surveillance. En route, I could hear the radio traffic between the surveillance aircraft and the ground teams, and I immediately realized we were in for a big day. The plane had the foursome squarely in sight. They had already stopped at a party supply store, where they purchased disguises, and as I listened to the radio traffic, I learned they were cruising a parking lot, obviously looking to steal a car.

"Yankee 1 to ground units," called the plane, "subjects are cruising a mall parking lot outside the Sears store on Route 1 in Revere. They are still in the gray Chevy sedan but seem to be interested in a brown Toyota located at the far end of the lot closest to Route 1, copy?"

"We copy Yankee 1 and have the subjects in sight at this time," replied Yankee 6, one of the surveillance agents located in a van disguised as a commercial painting contractor.

"Yankee 6 to all units, one of the male subjects just popped the door on the brown Toyota. This is it!"

"Yankee 6 to all units, the subject is bent over in the front seat; he has started the car and is backing out now. A second male subject has exited the Chevy sedan and jumped into the passenger seat of the Toyota. The Toyota is moving through the parking lot and heading for the exit to Route 1."

"All units, this is Yankee 1. The Toyota is southbound on Route 1, say again, southbound on Route 1 in the right lane, moderate speed; this is now our primary target vehicle."

"Yankee 5 to all units, I have an eyeball on the Toyota. The Chevy is two cars behind the Toyota; both vehicles are southbound on Route 1."

This dialogue continued for about seven minutes with various Yankee units moving in close to the bank robbery suspects and then backing off to avoid suspicion. Eventually, the plane reported both suspect vehicles on Main Street in the town of Medford, located north of Boston. They seemed to be interested in a bank on Main Street.

"Yankee 1 to all units, both suspect vehicles are circling the bank on Main Street. This may be a new target."

This was not good news as it created a situation we were not planning on. We did not have information that the gang was interested in this bank and were not prepared in case they decided to hit it, but we would react no matter what.

"Yankee 1 to all units, the Toyota is heading west on Main Street, and the Chevy is following. It doesn't appear they are going for the Main Street bank after all."

At this point, Peg came on the air: "All units, it looks like they are heading for the original target bank on Alewife Parkway in Cambridge."

As luck would have it, I was situated near the Alewife bank and decided to hide among the cars in the large parking lot. As I listened to the surveillance, it became clear that the subjects were approaching my location; in fact, they were heading directly for the original bank. Since I had not been able to actually observe the subjects or either of the suspect vehicles, I parked in the lot close to the front of the bank.

"Yankee 1 to all units, the Toyota has pulled into the parking lot on Alewife Parkway and is driving past the front door of the bank at this time!"

I was in the right spot at the right time and clearly observed the Toyota as it passed my parking spot in front of the bank. It didn't stop but just kept going past. I was able to observe two men in the front seat but was unable to get a good look at either one of them. I really couldn't tell what they looked like.

Seconds later Peg called me. "Victor 6, are you near the bank?"

"Affirmative, Peg, go ahead," I responded.

"Since you are wearing a business suit today, I want you to go into the bank and stand by there. You'll hold the doors shut when the suspects pull up," Peg instructed.

"Got it, Peg. I'm going inside now," I responded.

With that I quickly made my way into the bank. The bank consisted of a vestibule with an ATM machine. Customers had to pass through a second set of doors to enter the main area of the bank where the tellers were located. I positioned myself in the vestibule and kept a sharp eye out for the Toyota. I was not able to use a portable radio inside the bank for fear of being obvious. The only means of communication I had was a squad cell phone. I pretended to use the ATM while keeping a lookout for the Toyota. According to our plan, as soon as the Toyota pulled up in front of the bank and the passenger got out of the car, I would lock up the double doors leading into the vestibule from the street. The rest of my squad would surround the suspects and jump them.

Sometimes the plan doesn't go exactly the way we expect it to. After about five minutes inside the vestibule, with no sight of the Toyota or my fellow agents, I called into the office and got our command post.

"Hey, this is Nadolski. I'm in this bank with no sign of the subjects or any of our guys. What's going on?" I asked.

"Dave, I don't know. I haven't heard anybody on the air for several minutes now," the command post agent responded.

"Okay, reach out for Peg. Find out what the hell is happening. I don't like hanging out in the wind like this," I demanded.

"Stand by, Dave," replied the command post.

A couple minutes later, the command post called back. "Dave, nobody's answering on the radio; we're in the dark here. You're on your own at this point. I don't know what to say."

We've got a plane up, two surveillance squads, and the whole freaking Bank Robbery Task Force out here and suddenly I'm on my own? *Fine. Improvise, adapt, and overcome*, I thought, trying to steady my nerves.

Another couple of minutes pass, and I happened to notice a guy walking from the middle of the shopping center parking lot heading for the bank. Something about him looked pretty weird. He had a baseball cap, sunglasses, and straw-like hair sticking out from under the cap. He was about six feet tall, fairly muscular, and about twenty-five years old, I figured. He was wearing a short beige-colored jacket, and both his hands were in the pockets. I didn't like the looks of this guy one bit. He could be one of the suspects, but I couldn't tell for sure since I had not gotten a good look at any of them. If he was one of the suspects, he should have a dozen agents on his tail, but he was obviously alone. I had to make a decision, so I decided to let him in. As he entered, I stepped aside and pretended to be using the ATM.

He walked past me, through the second set of doors and into the main area of the bank. I followed close behind and positioned myself at a desk just inside the door where I pretended to fill out a deposit slip, all the while keeping an eagle eye on this guy. At this point, I scanned the interior, taking note of where the tellers and customers are standing. The subject got in line behind two other customers, his hands were still in his pockets, and I'm getting nervous. This doesn't feel right. I line myself up to draw and shoot if need be. My mind is racing, and I'm trying to decide at what point to pull my gun. I finally decide that if this is the guy and he pulls a gun, I'm going to draw and shoot him in the chest. My hand is on my gun, my breathing is under control, I'm laser-focused on his hands, and I'm not going to wait for him to kill a teller before I fire. I hope to God I'm right!

Finally, the subject is at the counter. He removed his hand from his left pocket, and I started to draw my pistol. Thank God, no gun, but he does have a piece of paper. As I secure my pistol back into my holster, I observed him handing the teller the paper; she read it and looked shocked. She started shoveling money into a bag and pushed it to the suspect. The suspect quickly scooped up the bag and started for the exit doors.

At this point, I stepped in front of the guy and pretended to be looking at a paper in my hand. I'm walking slowly for the exit doors. The suspect is practically pushing up behind me; he is clearly in a hurry to exit the bank and no doubt thinking, *Why is this asshole walking so slow in front of me?*

I continued slowly through the first set of doors and stepped into the vestibule where I paused briefly, acutely aware of this man's breath behind me. I looked into the parking lot expecting to see fifteen FBI agents with guns drawn, but the only thing I see is the Toyota, motor running in the parking lot with the getaway driver behind the wheel. There are no FBI agents in sight!

It's clear to me now that there is only one agent between this guy and the getaway car, and that agent is me. As we moved through the second set of doors leading to the sidewalk outside the bank, I figured, *Fuck it.* I turned around and screamed, "FBI! YOU'RE UNDER ARREST!" and immediately hit him in the face.

The shocked look was priceless, but I didn't have time to admire it. As I heard the getaway car screech away, I grabbed for the suspect's head. The hat, hair, and glasses came off in my hand, and he started pounding me with his fists. I did my best against a bigger, younger opponent, but I started to slide for the pavement. On the way down, I grasped his waist area searching for a gun. Thankfully, I didn't find one. I comically slid all the way down to his ankles and had both of my hands wrapped around one foot as he was trying to shake me loose. He actually dragged me fifteen feet down the sidewalk before his tennis shoe came off in my hands and he started to bolt.

Just then, agent Dave Donahue ran up with gun drawn and demanded, "Stop right now asshole or I'll shoot you!"

Surprisingly, the bank robber must have tired himself out beating me up because it worked. He stopped and raised his hands in surrender. I managed to get to my feet and helped Donahue subdue, search, and handcuff the suspect.

"Dave, where the hell is everybody?" I asked incredulously.

"Nads, I have no idea. The surveillance guys suddenly went silent. I don't know where anyone is. I saw you go into the bank and have been waiting out here ever since. This place should be swarming with agents!" Donahue said.

While I was being dragged down the sidewalk, the getaway driver in the Toyota was making his exit. Unfortunately for him, he drove around the back of the strip mall into the waiting arms of three FBI agents, including Peg Cronin who cornered and arrested him. Two down.

At this point, we still had two suspects unaccounted for. They were the two who were parked at the far end of the strip mall in the Chevy. The plan had been for the bank robber to exit the bank, get into the Toyota, and then meet the Chevy. All four subjects would escape in the Chevy and leave the Toyota behind. Luckily for us, one of our more astute C-6 agents, Larry Travaglia, had the Chevy under surveillance. When he heard over the radio that the robber had been captured, he decided to move in on the Chevy.

Larry pulled his car in front of the Chevy, got out, and, with gun drawn, demanded the surrender of the two occupants. Unfortunately, they had other ideas and decided to screw. They smashed into Larry's car, pushed it aside, and exited the parking lot at a very high rate of speed. Larry hated the fact that they escaped and really hated the fact that they damaged his beautiful new Bureau car, so he took off after them. A high-speed chase ensued for about a half mile when the Chevy suddenly slammed on its brakes and pulled a 180 in the middle of the street. Larry was hot on the Chevy's ass and couldn't stop in time to avoid smashing into the driver's side of the car. The momentum of the crash sent both cars sailing over the sidewalk and into a chain link fence on the other side. Since the passengers of the Chevy were trapped in their car, Larry simply climbed out of his wrecked car, slid over the hood Hollywood-style, and stuck his pistol into the ear of the Chevy driver, demanding their surrender.

At this point, things could have gone very wrong because just as Larry was approaching the Chevy with his gun drawn, a uniformed Massachusetts state trooper pulled up. He happened to be driving past and had no idea what was going on. Luckily, Larry had the habit of wearing his FBI badge on his belt clip where it was visible and was able to convince the trooper of his identity. Larry was very happy to accept the trooper's help.

Meanwhile, back at the bank, Donahue and I placed our suspect into the back of Donahue's car. I noticed the money bag and was about to throw it into the backseat with the suspect when I decided it was too much paperwork. We didn't need the money to make the case.

"Dave, I'm going to take this money bag back into the bank. They can account for it," I said.

"Okay, fine with me," said Donahue.

As I was walking back to the bank, I heard a soft "click" inside the bag. I knew exactly what that sound was and threw the bag as far as I could into the parking lot. Five seconds later, it exploded into a purple haze of tear gas and dye. The teller had placed an exploding dye pack into the bag along with the cash.

The dye pack was supposed to go off twenty seconds after the bag cleared the outer door of the bank. In this case, it went off a full ten minutes after the bag cleared the bank and ten seconds before I returned it to the bank manager, lucky for her.

I'm not sure how we managed to avoid attracting the attention of the TV news crews that day with a bank robbery, exploding dye pack, high-speed chase, and car crash, but thankfully they never caught wind of it. The worst part would have been trying to explain how a well-planned and executed surveillance went to shit the way it did.

Later during the booking process, I asked the bank robber why he didn't just surrender when I announced he was under arrest after leaving the bank.

He took on a surprised look and said, "I just thought you were a crazy civilian. Sorry, dude."

This was a classic example of Murphy's Law—whatever could go wrong did indeed go wrong. The entire operation went like clockwork but broke down at the very end. Miscommunication between the surveillance squads and the task force agents for a crucial ten minutes left me alone except for agent Donahue, and I thank God for him! Both teams assumed the other was keeping a close eye on the front of the bank, and as it turned out, nobody was. Luckily no harm, no foul this time, and we all learned a valuable lesson that day about timing, communication, and caution. We didn't know it then, but what we learned would play a significant role for us in the future.

Still . . . what a day! I was riding high on the adrenaline rush of a cops-and-robbers game where the good guys won when I burst through our back door, talking nonstop, feeling like a frickin' superhero. Linda gave me a warm welcome and a stiff drink, but I noticed that she was pale and moving slowly. She had been feeling poorly for a few weeks with no apparent cause.

"Linda, are you okay?" I asked. "You look worse than when I left this morning,"

"Dave, before I go to the doctor, I want to check something out," she informed me.

"Like what exactly?" I asked

"I need to buy a pregnancy test kit," she said.

"What?! That's not the problem; you're just coming down with the flu!" I said.

"I don't believe that's it. Go to the drug store and get a reliable test kit. I don't feel well enough to do it myself," she said.

"Okay, okay, I'll get the best one available. Do they have flu test kits now? That's what you really need. You'll see," I said.

I was back an hour later and handed the package to Linda, who crossed her fingers and went into the bathroom.

Ten minutes later she called out to me, "Dave, come in here."

"I wasted $7.50, didn't I? No need to apologize," I said.

I went into the bathroom and she handed me the test strip. It was blue.

"See, I told you," I said.

"Oh, really? Start thinking of a baby name. I'm thinking Baby Oops." Linda was actually smiling.

I had to sit down. In fact, I had to lie down.

"Oh my God! After everything we went through with your last pregnancy? We might have to do it again at our age?" I whined.

"Well, I'm afraid so!" Linda informed me.

This was serious. Suddenly my superhero cape dissolved, and all I could think of was what Linda had endured during her last pregnancy. I felt powerless and scared. Taking down a lowlife bank robber pales in comparison to a woman's journey through a high-risk pregnancy—now that's heroic.

Three days later, we found ourselves in the office of Dr. Karen McCreedy, Linda's doctor who was part of an all-female OB practice in Newton, Massachusetts.

"Well, guys, the test results and my examination are conclusive: you're having a baby! Congratulations! However, given the fact that you're forty-two years old, Linda, and the difficulties in your last pregnancy, we will need to take special precautions this time. I need you to stay in bed as much as possible starting two months from now. Hopefully we will be able to prevent a repeat of the problems you had during your pregnancy with Kate. I need to examine you every couple of weeks from here on and eventually every week as the pregnancy progresses. I feel confident we are doing everything that can be done to avoid a miscarriage," Doctor McCreedy said.

"Oh God, not again," Linda moaned. She looked me right in the eye and asked, "One question, Karen: can you recommend a good doctor for Dave's vasectomy?"

As it turned out, Linda experienced the same problems and was once again confined to bed rest, and the last four months of her pregnancy were pretty horrible. Eventually Linda made it to the finish line and delivered another beautiful baby girl, whom we named Meredith. Linda has proved time and time again to be the backbone of our family. She put herself through hell to ensure our unborn daughters survived. At the same time, she selflessly gave up a career of her own to follow me from Detroit, to Atlanta, to Connecticut, and finally to Massachusetts and to raise our daughters into the fine women they are today. None of this would have been possible without the love of my life at my side.

8

THE LIBRARY CARD

QUINCY, MASSACHUSETTS

On Monday, November 11, 1996, I had just arrived home after a long day at work when I received a call from the office to turn around and head to the city of Quincy for a break-in and theft of irreplaceable books from the personal library of John Quincy Adams located on the grounds of the Adams National Historic Site. Upon arrival, I found a beehive of activity at the site, which consisted of the stand-alone Stone Library building that housed the personal book collection of President John Quincy Adams and an adjacent house once occupied by the president and his family.

Being a National Historic Site, the property is owned by the US government and administered by the National Park Service. The small Stone Library was crammed with hundreds of volumes of books collected over the years by John Quincy Adams. Since the property is owned by the US government, the break-in was being investigated by the FBI, and I was appointed as the case agent.

When word spread, it became big news. Several TV stations were conducting interviews. The Quincy PD brass were on hand, as well as a half dozen folks from the Park Service. My two Quincy PD detective buddies, Bill Lanergan and Tom Healy, were on hand and were investigating on behalf of Quincy PD. They were both very experienced and knew just about every felon on the South Shore of Massachusetts. I managed to buttonhole them long enough to get an update.

"Yeah, Dave, we already have some folks who saw a suspicious vehicle in the area despite it being dark and rainy," Bill informed me.

"Let's show Dave the scene," suggested Tom.

We went from the main house about fifty feet to a small stone two-story structure. Quincy crime scene techs had large, bright floodlights set up and were examining the oak front door of the building.

"This is the Stone Library, Dave; it's where the personal book collection of John Quincy Adams is stored," Tom reported.

I noticed the front door consisted of six wooden panels about two feet by two feet each. Lights were directed on the bottom right panel, which was missing.

Bill explained, "The suspect cut that panel with a saw of some type, probably a power saw. He or she—but I'm assuming it's a he—then crawled right in and under an electronic alarm beam, which was activated since the museum was closed for the night. He managed to avoid tripping it on the way in but wasn't as careful on the way out. The Park Service has already determined at least four very valuable and historic books are missing from the collection."

We walked into the building, where I observed all four walls were crammed with thousands of books from floor to ceiling. In the middle of the floor was a large wooden table with some of the more interesting and important books on display for the public to view. The table was surrounded by a red velvet rope indicating the books were not to be touched. I further noticed four empty spots where the missing books were formerly on display.

"Look over here, Dave," instructed Bill. "See the security beam the bum crawled under?" The security beam was only two feet above the floor. This guy did a squirm and low crawl to get into the door hole and slither under the beam.

"We have a contortionist on our hands, guys!" I commented. "Is the circus in town?"

"Since this story hit the evening news, we've gotten a couple solid leads already," said Tom. "Our K-9 officer Rich Churchill and his German shepherd, Oldo, tracked the suspect from the front door to a location about 150 yards away. That's where there's an opening in the stone wall surrounding this property. The track ended at a set of fresh tire tracks."

"Just before you got here, we learned of two more potential witnesses," Bill said as he flipped through his investigator's notebook.

"A witness reported observing a full-sized station wagon with four square-shaped headlights and wood-grained side panels parked with its lights off and pointed toward the street. Another witness drove past a few minutes later, and she reported a station wagon in the same spot. She thought it was beige, and it appeared to be an older model Chevy from the early '80s. Guess where the car was parked."

"I'm hoping you are going to tell me it's where the dog lost the scent," I informed the two detectives.

Bill and Tom both had huge grins on their faces. "Bingo!"

The next day Bill, Tom, and I met with Marianne Peake, superintendent of the Adams site. We were joined by Special Agent Jeff Cady, a new agent on C-6. My supervisor, Tom Powers, had assigned Cady to assist me with this case. Cady was a smart, wisecracking kid who was anxious to work on this case, which was just fine with me because I could use him.

Marianne began the meeting. "Welcome, guys, and thanks so much for devoting your resources to this burglary. We don't have the investigative resources in the Park Service that will be needed for this. I can now tell you what is missing from the library. There were four books taken from the table. I have pictures of them for you.

"The first one is a 1772 English Bible that belonged to John Quincy Adam's wife, Louisa Catherine Adams. The second book is a Latin version of the King James Bible that dates back to 1521 and was the oldest book in the collection. The third book was Bloch's *Ichthyologie*, an eighteenth-century book of valuable, hand-painted color plates with fish illustrations. It was printed in French. The final book, and probably the most historically significant, is the 1838 Mendi Bible, given to John Quincy Adams by fifty-three Mendi tribesmen he helped free after they mutinied while being transported on a slave ship from Cuba. Adams personally represented them before the US Supreme Court and obtained their freedom and repatriation to Africa. Word is there may be a movie in the works concerning this historic event!

"We do not know if there is a reason why these particular books were selected by the burglar as they are all extremely valuable and important to our history, but they cannot be sold to anyone without causing suspicion. No one in the art world will touch these books," Marianne said.

We put the word out to the art world, and the local TV stations did their best to keep the story alive, but after four days, we were mainly spinning our wheels. The car description was pretty good, but without a license plate, we didn't have much. Informants were pressed for information but came up short, until the call finally came in.

I received a message from Walt Steffens, an agent on the Organized Crime squad, that a guy in Concord Prison was looking to speak with the case agent on the Adams break-in. Walt had been contacted by a Massachusetts state trooper assigned to the Concord barracks, which are located directly across the street from Concord prison. The trooper had a guy who claimed to know exactly who broke into the Adams site.

I reached out to trooper Zach Leach. "Hello, trooper, this is Special Agent Dave Nadolski from Boston FBI. I'm handling the Adams break-in, and I understand you are in contact with someone who claims he can help us out. Is that correct?" I asked.

"That is correct, Dave. Our barracks are located across the street from the prison, as you may well know. We use prison inmates to clean up and do certain work details over here. I've gotten to know one inmate who is a mechanic and is trusted with working on our patrol cars. He's a pretty good guy; we've never had a problem with him. He's had problems with drugs in the past, which led to him sticking up gas stations and such with a toy gun. He never actually hurt anyone as far as we know. He's over here today, and he's working on a couple cars. If you can make it out here in an hour or so, we can arrange for you to speak with him privately. He prefers to be away from the prison for the meeting because he can't trust anyone on the inside, including the correctional officers," Trooper Leach confided.

"Okay, Zach, let me get ahold of one of the Quincy detectives and I'll do my best to get there within an hour. Thanks for the call."

I happened to be working with Tom Healey, so I grabbed him and ran down to the garage for my car. On the way out to Concord, we discussed the likelihood that this guy had something solid. Ultimately, we determined there was no way to know for sure, but if the Massachusetts State Police trusted him, I guessed we should too.

We arrived at the barracks in fifty minutes. At the front desk, I asked for Zach Leach. Trooper Leach was down in three minutes. He stuck his hand out and said, "Thanks for coming, guys. We have the inmate in an interview room. He was recently transferred to Concord from another prison and just started working on our cars. We don't know him very well, but he is a good mechanic. Unfortunately, we have to get him back to the prison within forty minutes, so we better move it."

The trooper led us to the interview room, opened the door, then excused himself. Sitting in a wooden chair examining the ceiling was a skinny guy, midthirties, dressed in prison dungarees. He had a short-sleeve shirt on, and his arms were covered with prison tattoos. This was before tattoos were popular. His black hair was greasy and fairly long; his hawkish face sported a prominent nose. His face was clean shaven, and he wasn't making eye contact. I walked directly up to the inmate and extended my hand.

"Hi, my name is Dave Nadolski. I'm a Special Agent with the FBI. This other handsome fella is Detective Tom Healey from Quincy PD."

The inmate looked us over slowly. "Quincy, huh? My hometown," said the inmate. He didn't move to shake my hand.

"Well, that's good to know. I don't believe I caught your name," I said.

"No, you didn't because I didn't give it to you," replied the inmate, looking back at the ceiling.

What's this jag-off playing at? I wondered. I looked at Tom, and he had a blank expression on his face.

"Okay, well, anyway, I know you have to get back to your cell pretty soon so it's our understanding that you may have some information to share regarding the Adams burglary. I'm the agent assigned to the case, and Detective Healey and I are working together on this. I'd be very happy to talk to you for as long as you are available today, but if this is a bad time, maybe we should postpone this chat," I said coyly.

With that we sat down and just looked at the inmate. The inmate finally took his eyes off the ceiling and broke into a slight grin. "My name is Tony Romano," said the prisoner. "The guy you are looking for is Kevin Gildea."

I looked at Tom and saw him crack a smile.

"Interesting name. The same Kevin Gildea from Quincy perhaps?" asked Tom.

"One and the same, detective," Romano answered, the smile growing on his face.

"If I may ask, what makes you think Gildea has anything to do with this burglary?" I asked.

Romano looked me over and said, "Because he planned it while doing time with me here in Concord prison. Check on him and you'll see he's out and around. He's got a sheet for burglary and has been planning a museum score for some time. Kevin and I go way back, and I've been waiting for the day when I could stick it to the prick. This has Kevin written all over it."

"Why do you think he would take something so high profile that he can't possibly get rid of?" I asked.

"Well, Kevin is a friend of Myles Connor. Ever hear of him?" Tony asked.

I had heard of Myles Connor in connection with the unsolved 1990 Gardner Museum robbery in Boston. The largest private-property heist in history, in which thirteen pieces of art valued at $500 million dollars walked out the door, but I couldn't see the connection with the Adams theft.

"So what is he looking to get?" I asked.

"Connor and Gildea are asshole buddies, and they're both fucking crazy. Connor has been known to steal artwork in order to make a deal for a lower sentence on some other charge. It worked for him in the past, and I think Gildea may be doing the same thing here," Tony said.

"Well, thanks for that, Anthony; we will certainly check this out. Furthermore, it may interest you to know that if your information pans out, you may be eligible for the $5,000 reward being offered by the Park Service," I replied.

"I like the sound of that, agent, and I'll hold you to it," Romano replied with a sly grin.

"Anthony, is there any way for me to get in touch with you that won't arouse suspicion?" I asked.

"Yes, there is, but first you can start calling me Tony. You're not my father," Tony wisecracked.

"Fair enough, Tony," I responded.

"You can reach out to Lorraine at this number; she's my ex-wife. She will reach me."

With that he handed me a folded piece of paper with a phone number.

"Okay, Tony, nice chatting with you. We'll be in touch."

We took our leave and headed for the door. "One second, Mr. FBI man," Tony called out. "You'll find my information to be spot on, but I wasn't planning on giving it to you unless you earned it. You're not a prick. I like that," he said with a grin.

I nodded my head and walked out.

On our way back to Boston, we talked about Tony and speculated about the information he gave us. Tom had heard of Gildea and, in fact, knew he was a burglar by trade.

"This information makes sense at least. We'll have to figure out what he's been up to lately. I thought he was still in prison," Tom said.

With that, Tom's beeper went off, and as he looked at it, he said, "Shit, 9-1-1. Call the office."

We found a pay phone, and Tom called in. He spent a few minutes on the phone taking notes. When he got back to the car, he said, "We may have another break. There's a defense attorney in Quincy by the name of Robert Jubinville. He's looking for me and has information on the case. He wants us to come by his office as soon as possible."

"Okay, let's contact Lanergan and Cady first. They're at the FBI office," I said.

Later that afternoon, the four of us found ourselves sitting in front of attorney Robert Jubinville, who had been a Massachusetts state trooper before going to law school, after which he quit police work in order to practice law. Tom and I hadn't gotten a chance to brief Bill or Jeff on what we learned earlier that day.

"Okay, guys, I've got some hot information regarding the Adams break. I can't give you all the details due to attorney-client privilege, but I can say that I am in contact with someone who knows where the books are and needs to work out a deal with you for their safe return. My guy says he didn't steal the books but has access to them. The thing is he was busted recently burglarizing a gas station. He's on federal probation for a gun conviction down south and is looking at five years for the probation violation not to mention the gas station burglary. He needs to get out from under those charges," Attorney Jubinville said.

This was starting to make sense. I looked over at Tom. We smiled at one another, and I said, "Déjà vu all over again, Tom!"

Tom laughed out loud.

Jubinville looked confused. "What are you talking about, agent?"

"What's the name of your client, Mr. Jubinville?" I asked.

"I can't divulge that until we have a deal." Jubinville responded.

"Okay, how about this?" I asked. "You tell Kevin Gildea to surrender himself to our custody with the books, or we'll hunt his ass down and he'll never see the light of day again!"

Jubinville actually put his hands on his desk and pushed himself up. "How do you know his name?" he demanded.

We stood up, and I signaled Jeff and Bill that we were leaving. I handed Jubinville my card and told him to get Gildea to call me to arrange his surrender. Once we were in the parking lot, Tom and I filled in Jeff and Bill about our prison visit. I'm sure Jubinville could hear us laughing from his office!

Things were starting to look up for this case. We finally had the identity of the suspect, and the next step was finding him and recovering the books, so that's exactly what we set out to do. A criminal record check for Kevin Gildea revealed burglary to be his crime of choice. There was a federal charge in Fort Lauderdale, Florida, for "knowingly making a false statement to a federal firearms dealer" and also a second count of "receiving a firearm shipped in interstate commerce while being a felon." He was sentenced to five years on the false statement charge and was given five years' probation for the receiving a firearm while being a felon charge. The probation was still in effect and, to our way of thinking, may have been the reason behind the theft for ransom theory. More interesting was an outstanding warrant for violation of a restraining order by a woman by the name of Katrina Klein, who lived on Condor Street in East Boston. We wondered who she might be, but given the fact that her date of birth was close to Gildea's, we assumed she was a former girlfriend. We decided to give Katrina a visit to see if she could provide some information that would help us locate Gildea.

Katrina lived in a two-story apartment building in East Boston. East Boston is a very old section of town with row houses jammed close together. Parking is very scarce as the vast majority of the homes have no garage or driveway. The apartment Katrina lived in was ground-floor and at the rear of the building next to a small parking lot. The parking lot and driveway was shared with a business called Taxi Master, which did auto repairs for the taxi trade in Boston.

Tom Healey and I parked behind Katrina's apartment, located her door, and knocked. After several attempts, it was apparent that she wasn't home or wasn't answering the door. We then walked over to Taxi Master and introduced ourselves to Mark Thompson, owner of the business.

"Hi, Mr. Thompson, my name is Dave Nadolski," I said while producing my credentials. "This is Detective Tom Healey of the Quincy Police Department, and we were hoping you had a few minutes to help us with an investigation we are conducting."

Mark Thompson was middle-aged; about five feet, eight inches; and had the strong sturdy look of someone who worked with his hands. He was dressed in a gray mechanic's uniform, and his sewn-on name tag said "Mark." After wiping the grease from his hands, Mark said, "Sure, be glad to help the FBI and police. What can I do for you?"

"Have you been watching the news lately, specifically regarding the break-in at the John Quincy Adams Library in Quincy?" I asked.

"Oh yeah, I sure have. Quite a caper!" replied Mark enthusiastically.

"Well, that's what we are investigating, and you may be able to help us," I advised him.

"Fire away. I'll do whatever I can to help," said Mark.

Tom reached into his folder and removed two driver's license photos of Kevin Gildea and Katrina Klein. Tom held them up for Mark to view and asked, "Have you ever seen these two people before?"

Mark took a close look at both pictures and handed them back to Tom. "Yeah, that's Katrina Klein and her boyfriend, Kevin. I know those two real well. Katrina lives in the apartment over there," Mark said, pointing to the door we had knocked at.

"Kevin is around now and again. I'm always fighting with them over the parking here. As you can see, it's real tight, and I have to share space with the tenants of that apartment building. I need room to get cars in and out and that causes conflict," Mark said.

"Mark, have you seen Kevin around here lately by any chance?" I asked.

"Well, not lately; they've both been keeping a low profile, I guess. Are they involved with the robbery?" Mark asked.

"Actually, we are not sure, but we are very interested in talking to them. You're a car guy, so can you tell us what Katrina is driving now?" I asked.

"Oh, she's been driving a four-door Mercury Sable. Piece of shit."

"Okay, what about Kevin? What's he drive?" I asked.

"Well, Kevin has a different rental all the time, usually nice new cars. Recently though he's been tooling around in a Chevy Caprice station wagon."

"Mark, can you describe what the station wagon looks like?" I immediately asked.

"Oh, hell yes. It's beige with fake-wood panel sides. It's a 1985. I've been having some words with Kevin about that car, and I even wrote down the license plate. Do you want that?"

I looked at Tom, and his mouth was open.

"Sure, Mark. That would be very helpful, thanks!" I said with a huge grin.

As Mark was retreating to his small office at the rear of the business, I grabbed Tom. "Can you believe this shit? He's got the license plate!"

"Here you go, agent." Mark handed me a torn corner of a piece of lined notebook paper. Written on the paper was 7940BR, Gildea's license plate.

"This is very, very helpful to our investigation. If you don't mind, I'd like to keep this piece of paper. Is that okay with you?" I asked.

"Of course! Glad to be of help," replied Mark.

"One more thing, Mark: have you seen this station wagon around here since the Adams burglary last week?" I asked.

"Actually, now that you mention it, I haven't," answered Mark.

"I'm going to give you my number and Detective Healey's number. If you see Kevin or Katrina or that station wagon back here again, please give us a call. Don't do anything except keep an eye on it for us and don't be too obvious about it. Can you do that?" I asked.

"You bet!" Mark said. He was beaming from ear to ear.

We huddled back at the FBI office with Bill Lanergan and Jeff Cady, then got busy putting a lookout order out to local law enforcement for the station wagon and for Kevin Gildea as well. A check of the license plate on the station wagon revealed it was registered to Robert Conners, born in 1968 and residing at 31 Saint James Avenue, Apartment 1, in Boston. A quick check revealed that address to be a mail drop. Specifically, they rented out private mailboxes with a residential address.

At this point, we pretty much figured Gildea had assumed the identity of Robert Conners, so Jeff and I went into the business and spoke with the manager, Roger Guilford, who informed us the mailbox using the address of 31 Saint James Avenue, Apartment 1 was, in fact, rented by Robert Conners.

"So have you ever seen the guy who picks up the mail at this box?" I asked Roger.

"Oh yeah, he comes in here. Is there a problem?" asked Roger.

"As a matter of fact, there is a rather big problem, and I need your cooperation in order to handle this quickly and quietly," I said to Roger.

"By all means! You can ask me anything. and I will give you my full cooperation!" replied Roger.

"Good, glad to hear that. I'm going to show you a picture, and I'd like to know if you recognize the person." I then showed Roger the picture of Kevin Gildea.

"Sure, that's Robert Conners," Roger immediately responded.

"Okay, and how often does Robert come in here?" I asked.

"Probably every day, though I couldn't say for sure."

"Has he been in here today?" I asked.

"Yep, I saw him around 1:00 p.m. When he comes in, it's usually right after lunch."

"Okay, Roger, you've been a big help, and I'd like you to keep this conversation to yourself. Can I count on you to do that?" I asked.

"Absolutely, agent; you can count on it."

Later that day I called a squad meeting.

"We need to do a full-court press on this mail drop on Saint James Avenue tomorrow. Chances are Gildea will be there to pick up his mail. I don't know what he has going on, but he stops in there just about every day to clean out his box. I want to cover the place all day with agents and cops and grab him after he cleans out the box. I've talked to Assistant United States Attorney Jim Lang and filled him in on everything we know about Gildea. He's getting an arrest warrant," I explained.

The next day, fifteen invisible special agents and detectives surrounded the mail drop as soon as it opened. Jeff Cady; our supervisor, Tom Powers; and I maintained a direct line of sight on the front of the building from an office lobby across the street. Although it looks pretty exciting in the movies, surveillance can be very tedious after a while. It's easy to lose concentration, especially after a number of false sightings. Luckily my years of surveillance experience as a police detective and in the New York FBI office helped me remain focused, but it wasn't easy. The morning dragged on, and finally noontime was approaching. The business in the mail drop picked up as office workers poured in and out around lunchtime. It was difficult to eyeball everyone as sometimes a small group would enter all at once.

"Shit, look at that bunch going in," I said to Jeff and Tom Powers. I didn't see everyone in the group and decided I needed to get inside and eyeball the mailbox itself.

"Tom, I'm going in to check that last group. If he's not in there, I'm staying to keep an eye on the box. Gildea has never seen me, so he won't suspect me when he walks in. I'll radio with a description as soon as he leaves and follow him out," I said.

I trotted across the street and into the building. Luckily, nobody was near Gildea's box, so that was good. I had my Bureau radio concealed inside my jacket and a very unobtrusive earpiece in my right ear. I also had a wire microphone in my jacket sleeve. My call sign was Tango 11.

"Tango 11 is inside the building; the target box has not been opened yet. I'm maintaining an eyeball inside." Numerous clicks came over the speaker in my ear indicating the agents and cops read my message and were confirming.

A half hour led to an hour. One hour led to two, and I was beginning to think today wasn't going to be the day when suddenly a familiar-looking guy walked in the door and directly to Gildea's box.

"All units," I whispered, "this is Tango 11. Target is clearing the box now. He's wearing a blue denim jacket and gray work pants. Brown hair and glasses. He's five feet, ten inches, medium build. He's exiting onto the street now and heading toward Berkeley Street. He's alone."

The air came alive with several units checking in. "This is Tango 4. I've got an eyeball, and he's turning right onto Berkeley Street now!"

With that announcement, I bolted out the door and fast walked to Berkeley Street. I rounded the corner and observed Gildea a half block ahead and moving quickly. Suddenly he made a sharp right turn onto Newbury Street. As I was running toward Newbury Street, I heard more radio traffic.

"All units, this is Tango 10. I've located the station wagon parked on Newbury Street about a half block down from Berkeley, and I've got an eyeball on the subject. He's reaching into his pocket; I think he's pulling out his keys! Affirmative, he has his keys in his hand and is approaching the driver's side of the station wagon."

After hearing this, I kicked it into gear and bolted down Newbury Street. I reached the car as Gildea was pulling the driver's door open.

"Kevin, hold up there!" I yelled.

A very startled Kevin Gildea froze and looked at me. He hesitated a moment too long, and I was on top of him.

"FBI, Kevin! You're under arrest!" I shouted.

"What the fuck!" were the first words out of Kevin Gildea's mouth.

I had his hands behind his back and the cuffs securely attached to his wrists before he knew what hit him.

A two-man Bureau car pulled up with its blue light activated and blocked the station wagon, plus most of the other traffic on busy Newbury Street. I led Kevin to the backseat of the Bureau car and eased him inside.

Jeff Cady had just arrived.

"Jeff, secure this station wagon and get it towed to the Bureau garage. Follow it in and wait there with it. Notify Jim Lang at the US Attorney's office that we need a search warrant. We may have the books back by tonight!" I said.

Jeff was thrilled, as was the squad supervisor—and everyone else for that matter. It had only been a few days since we learned of the identity of the Adams burglar, and now he was in cuffs in the backseat of a Bureau car. Sometimes life is so good.

I rode with Gildea to the FBI office at One Center Plaza. We parked the car in the underground garage, and as I was leading him up for booking, I contemplated my interview plan. I decided to just play it like we had all the answers and didn't need anything from him. Truth be told, this case was locked up.

Upstairs I had Gildea empty his pockets. I found a notebook containing a bunch of names, addresses, and phone numbers. In his wallet was a temporary Massachusetts driver's license in the name of Robert Conners. Gildea's picture was on the license. There was a bill of sale dated November 7, 1996, for a 1985 Chevy station wagon and a check in the amount of $300 from the account of Robert Conners, with an address of 265 Route 28, Orleans, Massachusetts. I picked up a Gold's Gym, Portsmouth, New Hampshire, membership card in the name of Robert Conners with Gildea's picture on it.

There were a lot of receipts and a membership card from Foxwood's Resort and Casino in Gildea's actual name. There was a torn piece of paper with handwritten numbers: 11-14-6-9. That paper would eventually become very important.

After the booking process was complete, I had Gildea brought into an interview room, where I had the contents of his wallet and pockets spread out on the table in front of me.

"Kevin, I'm Special Agent Dave Nadolski. I'm investigating the Adams break-in. Right now, you're being held on a federal probation violation, but the US Attorney's office in Boston will be charging you with the break-in and theft of books from the Adams library. You have the right to remain silent. Anything you say can and will be used against you. You have the right to an attorney. If you cannot afford one, one will be appointed for you by the court. Are you willing to answer my questions without an attorney present?" I asked.

During the warning, Gildea was looking over my head at the wall behind me. I wasn't sure he was listening. "I don't use lawyers. I generally represent myself," he replied.

"I'll take that as a yes," I said. "You seem to be living a rather unusual life, Kevin. You have a rented mailbox in someone else's name. You have a Massachusetts driver's license in someone else's name; you have a car registration in someone else's name; and here's a weird one: a Portsmouth, New Hampshire, gym membership in someone else's name. Seems like a long way to go to play paddleball. By the way, who the hell is Robert Conners?" I asked.

He looked back at the wall and remained silent.

"You've been trying to ransom the books for a pass on your federal and state legal troubles. I know that's a play out of the Myles Connor playbook, and it did work for him. I'm just here to tell you that it won't work for you. We really want to recover the books, and we will recover the books. I work for the Federal Bureau of Investigation, and that's what we do. It would be nice if they were stashed in your car, but I think that's a little too obvious for you. Why would you want to be caught red-handed like that, right?" I asked.

Gildea smiled and looked at me. "That would be a rookie play," he said.

"For sure, and you're no rookie. So I propose we cut to the chase and you let me in on exactly where the books are, and I'll tell the prosecutor you've finally come to your senses," I said.

Gildea looked amused. "So, assuming what you said is true, and I'm not saying it is, what would I get out of it?" asked Gildea.

"Unfortunately, not as much as you'd like. The thing is we won't deal on your federal parole violation from Florida or your state charge for the Cape Cod burglary, and we will still charge you with the theft of the books, but you're in handcuffs right now and not in a very strong position. By the way, I think Katrina might have some exposure here. A witness claims a woman was driving the car during the burglary, and I know you and she are back together. If you love her, take care of her. So chew on that and maybe we will talk again soon. It's up to you," I said.

As I started for the door, I stopped and turned around to face Gildea and said, "One last thing, Kevin: I've got a message from Tony Romano. Payback's a bitch."

I noticed he no longer looked amused.

I joined Jeff, Bill, and Tom at the FBI garage. Not surprisingly, a search of the car failed to reveal the books, but there was a ton of other stuff. It looked like Gildea was living out of his car. We found power tools (that was a good find), boxes of clothes, newspapers, food wrappers, a box of unlabeled cassette audio tapes (interesting), personal papers, more Foxwoods Casino papers. Along with those items, fabric samples and fiber samples were removed and preserved as evidence. The boys had done a pretty thorough job.

"Okay, everyone, let's saddle up and go pay Katrina Klein a visit. It's starting to get dark and maybe we'll finally catch her at home," I said, ready to pounce into action.

We arrived at Katrina's apartment and found her Mercury Sable parked behind her apartment. Good news.

Katrina answered our knocks with "Who's there?"

"FBI, Ms. Klein. Please open the door," I announced.

"Oh shit," she said. "Okay, hang on."

The door creaked open a few inches to reveal a woman in her early to mid-thirties with long, stringy brown hair; a medium build; and somewhat glassy eyes.

"Ms. Klein, my name is Dave Nadolski and I'm an FBI agent. These fellows are also with the FBI and the Quincy Police Department," I explained as we all presented our array of identification. "We would like to come in and talk with you about Kevin Gildea. May we do that?" I asked.

"Do I have to?" she asked.

"Of course not, but as you are probably aware, Kevin was arrested this afternoon and we know he has been staying with you. We are looking for property removed from the John Quincy Adams library, and Kevin is being charged with taking that property," I said.

"Okay, come on in. Sorry, I'm not a good housekeeper," she said.

We all squeezed into the front room of the apartment. A half-empty whiskey bottle was on a table with a glass next to it. It was furnished in modern thrift-shop style, but there were some rather stunning framed pen-and-ink drawings on the wall.

"I know Kevin was locked up today, and I'm very worried about him. I've had a few drinks," Katrina told us.

"Sure, no problem, but please don't have any more while we are here. We've got to ask you a few things and need you clearheaded. Can you do that?" I asked.

"Yeah, okay," she said.

"That's great. First off, I've got to tell you we know Kevin stole four very valuable books from the John Quincy Adams Library in Quincy. You've heard about the burglary, right?" I asked.

"Of course I did! I don't exactly live under a rock, you know. But if Kevin did it, I don't know anything about that!" she exclaimed.

"We found out about you because you filed a restraining order against Kevin awhile back. Something about him beating you up pretty good," said Tom Healy.

"Yeah, we got into a fight; he thought I was stepping out on him with a guy I used to date. We made up," she said.

"So how much do you know about his business?" I asked.

"Not much apparently," she responded. "I do know he's a very talented artist and actually sells his art. Want to see something he drew?" she asked.

"Why not?" I responded.

With that she went into another room and returned with a large portrait of Mother Teresa. It was very lifelike and looked professionally done.

"Kevin did this ink drawing." Katrina beamed.

"Wow, that's shocking. The guy has a talent for sure," said Tom.

"Okay, Katrina, nobody is saying you would know about the theft or be a part of it, but since he's been staying here, maybe he hid the books here right under your nose. Could we look around for them?" I asked.

"I really don't think he could have done that, but I'll let you look around if you need to," she agreed.

With that we obtained a written consent to search and spread out looking in all the rooms and closets and under the furniture. To say she wasn't much of a housekeeper was an understatement. While we were doing our thing, she started pouring more whiskey.

"Katrina, please don't continue drinking while we are here," I said.

"I'm thirsty," she said and downed the whiskey.

We covered the entire apartment in about five minutes.

"Okay, it doesn't look like anything is stashed here in the apartment. The only other thing I'm going to ask of you is permission to search your car. It'll take about three minutes," I said.

"What if I said no?" she burped out.

"We'd wonder why," said Bill Lanergan.

"Okay, fuck it. Gimme the paper. Search the car, then get the fuck out!" Katrina said in a surly tone.

The search only took three minutes, and we came up empty.

"All right, Katrina, we are leaving now. I'm leaving my card behind in case you hear anything or remember something later. Believe me, this is a big deal, and Kevin is in a world of shit over it. Don't do anything to join him," I warned.

"Fuck off!" With that she slammed the door in our faces.

"I thought that went pretty well," said Jeff Cady.

The next day we decided to split up and check some of the leads that had been looking us in the face since the arrest. Bill and Tom headed to Cape Cod to locate and speak with Robert Conners in the town of Orleans. They found Robert at a rooming house. It turned out Robert was special needs. Tom and Bill interviewed the owner of the property and discovered Kevin Gildea had been living there until a few months earlier. He had been working at the Chatham Sign Shop in the neighboring town of Chatham. Robert and Kevin knew one another but did not share a room. Robert was unaware that his identification was missing and that he was also missing several checks from his checkbook. He considered Kevin to be a friend and was very upset to find out his trust was misplaced.

Meanwhile Jeff and I headed to the Gold's Gym in Portsmouth, New Hampshire. Upon arriving at the gym, we identified ourselves to the front desk person and asked to speak with the manager. Manager Jill Harper showed us into her small office. "What can I do for the FBI?" she inquired.

"Jill, we are investigating the theft of valuable books from the John Quincy Adams Presidential Library in Quincy, Massachusetts. Did you happen to catch anything about that on the news?" I asked.

"Well, I'm not much on following the news so I don't believe so," replied Jill.

"The theft occurred during the evening of November 11. The thief cut his way through the front door and stole four very valuable and fragile antique books. The reason we are here is this gym may be connected to that theft in some way," I said.

"What?!" exclaimed a very shocked Jill.

"I'm not saying anyone working here is involved, but there may be a connection to one of your members," I said.

"Oh my God! What can I do for you?" Jill volunteered.

I produced the gym membership card with Robert Conner's name on it that was retrieved from Gildea's wallet when he was arrested.

"Jill, do you recognize the picture of the man on this membership card?" I asked.

"No, I don't. He's not a regular, that's for sure!" said Jill.

"What's your process for checking in members?" I asked.

"When a member arrives, they show their card and sign in at the front desk," replied Jill.

"Do members have their own locker at the gym or does the member take whatever locker is vacant at the time?" asked Jeff.

"We do not assign lockers. Members take what's available at the time," replied Jill.

"Can a member use a locker for a number of days? Just leave their workout clothes locked up in a locker?" I asked.

"No, that's not allowed. They have to take everything with them when they are done using the gym, including their lock. Our policy is to cut off locks that are left on lockers. Otherwise we'd end up with a bunch of lockers with abandoned locks," said Jill.

"I see, good policy. What happens if you cut a lock and remove someone's property from inside?" I asked.

"Well, in that case, the property goes into the lost and found, which is just a locked room. If somebody comes back looking for their stuff, we let them into the lost and found room," Jill said.

Jeff and I looked at one another and smiled.

"Jill, we are going to need to see some paperwork. Could you provide us with the membership agreement for Robert Conners plus all the sign-in sheets for the dates of November 12 through yesterday please? This could be very important to our investigation," I said.

"Of course. Please wait here; I'll be right back," Jill said as she left the room.

"Jeff, can you believe this? What if the books are in a locker or in the lost and found?" I excitedly asked.

"It couldn't get any simpler than that. So I'm sure it won't happen!" said Jeff.

"Yeah, but think about it. Why go to all the bother of stealing an identity and using it to open a gym membership unless you're hiding something?" I asked.

"My fingers are double crossed!" exclaimed Jeff.

Sitting waiting for Jill to return was tough. I began pacing the office and was about to break out and hunt her down when the door finally opened and she walked in with a stack of papers.

"Here we go. Here's Robert Conner's membership agreement, and here's the sign-in sheets you asked for," said Jill.

Jeff and I both went immediately for the sign-in sheets, and I grabbed November 12 first. We started down the list of signatures, and then at 1:00 p.m. we hit pay dirt! The familiar signature was right there. Robert Conners!

Jeff and I both leaped up and high-fived. Jill was staring at us open-mouthed.

We continued down the list to see if he signed in again, and luckily, he didn't.

"Jeff, the books are here someplace. Either still in a locker or in the lost and found. They've got to be!" I shouted.

"Jill, take us to the lost and found right now!" I demanded.

We held our breath as we entered the room and flipped on the light. It was kind of surprising the amount of property in there, but we were looking for a piece of luggage or something like that. Suddenly Jeff grabbed my arm. "Over in the corner, it looks like a backpack," said Jeff.

I shot over to the corner. Sure enough, there was a green canvas backpack. I lifted it by the shoulder straps. It was heavy!

"Jeff, go get my camera in the car. Get two pair of cotton gloves and some paper evidence bags as well. Everything is in the trunk. I'm going to stay right here," I said.

Jeff returned in about three minutes. We slipped on gloves, and I photographed the backpack and the interior of the room.

"Jeff, open the backpack and flip the lid back. I need to see inside," I instructed.

He opened the backpack and slowly lifted the cover. "Okay, Jeff, hold it," I instructed. I took several more pictures. Inside the backpack was something wrapped in plastic. On top of the plastic-wrapped object was a cut padlock. I made sure to clearly photograph the contents before going further.

"Okay, now reach down and take the padlock out by the hasp and place it into this evidence bag," I instructed Jeff.

"Good, now peel back the top layer of the plastic wrapper very slowly and stop as soon as the contents are revealed. I need to take more photos," I told Jeff.

Jeff slowly peeled the plastic wrap to reveal the contents beneath. We saw at least two large books side by side in the backpack!

"Holy cow!" I exclaimed.

"Unbelievable!" shouted Jeff.

That's as far as we went with the unwrapping process. At this point, I picked up the backpack by the shoulder straps and carefully carried it to my car. Jeff opened the backseat, and I gently placed it inside along with the evidence bag containing the padlock.

"Jeff, stay with the car. I have to call the office," I said.

I called Tom Powers and gave him the big news. I also called Tom Healey and told him to grab Bill Lanergan and meet us at the FBI office. We were bringing home the goods!

We decided not to go any further with the removal process. The Park Service had warned us not to unwrap the books if they were found. They had a professional who was to take over removal of the books from the backpack, so upon arrival at the office, we took the backpack to our evidence room and secured it there.

The next day at 9:00 a.m. we all reconvened at the FBI office. I had set up an examination table in a spare room down the hall from the evidence room. It was a little crowded with Jeff; me; Tom Healey; Bill; my supervisor, Tom Powers; our photographer, John Green; plus Marianne Peake and two other folks from the Park Service. One of the Park Service folks was June Andrews. June was an expert when it came to handling fragile antiques. Over the aluminum examination table, we had laid fresh white butcher paper. The green canvas backpack was sitting on top of the table and the top flap was open revealing two books. Slowly and carefully, June peeled back more of the plastic surrounding the books and finally reached inside with gloved hands and slowly lifted one leather-bound book out and carefully laid it on the table. The cover was now visible, and Marianne Peak announced that it was the "Mendi Bible." Applause broke out in the room, and the agents exchanged high fives all around! "Thank God it's not the Boston phone book!" I exclaimed to the laughing crowd.

The process continued until all four books were lying side by side. Unfortunately, the 1772 English Bible and the 1778 Bloch's *Ichthyologie* suffered some water damage and were going to require restoration. Despite that setback, the mood was one of jubilation, and the Park Service was extremely happy to have all four books back in their possession. Finally, we could focus on preparing the case for court.

Preparing the case for court was mainly the job of AUSA (Assistant United States Attorney) Jim Lang and required a number of meetings with Jim. Jim stressed that we had very good circumstantial evidence against Gildea but wished there was better physical evidence to directly tie Gildea to the case.

"Jim, I just thought of something that's been nagging at the back of my brain until now. The day Gildea was arrested, we recovered a small piece of paper with some numbers written on it. I didn't think much about it until now, but what if those numbers were actually the combination of the padlock we recovered along with the books?" I asked.

"Well, that would definitely tie Gildea to the lock from the locker where the books were found. That would be damn powerful!" exclaimed Jim.

"Okay, I'm going to call the FBI lab in Quantico. Let me borrow your phone," I said.

Fifteen minutes later, I had my answer.

"Jim, according to a laboratory specialist, they would be able to take the lock and conduct an examination on it and, in most cases, be able to come up with the combination despite the fact that the lock had been cut off of the locker with bolt cutters. They want me to submit the lock right away. Additionally, I am not going to give them the numbers we recovered. This has to be a blind test," I said.

"Of course, that's the way it has to be done. If we provide them the numbers first, it would invalidate the evidentiary value of the test," advised Jim. "Let's get it done, Dave."

I overnighted the lock to the FBI lab. Three days later, I received a phone call from lab specialist Donna Nickerson.

"Hi, Dave, this is Donna from the FBI lab. Regarding that lock you submitted, I have some news. I was able to successfully recover the combination. Are you ready to hear the numbers?" Donna asked.

"Oh, you bet, Donna! I'm on pins and needles!" I replied.

"I found the combination to be 11-14-6-9," replied Donna.

"Are you sure about that, Donna?"

"Absolutely," she replied.

"Donna, I could kiss you right now! Those are the exact numbers I was hoping you would come up with! You have just locked this case down," I happily responded.

"My pleasure, agent. I'm just glad we were able to help," replied Donna.

Jim and the rest of the team were thrilled with the news.

"Dave, this puts the cherry on the top! I'm going to call Gildea's attorney and inform him of this new development. He'd be nuts to go to trial now," Jim stated.

As it turned out, there was no trial. Gildea pleaded guilty to the theft and was sentenced to two years' incarceration and two years' supervised release after doing his prison time.

Eventually we decided we just didn't have enough to charge Katrina Klein with the robbery or anything else connected with the crime. I didn't feel too bad about that because the main actor was definitely Gildea.

9

PATHS CONVERGE

FBI, BOSTON DIVISION

Shortly after the conviction of Kevin Gildea, I reached out to Tony's ex-wife, Lorraine, and asked her to pass a message to Tony. I wanted Tony to call a particular number at the Boston FBI office. My instructions were for him to identify himself to the person who answered the phone as "Tony" and to further say he needed to get in touch with Dave Nadolski. He was to wait on the line until he was connected directly to me. Lorraine agreed to do this. I further instructed Lorraine to tell Tony that this would be the method of communication between Tony and me going forward. If I needed to speak to Tony, I would contact Lorraine. If Tony needed to speak to me, he could call the number I provided him.

This method of communication put contact into Tony's hands. I would never reach out to him directly. Tony would have to contact me from a phone within the prison that was not recorded if he felt there may be a problem using a recorded line, or wait until he was at the state police barracks and use a phone from there.

Initially, in order to set up this communication link, Lorraine had to visit Tony in Concord Prison and spell it out for him. I felt this would be a good first test for Tony. If he couldn't get this process straight, we had a short future together.

My first call from Tony was at 7:10 p.m., June 13, 1997.

"Tony, nice to hear from you again; it's been awhile," I said.

CHAPTER 9

"Yeah. I've been watching the news, and it looks like my information paid off, Agent Nadolski."

"It did; thank you for that. Going forward just call me Dave, okay?" I asked.

"You bet, Dave," replied Tony.

"Listen, Tony, first off I was serious about getting you the reward money. I've already put in a claim on your behalf with the Park Service. I informed them, without using names at this point, that a source identified Kevin Gildea specifically and that source was the first time Gildea's name was mentioned. I can't see how they can ignore that, nor will I let them," I said.

"Thanks. I appreciate what you are doing for me," said Tony.

"You deserve it, Tony, and I want you to use this phone number to get in touch with me going forward. I'm interested in any information you may have about criminal activity that may be of interest to the FBI. In the meantime, is there anything I can do for you?" I asked.

"Actually, I'm up for parole at the end of this year. That would mean doing a certain amount of time at a halfway house in Boston. From there I would be able to get my own place and maintain my freedom for as long as I keep a job and don't reoffend. I won't lie to you; I've slipped up before and got back on drugs. My drug addiction is the source of all my problems. I'm not a violent person. I haven't had a fight since high school, and I've never physically harmed anyone. Unfortunately, my record doesn't reflect that with all the armed robberies. The thing is the robberies were with a squirt gun I made to look like a real gun. I realize that doesn't matter in the eyes of the law, but I just wanted you to know I'm a chickenshit!" explained Tony.

"Good to know. I've done some homework on you and came to that conclusion already, but I appreciate you telling me this on your own," I said. "Listen, I'd like to share what you did for me with the parole board. I'm not advocating for anything on your behalf, but I'm sure it couldn't hurt for me to let the board know what you did for the FBI," I said.

There was silence on the other end of the line, so I finally had to ask, "Tony, are you still there?"

After a few more seconds, I heard, "Yeah, I'm still here. I don't know what to say to you other than nobody's gone to bat for me in a hell of a long time. If you were to talk to the parole board, I'd be forever grateful."

"Consider it done. Keep in touch," I said as I signed off.

The next day I telephoned Sheila Hubbard, chair of the Massachusetts Parole Board.

"Ms. Hubbard, my name is Dave Nadolski. I am a Special Agent of the Federal Bureau of Investigation. I am the case agent on the robbery that took place at the John Quincy Adams Library, and I am calling to advise you of valuable information provided to me by a Concord prison inmate by the name of Anthony Romano," I said.

"Thank you, agent; that is gratifying to hear. What was the information provided to you?" asked Hubbard.

"Ms. Hubbard, Anthony provided the name of Kevin Gildea. I had never met Anthony prior to that call and was very happy to receive the tip. If you have followed the news, you may be aware that Kevin Gildea has pleaded guilty to that robbery and is currently incarcerated. Without the information provided by Anthony, I'm not sure we would have been able to make an arrest. Furthermore, Anthony has not asked for anything in return, but I am recommending that he receive the reward money offered by the Park Service for information leading to the arrest and conviction of the perpetrator of the robbery. The purpose of my call today is to inform you of the service provided by Anthony and to personally commend him for his actions in this matter. I thought you should be aware of his contribution," I said.

"Mr. Nadolski, this is very good news, and I appreciate you bringing it to my attention. Normally when I receive a call from a federal law enforcement agency, it's not to report something laudable about one of our parolees or inmates. This is a pleasant surprise! Thank you," Hubbard responded enthusiastically.

10

HEARTBREAK IN CAMBRIDGE

FBI, BOSTON DIVISION

Friday, October 3, 1997, 5:00 p.m.

The mood on C-6 was upbeat as agents prepared to call it a day and start heading home for the weekend. "Rob, what do you have planned for the weekend?" I asked Rob Carrol.

Rob was a hard-charging C-6 agent. Always ready to volunteer. He was once described to me as the guy you would call if you were across the country and needed someone to bring you $5,000 for bail money. He'd be there the next day with the cash, no questions asked. I loved working with Rob and considered him a close friend.

"I don't know. I might go apple picking with my daughter. How about you?" he asked.

"Sounds like our plans as well, except I'm on call this weekend. Keeping my fingers crossed that the bad guys give me a break," I replied.

Since C-6 is a reactive squad, we had an agent assigned to respond to all emergency cases 24/7. This weekend was my turn so that meant I had to be available all weekend.

"Well, good luck with that, Nads," said Rob with a sly grin.

No sooner had Rob and I had that exchange when John Trahon walked into the squad area and addressed the squad, "Attention, everyone. I just received a call from the captain of detectives at Cambridge PD requesting our help with the missing boy case. They've had a development, and our SAC has ordered us to head there right now, so let's roll."

Rob and I looked at one another. No apple picking for us this weekend.

For the past two days, police and volunteer citizens in Cambridge, a city located across the Charles River from Boston and home to Harvard University, had been fanned out all over town searching for a missing ten-year-old boy by the name of Jeffrey Curley. Jeffrey was last seen by his grandmother around 4:00 p.m. on the first of October. He had popped his head into her kitchen and said he was leaving the yard to go do something and would be back. He never made it home, and no one knew where he was. Short of evidence of foul play, the FBI doesn't routinely enter missing person cases unless requested by the local police. We now knew this case had entered a very ominous phase.

John Trahon approached and said, "Dave, hold up a second. I'm not sure what we are getting into here, but since you have the helm this weekend, you are officially assigned as case agent on this. You might as well warn Linda not to hold dinner."

That was fine with me and every other agent in the room. Anyone who serves as a first responder, in whatever capacity, develops an instinctive response to tragedy, becoming laser-focused on jumping to the call. We were all ready, willing, and anxious to get involved; any thoughts of a family-focused weekend instantly dissipate. Personally, I was saying a silent prayer that we were still in a position to find this boy alive.

Once the squad arrived at Cambridge PD, John and I met with Detective Sergeant Patrick Nagle, who filled us in on the latest.

"Thanks for showing up in force, guys; we appreciate it. We've developed at least one person of interest and could use the help of the FBI. As you may know, we set up a command post at Jeff Curley's house from which we have been directing the search effort. Yesterday we were approached by a local guy, a small-time troublemaker by the name of Sal Sicari. Sal told us he may have been the last person to see Jeffrey before he disappeared, and he wanted to help out with the search effort. One of the officers asked Sal what he was talking about, and Sal told him he was walking down the street in front of Jeffrey's house around 4:00 p.m. on Wednesday. According to Sal, he saw Jeffrey, whom he knows, playing with his dog in his grandmother's yard. Sal claims he called out to Jeffrey, who opened the gate and ordered the dog to attack him. Sal yelled out at Jeffrey to stop the dog, but Jeff just laughed. Sal said he ran for his life and managed to get away. He said he didn't see Jeffrey again but thought that was about the time Jeffrey was last seen," Sergeant Nagle recapped.

John and I looked at one another. What a coincidence.

Sergeant Nagle continued, "At this point, one of Jeffrey's brothers entered the command post and observed Sal. The brother started screaming at Sal and claiming he had something to do with the disappearance. He said Sal had been hanging around with Jeff and claimed Sal was a piece of shit and somehow involved. Our officer had to restrain the brother before he attacked Sal, who of course denied everything and said he just wanted to help find the kid. Sal took off at that point."

John looked at Sergeant Nagle and asked, "What happened next?"

"Well, it got really weird at this point. This morning Sal shows up again at the command post and wants to speak with the detective in charge. So I went over to the command post to meet with Sal. I asked him to meet me at the station. Sal showed up, sat down with me and Detective Silverio Ferreira, and told us he suspects his friend Charles Jaynes may have something to do with the disappearance of Jeffrey," Sergeant Nagle said.

"Good, so is Sicari still here?" I asked.

"Yeah, he's cooling his heels in the interview room. I thought we'd wait for you guys until we go any further," replied Sergeant Nagle.

"Okay, so show me where he is," I replied.

I entered the interview room, which was actually more of a meeting room with several tables and a number of chairs. The room had windows overlooking the busy street below. Sal Sicari was sitting on one side of a large folding table. He was in his midtwenties, about 160 pounds, and maybe five feet, eight inches tall. He had angular features; thick, black, curly hair; and a short, black goatee. He was wearing an old, dark-gray work shirt and was sitting calmly with his hands folded in front of him on the table. Detective Ferreira was sitting across from him; neither one was talking.

I introduced myself. "Hi, Sal, my name is Dave Nadolski, and I'm an FBI agent."

"FBI? Why are you here?" asked Sal with obvious concern in his voice.

"Well, Sal, the Cambridge police department asked us to join the investigation. I understand that you may be the last person to see Jeff before he disappeared, is that right?" I asked.

"Yes, sir, I may have been. It was the night before last, and I saw him playing with his dog in his grandmother's yard. I called out to him and he told the dog to get me, so I took off. He thought that was a big joke. I could hear him laughing as I ran down the street," Sal said.

"All right, Sal, maybe you were the last person to see Jeff. How well did you know the boy?" I asked.

"I live in the neighborhood, and I knew the kid since he was little. He was always running around the streets, and I used to talk to him from time to time." I wondered why Sal was referring to Jeff in the past tense.

"Where exactly did you run into Jeff?" I asked.

"Oh, you know, at the neighborhood parks for the most part," responded Sal.

"So for the most part you met him at neighborhood parks. Where else?"

"My friend Charles Jaynes has a car, and sometimes Jeff would bug us to give him a ride here or there, so Charles would do that for him."

"So Jeff would ride around with you and Charles in Charles's car? Is that right?" I asked, not liking where this was heading.

"Yeah, sure, the kid thought he was a hot shit hanging around with older guys. He liked to go cruising so we just humored him," Sal replied.

"Sal, how many times would you say Jeff drove around with you and Charles?" I asked.

"I don't know, a bunch."

"Sal, where is Charles Jaynes right now?"

"He and his dad have a car-detailing business. They detail cars that come into dealerships as trade-ins, so the dealer can sell them. I think he's working at a dealership in Newton today." Sal stopped looking at me and focused on his folded hands.

"Sal, tell me why you think Charles Jaynes may have something to do with the disappearance of Jeffrey."

"It's just a feeling, but I'm pretty sure he liked the kid more than is healthy, you know?" responded Sal, his head only a few inches from the tabletop.

Alarm bells are clanging in my head!

Detective Ferreira slipped me a note: *We found Jaynes at the dealership and arrested him on outstanding warrants. He wants a lawyer, will not talk.*

Okay, so Jaynes is out of play, but Sicari is talking, sort of. Time to put some pressure on Sicari.

"Sal, it seems to me you suspect your friend Charles of doing something to Jeff, but you weren't involved, is that right?" I asked.

"Yeah, exactly!" Sicari sat up and looked directly at me.

"That's good to hear, Sal, and I know it's hard to point a finger at a friend, but this is really important and I appreciate you helping us. What I want to do now is administer a polygraph test to show you are telling us the truth and had nothing to do with whatever happened to Jeff. Can we do that right now?" I asked.

"Yeah, sure, I want you to know I had nothing to do with this," responded Sal.

I excused myself and joined the rest of my team outside the interview room. I briefed John, Rob, the other agents, and Sergeant Nagle on what Sicari was telling me and quickly got ahold of our polygraph examiner, agent Tom Donlan, who was at home by this time.

"Tom, this is Dave Nadolski. I've got a possible suspect regarding the missing Cambridge boy. He's agreed to a polygraph, and I need you at Cambridge PD as fast as you can get here," I said.

"Okay, Dave, I'm wheels up and out the door. I'll be there as soon as possible!" responded Tom.

The polygraph, in and of itself, is not a truth or lie detector. It measures heartbeats, respiration, and perspiration and charts when these physiological reactions increase, decrease, or stay the same. When someone tells a lie, knowing it's a lie, and is worried about it, the machine will reveal "hits" on the physiological reactions. The person administering the test can tell which questions are giving the subject real problems and will run more than one test focusing on the problem questions. The person taking the test can figure out he's blowing it and will continue to react. It's practically impossible to control. At this point, the polygraph examiner will sit down in front of the subject and show him the reactions to the test questions. He will explain what the subject already knows: he wasn't truthful. This is the point where the examiner earns his pay. The subject knows he's been lying and isn't getting away with it, so it's the examiner's job to get a confession. A failed polygraph test is not admissible in court, but a confession is.

Tom worked on Sal in private for a couple hours while I sat with John, the Cambridge detectives, and the rest of C-6. The tension was palpable in the room. Eventually Tom walked out of the interview room and joined the rest of us. He was exhausted, I could tell right away. A polygraph test is very taxing on the examiner and the subject. Tom grabbed my arm and led me to the side of the room.

"Dave, Sal blew the test; he is definitely involved with the disappearance of Jeff Curley. Sal is sticking to the story that he thinks something bad happened to Jeff, but if anything bad happened, it was Charles Jaynes who was responsible, not him. So far, we have half a loaf," Tom said.

At this point, we received some important information. Cambridge and Massachusetts State Police detectives arrested Charles Jaynes and executed a search warrant on his car. Inside the car they found a receipt from Home Depot dated Wednesday, October 1, at 9:30 p.m. The receipt was for bags of lime and concrete. Another October 1 receipt for a fifty-gallon plastic container was also found in Jayne's car. This was explosive information and tough to explain. So was what happened next.

Armed with the receipts, Sergeant Nagle stormed into the room where Sal was still sitting at the table with his head in his hands and appeared to be silently weeping. Sergeant Nagle threw the receipts down in front of Sal and asked, "Sal, what the hell is this? Receipts for a fifty-gallon container, cement, and lime! How do you explain this?"

Sal removed his hands, stood up, suddenly stopped crying, and yelled, "FUCK IT, you got me now!" With that he reached down and overturned the table in front of him and started wailing.

At this point, Sergeant Nagle left the room, and I was joined by Detective John Fulkerson and Trooper Al Hunte, who had previously been speaking to Charles Jaynes and had just arrived at the Cambridge police station. Fulkerson and Hunte were very big men. Al Hunte was a muscular African American who stood over six feet and was at least 210 pounds. They walked into the room and approached Sicari directly. Sicari remained very emotional and disturbed, and before the detectives entered the room, he hid his head behind a curtain next to the window in the third-floor room. I was really hoping he wasn't planning to go OUT the window!

Al Hunte spoke softly to Sal. "Sal, I'm Detective Hunte. I'd like you to look at me. We want to ask you some questions. Is that okay?"

Sal removed his head from the curtain, looked at Al Hunte, and said, "I'm not talking!"

"Come on, let's sit down now, Sal. We have some things to talk about, okay?" responded Al in a very controlled and soothing manner.

Eventually Sal did come out from behind the curtain, and we got him to sit down and tell us the whole story of what happened the day Jeff Curley disappeared. Once Sal began talking, he reacted as if a gigantic weight was lifted off his chest. He stopped crying, calmed down, accepted some water, and became very cooperative, answering all the questions put to him. The story he told was the most disturbing story I have ever heard from a suspect.

Sal Sicari and Charles Jaynes lured Jeff Curley into Jayne's car the day of his disappearance with the promise of buying him a new bicycle. Sicari was driving, and Jaynes was in the backseat with Jeffrey. At one point, they stopped at a gas station to fill the car. Jaynes produced a cloth rag and soaked it in gas. Once he got back into the car, Sicari started driving and Jaynes told Jeffrey he wanted to have sex with him. Jeffrey put up a fight but was unable to overcome the 250-pound man. According to Sicari, Jaynes stuffed the gas-soaked rag in Jeffrey's mouth and sat on him until he was dead. They then stopped at a hardware store and bought a blue tarp and a roll of duct tape. Sicari used the tarp and tape to wrap Jeffery's body and place it in the trunk of the car. Later that evening, they purchased the fifty-gallon plastic container, lime, and cement to dispose of Jeff's body. The lime and concrete were to be added into the container for weight and to aid in decomposition of the body. All this was accomplished at Charles Jaynes's apartment in Concord, New Hampshire, but not before Jaynes sexually assaulted the boy's body.

Sicari and Jaynes loaded the fifty-gallon container with Jeffrey's body into the trunk of Jayne's car and headed for a river in Maine. Jaynes was driving and had a particular location in mind. After about an hour of driving, Jaynes stopped on a small bridge over a stream and announced they had arrived. All Sicari knew was that they were somewhere in Maine. It was pitch black, and the road they stopped on was in a rural area. It was a two-lane blacktop with metal guardrails. The river was about forty yards across, was slow moving, and had lily pads in it. There was a house just beyond the river that had a dog and an outdoor light on a motion detector. He knew this because when Jaynes turned around in the driveway of this house, the light came on and the dog barked. There was no further sign of life from the house, so Jaynes declared the location safe to dump the body. They stopped on the bridge, opened the trunk, and struggled getting the container out and on top of the guardrail and into the river below. They quickly left and returned to Jaynes's apartment. The next morning Sal and Jaynes drove back to Massachusetts, and Sal approached the police and volunteered to look for Jeff.

It was about 3:00 a.m. now in the interview room. Sal was asked if he could locate the spot where they dropped Jeff's body into the river. He wasn't sure but was willing to give it a try.

At this point, we had a meeting with everyone to lay out our plan for the rest of the night. Sal would ride with Detective Fulkerson and Trooper Hunte, followed by me and Rob Carrol in my car and the rest of my squad in their cars. We were notified there was a large contingent of press outside the police station and formulated a plan to deal with them. We screamed out of the police garage and took off at a high rate of speed, heading north. A couple of intrepid news crews attempted to give chase but were pulled over by squad cars and detained until we could make our escape. For the next four hours, we drove in a parade around southern Maine, with Sal providing the guidance. Eventually it was decided that Sal had no clear idea where to go, so Fulkerson and Hunte returned him to Massachusetts, where he was held in the Middlesex County Jail. Rob and I stayed behind in Maine to help establish a task force consisting of FBI, Maine State Police, Massachusetts State Police, and Maine game wardens. We set up a command post, and working with the description provided by Sal, we attempted to narrow down possible locations to search.

COMMAND POST, PORTLAND, MAINE

"Good morning, ladies and gentlemen. Thank you for your help bringing Jeffrey Curley home," I announced the next morning at the command post in Portland, Maine.

"Our mission is to locate and retrieve the remains of Jeff Curley and bring some type of closure to his family. We are searching for a two-lane bridge located in southern Maine. It is a rural area; the bridge has steel guardrails, and the water below is fairly slow moving with lily pads visible from the bridge. The bridge is approximately ten to fifteen feet above the water. Further, we believe there is a house next to the bridge that has a dog and a side-mounted floodlight activated by movement. Many of you are local officers who are obviously familiar with the roadways and bridges in this area, and we are asking that you provide possible locations that fit this description.

"Maine State Police have provided a team of scuba divers that are here and ready to search any possible locations. This recovery effort will be headed by the Maine State Police, assisted by the FBI Evidence Response Team. I'd like to invite anyone who may have an opinion as to where we may start our search efforts to raise their hands," I said.

Immediately a hand was raised and waved back and forth. The man was about fifty years of age, stout, and rugged looking. He was wearing a green uniform.

"Yes, sir, who are you and what is your suggestion?" I asked.

"I'm Maine Game Warden Jason LaPointe, and I have a location in mind that seems to fit this description," he said.

"We are all ears, sir; please continue," I replied.

"Well, there is a bridge in South Berwick that crosses the Great Works River. I'll be damned if it doesn't fit your description to a T," Warden LaPointe said.

This announcement caused a stir in the audience, and private discussions were taking place with a lot of head nodding.

Another hand shot up. "Trooper Al Peterson, Maine State Police. I second that location as a great place to start the search. I am personally aware of it and agree it fits the description."

The group engaged in further discussion of the location, and finally Maine State Police Captain Dan Elliott stood and clapped for attention.

"There is general agreement, so we will start with the bridge over the Great Works River. Our dive team will deploy there immediately and begin underwater search operations right away," Captain Elliott said.

Rob and I jumped into my car and started for the search location. Rob and I were both members of the FBI Evidence Response Team and would represent the FBI in that capacity. We were trained and experienced in evidence recovery and would make certain all protocols were followed in the event this became a federal prosecution.

GREAT WORKS RIVER, SOUTH BERWICK, MAINE

The location looked perfect. "Rob, look at this! A two-lane bridge over a river with metal guardrail. There's a house next to the bridge. There's even lily pads as described by Sal," I said.

"Man, this has got to be the spot!" Rob agreed.

Rob and I joined the rest of the group walking up and down the river looking for any sign of the blue plastic container along the shore or in the water. The dive team spent two hours in the water. They started immediately under the bridge and conducted a thorough grid search downriver for seventy-five yards. The current in the river created a lot of silting of the water causing poor visibility, but the river was only six feet deep and not particularly difficult to navigate. Unfortunately, we all came up empty. The divers felt they had done as thorough a job as practical, so we met at a Maine State Police mobile command post to discuss our options.

"We need to move on and start checking the other possible locations," announced Captain Elliott.

Everybody agreed but marveled at the fact that this location didn't pan out. It really seemed perfect.

"I don't get it," mused Jason LaPointe. "I was sure this was going to be the place."

"I agree, Jason; it looked good to me as well." I said.

For the next two days, the team searched five more locations throughout southern Maine with no success. We were beginning to suspect Sal was pulling our chain or hallucinating. We met at the command post on the fourth day to discuss our options.

"I believe we really need to go back to South Berwick and expand our search of the Great Works River," Warden Jason LaPointe said firmly. "It was the best place we've found, and I just can't believe we will find a place that better matches the description we were given."

Captain Elliott scratched his chin and looked around the room. "I can't disagree with that reasoning. Let's give it another go. This time I'd like the dive team to search at least one hundred yards downriver. I noticed there were some fallen trees in the water a little farther downstream. We may get lucky yet," he said.

October 7 was perfect for diving. It was a beautiful autumn day. The leaves were turning crimson and gold. There was a bright blue sky, and the temperature was in the high sixties. This was the perfect day for an autumn picnic, much too beautiful for the gruesome task we were engaged in, but maybe it was an omen of hope as well. Television station helicopters were aloft following our every move, as they had been for the past three days. The Maine State Police mobile command post was on scene, and every available diver was in the water. Rob and I were joined by other members of the FBI Evidence Response Team, and once again we patrolled the banks watching for any sign from the divers. This time Rob and I noticed the fallen trees in the water and observed there must be branches beneath the surface that would prevent the container from floating further downstream.

The divers had been in the water most of the morning and were now searching the area of the downed trees, which lay about ninety yards from the bridge. Suddenly, two divers surfaced and waved. We rushed to the area of the fallen trees to see what they were signaling about. The first diver removed his regulator and mask.

"We got it! It's caught up in the fallen tree. A blue plastic container!" he exclaimed.

Word spread like wildfire! Agents, officers, and troopers rushed to the bank. The divers pushed the container toward the shore, and six of us reached into the water and grabbed onto the blue plastic container wrapped in gray duct tape. Thank God!

Preparations had been made for the retrieval and transport of the container. The Maine Medical Examiner's transport vehicle was on scene and immediately drove down to the riverbank. Carefully, we lifted the waterlogged container from the murky water, and despite slipping and sliding on the muddy bank, we managed to lift and slide the container into the metal box on the back of the truck. We locked the truck as water escaped from holes in the plastic container and poured out the back. Finally, we had what we were looking for, albeit under grim circumstances, and could return this precious child—robbed of his innocence and robbed of his life—to his grieving parents.

I watched the medical examiner's truck slowly pull away with a full escort of Maine State Police vehicles leading and following the somber truck with their light bars flashing. Eventually, as the parade of vehicles disappeared down the lonely rural road, I rejoined the group of searchers who had gathered next to the command truck where ice-cold bottled water was being offered and thankfully accepted. I looked for Jason La-

Pointe and finally found him in an animated conversation with one of the divers who was still in his wet suit and chugging on a water bottle.

"Jay!" I called out as I walked up and extended my hand. "I want to formally thank you for suggesting this search location in the first place and also for sticking to your guns despite the first failed effort to find Jeff's body. If it wasn't for you, I don't know where we would be today."

Jay flashed a wide, toothy grin and accepted my hand with a hearty handshake of his own and exclaimed, "Hell, boy, what kind of game warden would I be if I couldn't come up with this location? The description was spot on!"

"It sure was," I agreed. "Next we have to put everything together for court. We still have a long road ahead."

As expected, the autopsy revealed that Jeff had been suffocated with a gas-soaked rag, which caused his death. This fact established legal jurisdiction in Massachusetts. The only other decision was whether the case would be filed in federal court or state court. While any murder in Massachusetts can be tried in state court, in this case the US Attorney's office also had jurisdiction because the defendants crossed state lines to have sexual relations with a child under twelve years of age. The big difference between the state law and the federal law is the penalty. When death occurs as a result of the crime, the federal death penalty kicks in—the state of Massachusetts had no death penalty.

The US Attorney for the District of Massachusetts and the Massachusetts Attorney General met to discuss which of the two jurisdictions should prosecute the crime. My money was on the federal prosecution because everyone's blood was up, and the general feeling among the people of Massachusetts was overwhelmingly in favor of having these guys die for what they did, especially when it was discovered that Charles Jaynes was a card-carrying member of NAMBLA (North American Man Boy Love Association). The name is an ironic description of its twisted membership.

Ultimately, the case was tried in state court, which meant that the most these defendants could get would be life in prison with no chance of parole. Assistant District Attorney David Yannetti conducted an excellent prosecution of Sicari and Jaynes, who were tried separately. I appeared as a witness in the Sicari trial to testify to the interview in the Cambridge Police Department and the recovery of Jeff's body. Sal Sicari was convicted of murder in the first degree and sentenced to life in prison with no chance of parole. Charles Jaynes fared better and was convicted of second-degree murder and is eligible to be considered for parole after twenty-three years. Jaynes, while clearly the instigator and person who actually killed Jeff, benefited by not talking to the police after being placed under arrest back at the car dealership. In reality, could there ever really be any just punishment for perpetrators of such evil? Makes you hope for that special place in Hell.

Pragmatically speaking, had the case gone to federal court, I would have been the case agent and would have been working this case full time for the next year.

II

PAROLE

HILLSIDE HOUSE, ROXBURY, MASSACHUSETTS

Tony finally became eligible for a parole hearing, and to his surprise, the board approved his first-time parole request and set a release date six months down the road. In the meantime, Tony was eligible for work release. Work release is a pre-parole condition where an inmate lives in a halfway house but is responsible for obtaining and maintaining a job during the day. He is still an inmate under the control of the prison system.

Tony was sent to Hillside House in the Roxbury section of Boston to serve his final six months before the parole became effective. Not a particularly good draw. His two new roommates at Hillside charged Tony "rent" to live in their room. One of the roommates sold heroin, and most of the residents were using—not particularly difficult because for fifty dollars you could obtain a "clean" urine sample. Tony picked up the needle again and quickly went downhill. He was working in his dad's auto shop during the day, and his wife, Lorraine (or Lo, as he called her), was living in an apartment located on the third floor of his dad's house. She was about to deliver Tony's baby at this time as well.

One Sunday morning Tony scored a furlough and planned to spend the whole weekend with Lo. It had been a couple days since he used heroin, and he was trying to kick the habit on his own because to seek help would have landed him back inside a walled prison and ruined his chance for parole. He needed just a little money to get enough heroin to "get the sick off," and so he robbed a kid in a gas station with a stick he picked up outside the business. As he was trying to get away, a state trooper chased him down. He managed to get away from the trooper by losing him in an apartment complex. Unfortunately, however, the Boston cops scooped him up in five minutes and deposited him at the county jail.

Tony soon found himself before a judge who sentenced him to ten years, and his next residence was Walpole prison.

Walpole was as tough and dangerous as ever. By this time Mello was back on the street and dealing cocaine and heroin. Lorraine was out of Tony's dad's place and looking for somewhere to live. Mello obtained a "partnership" in TRC Auto Electric located on Dorchester Avenue in Dorchester, a tough neighborhood of Boston. TRC was an auto-repair shop run by three brothers, Stanley, Eddie, and Joe Travers. Mello managed the business. Tony sent word to Lorraine to find Mello and see what he could do for her. She needed money and a place to live with the kids. Tony reached out to Mello and was assured Lorraine would be taken care of. With his domestic situation taken care of, Tony turned his attention to doing his time and staying alive in Walpole. Kevin Gildea, Tony's lock-picking buddy, had been singing the tune that Tony had turned him in and was responsible for Kevin getting busted on the escape attempt. In reality Tony was definitely responsible for a couple of arrests back at MCI Norfolk, but he never said a word about Gildea. Gildea's accusations required Tony to sleep with at least one eye open all night.

Lorraine had skipped a couple visits to Walpole, which got Tony concerned. When she finally did show up, she was distraught, had lost weight, and looked like shit.

"What's going on with you, babe?" asked Tony.

Lorraine just sat at the table looking at her folded hands, barely able to remain composed. Finally, she just blurted out, "Mello is making me mule drugs all over the goddamn city of Boston!"

With that confession, the dam burst and Lorraine began to sob. The guards looked over and started to move toward them. Tony quickly jumped to his feet and assured the guards that Lorraine was experiencing financial problems at home and was having serious personal problems. The guards had seen this a hundred times at least and to their credit backed off and let Tony deal with it.

"Listen, honey, you've got to get ahold of yourself! I want you to back away from Mello. I'll get my dad to take over the rent for the apartment you are in. Just take care of the kids." he told her.

After the visit, Tony returned to his cell and stared at the ceiling. *Don't worry, buddy. I'll take care of Lorraine.* Mello's words played endlessly in his head. *That miserable son of a bitch took care of Lorraine all right*, he thought.

Tony decided then and there he would make Mello pay some day. He'd play it cool with Mello until that time, but as soon as he was able, he was going to stick it to that lousy prick.

PARK DRIVE HALFWAY HOUSE, BOSTON, MASSACHUSETTS

My talk with Sheila Hubbard of the Massachusetts Parole Board may have made an impression because in September of 1997, I received a call from Tony informing me that he had received parole and was being assigned to the Park Drive halfway house located in the Fenway Park area of Boston. In order to qualify for parole, Tony would first need to demonstrate that he could be trusted, meaning he needed to obtain full-time employment, pass random drug tests, live peaceably in the group home environment, and most importantly obey all laws.

"So do you think you'll be successful this time around?" I asked him.

"Hell, yes. Believe me, I'm over the life I've been living. I want to change things; I'm getting too old for this shit. One drug slipup and I'm back inside. Park Drive is a great landing spot. It's well run, the staff takes no bullshit from anybody, and if there's a hint of drug use, the offender goes back. Under these conditions I think I can do well. Also, I landed a mechanics job in Dorchester working six days a week. The place is a busy shop on Dorchester Avenue called TRC Auto Electric. It's owned by three brothers who are good guys. The shop manager is an old friend of my father, a guy I did time with, believe it or not," explained Tony.

"Really? What's this guy's name?" I asked.

"Carmello Merlino. He goes by the nickname 'Mello,'" replied Tony.

"How old is Mello?" I asked.

"Around sixty," Tony responded.

"What did he do time for?" I asked.

"Just about everything. He robbed banks and armored cars, distributed drugs, did burglaries, home invasions; basically he'd do anything for a buck. Banks and armored cars were his specialty."

"Is he a made guy?" I asked, referring to his status as a member of the Mafia.

"No, he's not made, but he has a lot of Mafia friends and he'll do stuff with them from time to time," Tony explained.

"So you're going to be working with this guy?" I asked.

"Absolutely. He's my boss," replied Tony.

Of course, the thought going through my mind was this could be a golden opportunity!

"Okay, pal, let's stay in touch." I said.

"You bet, Dave," and with that, Tony signed off.

I did a full record check on Carmello Merlino, and quickly found out he was some kind of badass. His arrest record went back to 1950, before I was born, and had fifteen different arrest entries for state and federal crimes; most were violent crimes. He did state and federal prison terms, which broke up his crime spree. He was no longer on parole, which meant he was probably cooking up something new. *Life might get really interesting*, I thought.

About a week after the phone call with Tony, I was sitting at my desk when another call came in. The switchboard wanted to put Tony through to me again.

"This is Dave. What's up?" I answered.

"Can we meet tomorrow?" Tony asked.

"Yeah, no problem. When and where?"

"I get off work early tomorrow. There's a ballfield down the street from the halfway house. Can you meet me in the bleachers at 4:30 p.m.?" Tony asked.

"Okay," I responded. "What's this about?"

"It's about Mello. He's got something going, and I need to talk to you about it. Do you have the Gardner case?" asked Tony.

The Gardner case was a robbery that took place in the early morning hours of March 18, 1990, at the Isabella Stewart Gardner Museum located in Boston. Museum guards admitted entrance to a pair of men dressed as Boston police officers who said they were responding to a disturbance call at the museum. The two "officers" quickly overpowered the guards and tied them up. For the next hour, they collected and stole thirteen works of art valued at over $500 million. This was, and still is, the largest art theft in US history.

The FBI immediately opened a case, and despite investigating thousands of leads around the world, the perpetrators have not been identified and the artwork remains missing.

"No, I'm not assigned to that case. Why do you ask?" I replied.

"I don't want to talk about it over the phone, but bring whoever is working the case with you tomorrow, okay?" he asked.

"Sure, no problem. See you tomorrow." I signed off.

For the previous seven years, the Boston FBI office had kept one or more agents devoted to investigating the Gardner robbery. Veteran agent Neil Cronin was the current case agent in 1997. I walked over to Neil's squad area and looked around. I found Neil on the phone at his desk. Neil was a Boston native, an accountant, and a rather large man with jet-black hair. He was in his midthirties. I loved interviewing people with Neil. He would size a person up with the most deadpan expression on his face. He would listen to the whole story without interruption while taking meticulous notes. Nothing fazed Neil. During questioning, he would simply ask a question and then stop talking. The subject would get nervous while Neil just stared at the guy. Unable to stand the strain of silence, the subject would inevitably start babbling, and Neil would continue writing.

When not conducting business, Neil would hang around with fellow agent John Huyler. John and Neil were the office comedy team. Neil was often cracking jokes with John, hosting the office social events, and encouraging John to play the Marine Corps hymn over the FBI office public address system with his harmonica. It wasn't a party until Neil and John showed up.

I sat down at the empty desk next to his and waited for him to finish his conversation.

"What's up, Nads?" Neil asked after hanging up.

"Are you available to do an interview with me at 4:30 tomorrow? It's regarding the Gardner," I responded.

"4:30 a.m. or p.m.?" Neil asked wryly.

"Sure as hell not a.m.," I responded.

"Okay, that's good. Whatcha got?" asked Neil.

I spent the next ten minutes filling Neil in on Tony's situation and what he had done for me regarding the Adams case.

"So he comes up with this guy by the name of Carmello Merlino. Merlino goes by the nickname 'Mello.' He's an old-time mob associate and violent criminal who loves the big heists. He spent a lot of time in state and federal prison, and he's out now and working as the manager of an auto-repair shop in Dorchester. That's where Tony is employed as a mechanic. He and Tony have known one another for a long time and have actually done time together," I informed Neil as I slid Mello's rap sheet over to him.

Neil read it over and grunted, "Serious dude."

"So what I know so far is that Tony thinks Mello could be somehow involved with Gardner. Tomorrow we will find out more," I concluded.

"I'm in," Neil said quickly.

The next day Neil and I arrived ten minutes early for our meeting at the ball field and found Tony already sitting alone in the deserted bleachers. I liked seeing that. He wasn't late and in fact was early. Good sign.

I waved to Tony as we approached, and he signaled us to join him on the bleachers.

"I like this place; it's nice and private. I won't be running into anyone from the halfway house," said Tony as he looked over the vacant diamond.

"Tony, this is Neil Cronin. He's the case agent on the Gardner case," I said.

"Nice to meet you, Tony," said Neil as he extended his hand. Tony accepted it.

"I've filled Neil in regarding Mello already. I think Neil is pretty interested in what you have to offer us today," I said.

"That's right, Tony. Mello is certainly an interesting guy, and I'm anxious to hear what you have to say about him," replied Neil.

Tony didn't say anything at first and seemed to be making up his mind about Neil. Neil did his usual routine and didn't say another word and just sat looking at Tony. A full minute passed and I wanted to scream, but Neil just sat there with his trademark deadpan expression.

"Okay," said Tony finally, breaking the huge pregnant pause. "Dave may have told you already that me and Mello go back a ways. I first met him when I was a kid in my dad's auto-repair shop, and Mello and other thugs would meet in the back room where Mello was the master of ceremonies. He and I did time together in a couple spots here in Massachusetts. The thing is he's a fucking user and put my wife to work delivering drugs. That did it for me. He doesn't know it, but I hate his goddamn guts for doing that," Tony explained.

Neil nodded and continued listening.

"Every morning I meet with Mello in the shop at 5:30 a.m. He opens up before anyone else gets there, and he and I talk about stuff going on. He's been following the stories in the *Boston Herald* about the latest Gardner news and says things like you guys are going in the wrong direction and suggests that he may know the right direction. He doesn't get specific or anything, but he makes a lot of nonbusiness calls during the day and meets in the parking lot with some heavy hitters," Tony said.

"Who does he meet with?" asked Neil.

"Well, he's got a couple guys he does stuff with. It's almost like his personal crew. David Turner and Stephen Rossetti. They come by the shop every so often, and Mello meets with them in the parking lot," explained Tony.

Neil wrote the names down. "How old are Turner and Rossetti?" asked Neil.

"Thirties, I think," said Tony.

"Interesting. I wonder what they were up to when the Gardner was robbed," Neil mused.

"Yeah, if they were involved, Mello would know about it for sure. There's another colorful character who goes by the name 'Fat Richie.' He really lives up to his name. He's about five feet, seven inches and weighs in at around 350 pounds. He and Mello talk outside TRC, and I'm sure it's got something to do with the Gardner. Not sure what though; Mello hasn't clued me in," Tony said.

"I've heard of Fat Richie; he's a con man for the most part, but his name has come up in connection with the Gardner as well," replied Neil.

Tony leaned closer. "Listen to this, you guys: there's something else Mello is talking about. It's a new thing he's considering."

"What's that?" I asked.

"You know banks and armored car jobs are Mello's specialty. He likes dealing drugs, but armed robberies involving lots of fast cash are irresistible to him. Are you aware of the Loomis Fargo armored car vault in Easton, Massachusetts? South of Boston?" Tony asked.

"No. I never heard of it," I said.

"Well, Mello knows where it is. This is the place where the armored cars and all the money they transport are stored. It's a mini Fort Knox. He says it's a nondescript one-story cinder-block building with no windows or advertising of any sort. It's in an industrial park. Mello has been casing the place."

"No shit?" I replied.

"That's not all. His grand plan isn't to rob a truck. He actually wants to get someone on the inside. He wants an employee who is willing to go along with a robbery of the vault itself. He's even asked me if I know someone who can get a job there. He's obsessed with this idea. He likes how bold it is," said Tony.

"Jesus, why doesn't this guy just retire?" I asked.

"He'll never give up; prison doesn't bother him. Working a nine-to-five is worse than prison in his opinion, and the Loomis job is tailor-made for Turner and Rossetti too. Listen, I got to check back in at the halfway house now, so this meeting is over. I'll keep talking to Mello and let you know what I hear," Tony said as he jumped down from the bleachers and walked away.

On the way back to the office, Neil and I discussed the names and information given to us by Tony.

"Dave, this is good stuff. I think Tony may be on to something. I've heard of Turner before, and what I've heard about him isn't good. Stephen Rossetti is a new name to me, but there's a Mark Rossetti from East Boston who's a made guy and likes to rob armored cars. Could be related. We really need to stay in touch with Tony," Neil said.

"Believe me, I plan to, Neil," I replied.

Back at the office, I consulted with my supervisor, John Trahon.

"John, I need a few minutes. You won't believe the conversation I had with Tony Romano today," I began.

"Isn't he the guy you got the Adams tip from?" asked John.

"Yeah, good memory. I've stayed in touch with him since then, and he's out of prison and staying at the Park Drive halfway house now. As you know, inmates need to prove themselves by getting and holding a job, staying out of additional trouble, and essentially proving they can survive on the outside under looser restraints," I said.

"So how's he doing?" asked John.

"Pretty well so far. He landed a job as an auto mechanic at a garage in Dorchester. He's been working and keeping his nose clean. No drugs. He's toeing the line," I explained.

"That's encouraging," John responded.

"The really interesting part is his boss is Carmello Merlino," I said.

I filled John in on what Tony told us about Carmello Merlino, David Turner, and Stephen Rossetti. I went on to divulge the information about a possible Gardner connection and the fact that Neil Cronin was interested in pursuing that angle.

"The thing that really interests me, and by extension you, is this crazy man Carmello Merlino is actively planning to rob the Loomis Fargo vault facility in Easton."

"He wants to take a truck?" asked John.

"No, he wants to take over the vault," I replied.

"Really! How's he plan on doing that?" John asked.

"He has this notion that he can get someone on the inside of the facility who would be willing to assist with a robbery. He's been bugging Tony to try to come up with someone who can get a job at the vault and be the inside guy," I said.

"Sounds kind of out there. Is he serious?" asked John.

"Serious as a heart attack. Apparently, he seems to think it would be easy. He claims there's a lot of turnaround in that business. The guards aren't paid much, and jobs open up all the time. Besides just talking about it, Mello has been casing the place to determine the routine there. According to Tony, he also has a two-man crew he likes to work with, David Turner and Stephen Rossetti. I'd like to open an investigation based on this information and keep track of Mello through Tony," I said.

"Yeah, absolutely! Good work," John replied. "Get to it. Let's start by getting Tony formally opened as an informant. I got to go; my kid has a soccer game today."

The next day I started researching David Turner and Stephen Rossetti. What I found out about these guys was enough to make me believe Tony was on to something. Rossetti was the nephew of Mark Rossetti, a lieutenant in the Boston mob. Stephen worked as a self-employed general contractor and was married with kids but was no stranger to violent crimes.

Rossetti's adult criminal record started in 1977 when he was nineteen years old; the charge was breaking and entering. From there he went on to accumulate twenty-four additional charges for crimes involving burglary, drug distribution, possession of a dangerous weapon, possession of stolen property, conspiracy to commit armed robbery, and bank robbery. The crime he is most famous for was a Brink's armored car heist on April 26,

1982, which he committed with his uncle Mark Rossetti, relative Ralph Rossetti, and two other men at the Northgate Mall in Revere, Massachusetts. The men used stolen vehicles, were armed with shoulder weapons, wore masks, and, after overpowering the guards, made off with $280,892. They were all eventually caught and sentenced to prison.

David Turner was a single guy in his thirties with blond surfer hair, handsome and wholesome looking. His mug shot revealed a sly grin that made him look like he hadn't a care in the world. In fact, he had been a student athlete at Braintree High School located south of Boston. Turner had a prosperous business. He owned a trucking company called Two Sisters Trucking, which was located in Dorchester and was currently very busy hauling dirt for a gigantic public works project in Boston called the "Big Dig." He was bringing in big money. Unfortunately, he liked walking on the wild side, which included drug dealing and extortion, and he was the prime suspect in a murder of a witness who was scheduled to testify against him in a home invasion. His criminal history consisted of thirteen charges beginning in 1986 when he was eighteen years old. The charges were for shoplifting, drug possession, firearm possession, conspiracy to commit robbery, and armed robbery, among others.

I sat down and began to sketch out a game plan. The first thing that popped into my head was the realization that this case was tailor-made for an undercover operation. In fact, I couldn't think of any other viable option. Clearly, we needed to gather evidence, which would have to involve recorded conversations. These secret early-morning talks would have to be on tape, as would subsequent conversations that might take place outside the business. The big problem was I needed the involvement of Tony Romano, and I didn't think that would work for him. The way I saw it, we would need to provide the "inside guy" that Mello was looking for. The inside guy would actually be an undercover FBI agent, but since Mello wasn't going to advertise in the newspaper for a criminal conspirator, Tony would have to be the one to introduce the inside guy to Mello. Tony could step back at that point and let the undercover agent wear the recording device and record the conversations with Mello and anyone else who was inclined to get involved in the robbery. I envisioned our FBI undercover agent gathering all the evidence needed to prove the conspiracy and remaining involved up to the point where the gang comes together to actually rob the facility. At that point, the conspirators would be taken down with their guns, disguises, and stolen cars as they were about to commit the robbery.

After the arrest, the robbers would soon figure out that they had been infiltrated and that Tony did it; therefore, Tony would have to go away forever, as far away from Boston as possible. Everyone who watches TV is aware of the Witness Protection Program (actually called the Witness Security Program or WITSEC). WITSEC is administered by the US Marshals Service. The US Marshals Service goes way back to the Old West. In modern times, they are the primary security service for federal courthouses, prisoners, and witnesses. They also have other law enforcement functions such as hunting down federal fugitives within the United States and abroad. Each federal district has its own appointed marshal, and the worker bees are referred to as deputy marshals.

When witnesses enter the WITSEC program, they are immediately whisked away from the location where they conducted their service to the government (usually their hometown) and relocated to a different place within the United States. They are given a new identity and assistance making ends meet until they can land a job and support themselves. The protected witness cannot initiate any contact with anyone from their past. The protected witness is assigned to a deputy marshal who handles any communication between the witness and the people he or she left behind. If a witness breaks this strict rule, they can be dismissed from the program. Clearly WITSEC is a huge, life-changing experience for the witness and usually a tough sell for law enforcement.

Before I could get involved in that process, I needed to officially open Tony as an informant. Television cop shows typically portray informants as sleazy lowlifes, trading drug information for a few bucks or a break on a criminal charge. The FBI has a wide variety of folks with incredibly diverse backgrounds working as informants. An informant typically provides direct information or guidance to the FBI agents who are investigating a particular criminal violation. These people may in fact be career criminals, but just as likely they are business professionals who have never had a traffic ticket. What they all have in common is unique access to the targets of an investigation and a willingness to take risks to assist the FBI and US Attorney's office. This assistance could be as benign as listening to subjects of a criminal investigation talk and plan and then reporting what they heard back to the agents and prosecutors investigating the case. On the other extreme, an informant may actively assist in the gathering of direct evidence that would be needed in a criminal prosecution. This is typically accomplished by wearing a recording and/or transmitting device while in the presence of the criminal actors and recording their actual words. These recordings, along with the testimony of the informant, are then used in court to provide the most convincing and accurate evidence that can be obtained—the defendant's own words, on tape, talking, planning, and directing the criminal activity. With that type of powerful direct evidence, it wouldn't matter if the informant has a lengthy criminal history or even a history of lying. The proof is in the recorded words of the defendant. Not too many informants are willing to provide that degree of assistance.

At this very early stage of the investigation, I couldn't guess what Tony's involvement would be. He would maybe become and remain a person who merely reported the conversations he had with Carmello Merlino, without ever recording the conversations. This type of information is still valuable as it allows law enforcement to get an idea of what the criminal actor is planning to do. The informant may not want to go any farther than that. That's fine but may not be enough to bring a criminal prosecution, as something else would be required to supplement that information. I didn't know Tony well enough at this point to even guess what his future involvement would be in this investigation.

The first thing I had to do on my informant checklist was create a code name for Tony. It couldn't be a name associated in any way with his real name or one that accurately described him. For example, "Mechanic Man" would not be a good code name. My habit for naming an informant was to go to a Webster dictionary and, starting at the beginning, look at words. Eventually I'd find something I liked and could use. I was in kind of a hurry that day, so I only made it to the letter B. I selected Bird Dog. I thought it was fitting because a bird dog is a courageous and tenacious hunter. That's what I needed.

I got a message to Tony to give me a call. A few minutes later the phone rang. "I'm at a pay phone and don't have much money; what's up?" asked Tony.

"I need to talk to you directly. Let's meet at the Downtown Crossing subway stop on your way back from work today," I said.

"Okay, I can get off there at 6:10 p.m.," Tony replied.

"Good. Don't acknowledge me right off. I want you to walk toward the closest stairs to the street and start up. Stop halfway up and stand there for a minute, then look at your watch and walk to the nearest phone bank. Pick up a phone, pretend to put in money and have a two-minute conversation, then hang up and go back to the platform. Got it?" I asked.

"What's up with the spy shit?" Tony asked.

"It's the way I do things. Repeat back to me what I just told you," I said.

Tony repeated it all back perfectly. I was happy.

"Okay, so at the end of all that, I'll approach you if I feel it's safe. If I don't approach you, just get on the next train and get back to the halfway house. Don't look around!" I emphasized.

"Okay, okay, 007, Jesus! See you there . . . hopefully."

When the train entered the station at 6:10 p.m. today, I was on the platform and saw the throng of commuters pour out of the trains. Eventually I saw Tony step onto the platform. I immediately turned and walked over to the bank of phones on the wall and pretended to make a call. I saw Tony walk past me without acknowledging me. He went up the stairs, where he stopped looked at his watch and came back toward the phone bank. He chose a phone two down from me and turned away from me while pretending to make a call. I hung up the phone and walked past Tony and up the stairs. I waited at the top. After ten minutes I walked back down to the platform and, happily, found it was empty. Good.

Later that evening I got a call at home from the office. "Dave, I have Tony on the line. He says you know him," the FBI operator said.

"Yeah, Sue, put him through please."

"Yo, 007. This is 006. What the fuck?" said Tony.

I laughed. "Sorry, dude, I just didn't like the looks of the guy in the green jacket. Did you see him?" I asked.

"I didn't see anyone in a green jacket," said Tony.

"Okay, probably nothing. You did well. You and I are going to work together. Let's meet at the subway station tomorrow. This time we'll talk. I have some administrative details I have to go over with you. Okay?" I asked.

"Sure, 007. See you at 6:10 p.m. tomorrow."

"Over and out," I laughed and hung up.

At 6:10 p.m. the next day, I was once again waiting on the platform at the subway station. I observed Tony exit the subway car and step onto the platform. He looked at me, and I motioned for him to follow. We passed the phone bank and turned a corner where there were fewer people.

"Nice to see you, buddy," I said.

"Nice to be seen," Tony retorted.

"So here's the deal, Tony. I want you to know I do not cut corners, especially when it comes to your safety. Yesterday you couldn't have done better, congratulations," I said.

I saw the smile coming over Tony's face. I suspected he wasn't used to someone telling him he did a good job. Prison isn't exactly a supportive community.

We sat down on a bench. "I want to open you formally as an FBI informant. Everything we talk about going forward will be recorded by me in a written report," I said.

"Every single conversation we have?" asked Tony wide-eyed.

"Not every single conversation, just case-related information," I said. "I am officially opening a case based upon your information about Mello's plans. I want you to call me from a pay phone and fill me in on Mello's daily activities. I want to know about what you and he talk about in the morning before the shop is open and who he meets throughout the day. I don't care about legitimate customers at the shop, just the people you suspect are engaged in criminal activity. Can you do that?" I asked.

"Yeah, I can do that," replied Tony.

I took note of the fact that he didn't follow up that remark with "What's in it for me?" That was a good sign.

"In order to do this the right way, I want to open you as an official FBI informant. Are you okay with that?" I asked.

"Maybe. What's it involve?" asked Tony.

I thought that was a smart question. He didn't agree to something without knowing what he was getting into.

"Well, for starters, when you do things at my direction, you enjoy some protection from the US government as long as you don't break any laws. Second, we will reimburse you for expenses that you may incur as a result of your cooperation. Third, and most importantly of all, you will be at the pointy end of a very big spear. If this case develops the way it should, it will be because you stepped forward and agreed to undertake a dangerous assignment. Needless to say, this will be the most significant thing you've ever done and will literally result in lives saved. Mello is going to do this one way or the other. You're our only hope for getting ahead of the situation from the beginning. Without you, we have no information and will not be in a position to stop it from happening," I said.

Tony was listening and nodding his head.

"I want to involve you as little as possible. So at this point, I just need you to keep your ears open and let me know what Mello is thinking and doing. I don't want you to get too pushy with him. I want you to be a human tape recorder and just fill me in on what he's up to," I explained.

Tony looked up and grinned. "I can handle that. To tell you the truth, you're the first cop that's ever treated me like an equal. I'm not a criminal; I'm a recovering drug addict. I'm not proud of the crazy shit I've done to get drugs or for spending a large part of my life in prison. I don't want to be remembered for that. I want my son to remember me for something good," Tony said.

I put my hand on Tony's skinny shoulder and looked him in the eye.

"That's good to hear, Tony. I like your motivation. We'll take things slow at first and get a close look at Mello and his operation. You being my eyes and ears inside TRC Auto Electric is giving me a huge advantage. I appreciate it more than you know. Okay; now, your first lesson in government bureaucracy. We do things by the numbers; you'll have to get used to that," I warned him.

I withdrew a five-page typed form from the folder I was carrying and presented it to him.

"This is a formal agreement outlining your responsibilities as an FBI informant. As I said, it's all by the numbers. Want to read it?" I asked.

"No, I don't want to read it; where do I sign?" replied Tony.

"Right on the dotted line, my friend," I said grinning.

I handed Tony a pen, and as he moved to sign the form, I stopped him.

"One last thing: I changed your name to protect your identity. I need you to sign this as Bird Dog," I said.

"What!?" Tony exclaimed.

"Cool, huh?" I asked.

"Not fucking really! Where did you get that?" Tony asked.

"It was computer generated," I lied.

"Goddamn, get a new computer!" Tony complained.

"You'll get used to it. It's better than your prison name, BB67833," I joked.

12

UNDERCOVER AND UNDERDRESSED

TRC AUTO ELECTRIC, DORCHESTER, MASSACHUSETTS

If Tony was nervous about his new assignment, he wasn't letting on. He would later tell me he felt very good about what he was doing, though no one from his old life would agree. He told me he finally had a noble purpose and really didn't want to let me—or himself—down.

I was careful to meet with Tony in a safe location from time to time. For the most part, his reports came in to me by phone and I was recording the information in the form of an "Insert." An Insert was the name of a specific FBI report form by which investigative case information dealing with observations, perceptions, and routine data was recorded into the case file. Information derived from an informant was recorded on an Insert.

According to Tony, Mello was engaged in a variety of criminal endeavors and meeting with a lot of known criminals during an average workday. He was interested in somehow recovering the stolen Gardner Museum artwork in order to cash in on the five-million-dollar reward being offered by the museum. Mello would make suspicious phone calls from a pay phone located outside TRC.

I applied for and received a court order for a pen register on the pay phone. A pen register operates like a wiretap except no conversations are recorded. The only information a pen register records is the phone number dialed out or the phone number from which an incoming call originated. The length of the call is also recorded. The phone information would come directly into a special room at the FBI office. I then looked for those numbers associated with the time Mello was using that phone. My next step would be to find out who those numbers were registered to. This information had limited value, but if I were to develop probable cause with the pen register, I might be able to obtain a wiretap; however, that would be very difficult for a public phone, so my main purpose was to see if I could determine a pattern to his calling and possibly develop a broader picture of who he was dealing with. An investigator wants as much information concerning the target of an investigation as is possible to obtain. There are multiple ways to obtain information, and I was using two of the most popular methods of intelligence gathering, electronic and human.

The pen register on Mello's pay phone was the best electronic surveillance method available to me. Electronic surveillance is referred to as "ELSUR." The best ELSUR, in general, would be a concealed microphone in a room where criminal activity is discussed and/or a wiretap on a phone line used by the subject of the investigation to discuss criminal activity. It was clear to me, however, that this case would rise or fall based upon human intelligence, referred to as HUMINT. Tony was my HUMINT source. He was my eyes and ears inside and outside of TRC Auto Electric. He took his job seriously and provided almost daily updates on Mello's meetings and the conversations they had before the shop opened for business. Though still on parole himself, Mello was meeting with some very colorful underworld characters outside TRC: Richard "Fat Richie" Chicofsky, a lifelong con man; Bobby Guarente, a Boston mobster suspected of being involved in the Gardner Museum robbery; Dickey Joyce, another suspect in the Gardner robbery; and numerous others. He was willing to get involved with anything that would result in money in his pocket, but the one job he constantly talked about and really yearned to pull off was the takeover of the Loomis vault facility.

GROTON, MASSACHUSETTS

"Hey, Linda, I need a beer out here!" I yelled from my floating mattress in our backyard pool. Summer of 1998 was hot! We dug out the side of a sloped area in our yard and installed an above-ground pool. I was able to attach the pool to the lawn with a nice wooden deck, so the pool was essentially ground level. Not exactly an in-ground, kidney-shaped, Gunite beauty, but we liked it. I had been throwing little colored stones in the water while the kids looked the other way. I'd yell, "GO!" and Liz and Kate would dive in. Whoever recovered the most stones was the winner. Some fun!

"You don't have any more beer!" Linda shouted back.

"Oh crap. How about you get some from the liquor store in town?" I asked hopefully.

"How about NO?" she lovingly responded.

"Okay, I'll go, but the kids won't like it much. We're having fun," I tried one last time.

"You want dinner?" she asked.

"Never mind, I'll go! Jeez" was my sad response.

With that I jumped out of the pool, dried off, and went in for my favorite sleeveless tank top, car keys, and wallet.

"Hey, I've got zero money!" I complained.

"Well, the bank has plenty. You aren't wearing that bathing suit, are you?" asked Linda, aghast.

"Yeah, it's fine. It's Hawaiian. I'm just going to the drive-thru at the bank, and nobody at the liquor store cares," I said.

"Okay, mister professional FBI man, if you want to go into town looking like that, go ahead. Tell me you're not wearing those rubber flip-flops on your feet!" Linda said incredulously.

"Yep, see you later!" I shouted back.

With that, I jumped into the Jeep and drove the one mile into downtown Groton. Groton is an old town with a historic downtown area. Very picturesque and a great place to raise a family. Being thirty-five miles from Boston, there were no big city problems to worry about. The police department only had about fifteen cops total.

I approached the bank from a side street. The driveway led to the ATM machine on the side of the bank. I pulled up, stuck my card in, and retrieved twenty dollars—enough to last me all week. I put the car in drive and moved up to the front of the bank where I spotted a police car parked on Main Street in front of the bank. Surprisingly the car had its blue lights flashing.

That's weird, I thought to myself.

Suddenly another police car came flying up behind the first one, and the two cops jumped out and went into the bank.

"Oh, shit . . . the bank's been robbed!" I said to myself.

As a member of the FBI Bank Robbery Task Force, I couldn't just duck down and slowly drive away. FBI agents always respond to bank robberies, and Saturday is no exception. I knew the agent covering Groton was going to have to come from home and it was going to take him at least forty-five minutes to get here. I parked the car and walked up to the front door where Groton police officer Sid Snow was standing guard outside the locked front door.

"Hi, Sid. Is this what I think it is?" I asked.

"Yep, bank's been robbed. Are you coming to do the investigation? You guys are starting to dress rather casual, don't you think?" he said with a huge grin.

Linda is going to kill me.

"Yeah, new look since Hoover died. Open up, will ya?" I asked.

"Sure thing, boss. Love the flip-flops," Sid teased.

I walked into a typical post–bank robbery scene. A female teller was sitting in a chair with a glass of water in her hand, and another lady was fanning her face with a sheaf of papers. Cops were all over the place, chaos everywhere, customers were talking all at once.

"You'll be fine, Betty! I'll bet it wasn't even a real gun!" the fanning lady said.

I walked up to a man on the phone behind one of the desks. He looked up, covered the phone with one hand, and said, "I'm sorry, sir, I don't know why you were allowed in, but the bank is closed; you'll have to leave." he said.

I sat down at the desk and said, "You may find this hard to believe, but my name is Dave Nadolski, I'm an FBI agent, and I'm investigating this robbery." With that, he said, "I gotta call you back," and hung up the phone.

After staring at me for a few seconds, he said, "Are you sure about that?"

Luckily, Officer Snow came to my rescue, "He's an FBI agent, and you can talk to him. I think he left his suit at home. Dave, this is the branch manager, Pat Kelly."

"Thanks, Sid," I said.

I turned my attention to Mr. Kelly. "Obviously I wasn't planning to investigate a robbery today; otherwise I wouldn't be standing here in my bathing suit and flip-flops. Actually, I live in town and was making an ATM withdrawal when I observed all the excitement," I said.

Mr. Kelly responded, "Well, that's a relief. I thought you were a homeless person."

"I may be but just don't know it yet. However, if you don't mind, I'd like to talk to you about what happened here. First, I need to call my office; may I use your phone please?" I asked.

"Sure, sure, go ahead," responded Mr. Kelly.

I called the office and spoke with the duty agent. "Bill, this is Dave Nadolski. The Bay Bank on Main St. in Groton, Massachusetts, was just robbed. I'm not on duty today, but I happened to drive up to the bank just after the robbery so I'm going to cover it. You can call off whoever is covering the weekend," I said.

"You just did a huge favor for George DiMatteo. He's forty-five minutes away and will be relieved to catch a break on this one!" said Bill.

"I'll let him buy me a coffee," I said.

"One more call," I said to Mr. Kelly.

"Hi, Linda," I said.

"Where are you?" she asked.

"You won't believe what just happened. I was minding my own business trying to get some money from the ATM, when all of a sudden . . ."

"What happened?!" Linda cut me off.

"Well, the bank was robbed," I said.

"Get home *now!*" she said.

"Now, now, dear, I can't do that. I'm investigating the robbery," I said.

Long pause . . . "In your *bathing suit*?!"

"Well, yes, actually, but I just wanted to let you know what I was doing and I'll be home as soon as I can. Bye, sweetie," and, with that, I quickly hung up.

With that out of the way, I addressed the branch manager. "Nice to meet you, Pat. Would you mind giving me a pad of paper and a pen please?" I asked.

I spent the next hour interviewing employees and customers, prefacing every conversation with "I don't normally work in my swimsuit, but . . ."

This particular robbery had a little extra excitement because after brandishing a gun and getting cash from one teller, the suspect bolted out the door, jumped into a black Honda parked on a side street, and headed out of town in a big hurry. Luckily, a vigilant bystander caught a good description of the car and direction of escape allowing the police in Pepperell, the town next to Groton, to intercept and chase down the suspect. An arrest was made, and the cash and gun were recovered; no one was hurt.

After I wrapped up my interviews, I met Sid Snow and went outside with him. We were walking together toward my car when I noticed a news photographer shooting pictures of us.

"Sid, who's that guy with?" I asked.

"*Lowell Sun*," he replied.

Oh, shit, I thought, *that's our newspaper*.

"Well, Sid, I was planning to buy some beer, but I'm going to the florist instead," I said.

Sid nodded his head in response. "Good call."

The next day I grabbed the paper the second it hit the driveway at 7:00 a.m. Guess who was on the front page. Big Sid and Dapper Dave.

"Oh, crap, this isn't going to go well at all," I said out loud. Then I went back to bed.

Throughout the rest of 1997 and into 1998, Tony went about his dual role as confidant to Carmello Merlino and informant for the FBI. I debriefed him regularly and recorded his reports into the case file. As far as I could tell, and to the best of my belief, he was remaining sober. He must have been because his parole officer would show up at his apartment on a random basis and drug test him on the spot. He always tested negative. I kept in touch with the parole officer and made sure there were no issues. The parole officer was happy with Tony's progress, and between the two of us, we kept an eye out for any signs of unusual stress. So far so good.

13

STUFF IS GETTING REAL

DORCHESTER, MASSACHUSETTS

Fall 1998

Throughout all of 1998, Tony was faithfully reporting on activity at TRC. He reported the early-morning conversations with Mello, the activity regarding Mello's efforts to lay his hands on the Gardner paintings, and meetings between Mello and a large number of criminal associates. Most importantly, Tony reported Mello was conducting more surveillance at the Loomis vault and was constantly asking Tony if he could come up with someone to be the inside guy on a takeover of the vault. The pen register was a bust. Nothing of discernible value was obtained, and I was pretty sure I wouldn't be allowed to continue trapping calls. It was finally time to make a decision on this case.

I met with Tony at an Italian restaurant in the city of Quincy. I was sitting at the bar when Tony walked in and sat next to me.

"What's up, Dave?" asked Tony.

"I just had a conversation with my supervisor, John Trahon. He said this merry-go-round has gone on long enough. Either we open an undercover investigation and go all in or we shut down this investigation. Of course, I don't want to shut it down because it's clear Mello is intent on robbing the vault; but we have to go forward or we haul Mello in and tell him we're on to him. We can't just walk away and hope for the best," I said, sipping my beer and looking at Tony in the mirror over the bar. He did not look comfortable.

"So tell me again about this undercover operation you want to do. What are the details?" asked Tony.

"Basically, it's very simple. We have to introduce an undercover agent, posing as the inside guy who is willing to go along with a robbery. From that point on, the undercover agent will record the conversations with Mello. Of course, you will have to introduce the undercover guy to Mello, so when the arrests are finally made, Mello will know you were working for the FBI. You'll have to go into the witness security program and leave the state. You'll get a new identity, some money, and a fresh start far away from here. You'll probably have to testify at trial, but the undercover will do most of the testifying because he'll be wearing the recorder. That's the way it works if our undercover guy is accepted by Mello," I said.

Tony sat still and looked into the mirror for a full minute. "So I have to leave the state? Can you make that happen?" he asked.

"I can make it happen as long as the parole board goes along with transferring your parole to the US Marshals Service," I said.

"What happens if Merlino says he won't meet with the inside guy? He's not fond of strangers, you know," said Tony.

"In that case, you'll have to wear the wire, record the conversations, and testify in federal court. You'll still have to leave the state and never come back to Boston," I said, watching his reaction in the mirror.

Tony sat still for a full minute.

"I don't know about all this. I just moved in with a new girl; things are going well for me now," he said.

"Hey, I understand this is a huge ask, and it's dangerous work. Your life will change forever. I can guarantee I will do everything in my power to keep you as safe as possible and will always discuss moves with you beforehand. You would be the one on the hot seat for sure, but you'll be backed up by the biggest gang ever. If all goes well, this will be a huge case," I said, looking Tony straight in the face.

After a while, Tony said, "Let me think about it for a couple weeks. I've got permission to go on a cruise with my girlfriend, Patricia, and my brother and his wife. It's kind of last minute, and we are going next week. We'll talk again after I get back, and I'll have an answer for you then."

With that, he picked up his jacket and walked out the front door.

Tony returned from his cruise ready to get back to work. I left him alone for a while, knowing he needed to decompress and think about the road ahead. Was he going to be willing to stick his neck out and change his life or not? I hoped he would decide to join the team as a star player, but I fully understood the decision was Tony's—and Tony's alone—to make. I wouldn't want to be in his position, so I decided not to push him one way or the other.

A few days after returning, Tony finally called for a meeting at the Italian restaurant in Quincy. I arrived first and waited at the bar. As usual Tony was right on time. He walked up and took a seat next to me.

"Welcome home, dude. How was the trip?" I asked.

"Don't ask. Budweiser please!" he called out to the bartender.

"That good, huh?" I asked.

"Yeah, that good. Let's just say I'm glad to be home and leave it at that, okay?" grumbled Tony.

"Sure, whatever," I said. "Have you thought about where we are going regarding the case?"

"Actually, that's all I could think about, and it didn't make the cruise any better," Tony said.

After about twenty seconds of silence, I asked, "So are you letting me in on your decision or do I have to guess?"

He looked at me and grinned. "I'm in."

This was the turning point of the case!

"Okay, so you are in. You are agreeing to introduce the undercover agent, knowing full well that when all is said and done, you need to leave town permanently, right?" I asked.

"That's right. I need a change of scenery anyway," Tony replied.

"Furthermore, if Mello doesn't accept the undercover, you agree to wear the wire yourself, right?" I asked.

"That's right," Tony replied.

I couldn't stop the huge smile from forming on my face. "Welcome to the team, Tony," I said as I extended my hand. He shook it, and we returned to our beers.

I didn't know what went wrong on the cruise, but that night everything was suddenly going right. After Tony made his decision, I went into high gear. First order of business the next day was to meet with my supervisor, John Trahon. I met John in his office first thing in the morning.

"John, I met with Tony last night. He's agreed to go forward with the undercover operation. He's aware of everything involved, including relocating after the case is concluded, and is still willing to do it," I said.

"That's great news! Set up a meeting; we need to discuss how this is going to play out," John replied.

"I'll take care of that. I'm thinking of an undercover operation involving Dave Donahue posing as the inside guy," I said.

"Exactly who I was thinking of as well," replied John.

Dave had undercover experience and was perfect for the role in my opinion. He was a tall, good-looking guy; a couple years older than Tony; and a Boston native complete with the accent. He'd be the perfect fit for this assignment.

I walked over to Dave's desk. "Yo, Dave, let's talk a bit," I called out.

"What's up, Nads?" Dave asked.

"How'd you like to do another undercover assignment and not have to leave home?" I asked.

"I'm in, brother! What's the deal?" Dave enthusiastically responded.

I filled Dave in on the details of our plan.

"This will be the final jewel in my undercover crown if we can pull it off!" Dave responded.

"We can pull it off, my friend!" I enthusiastically replied.

I arranged a meeting between John Trahon, Dave Donahue, Tony, and myself at a bar in Quincy, far enough from TRC where we wouldn't have to worry about running into anyone who worked there.

At around 5:30 p.m., John, Dave, and I were in the parking lot of Pat Sheehan's Pub. We watched as Tony pulled into the parking lot and entered the bar.

"You guys wait here, and I'll check it out," I said as I climbed from the car.

I entered the dimly lit establishment where there were a couple of guys at the bar and another couple in a booth. The place was dark, perfect for our meeting. I located Tony in a booth for four in a far corner. I waited a minute or so to let my eyes adjust before looking around once again for anyone I might recognize. I didn't see anyone, and Tony didn't appear to be concerned so I approached the table.

"Are we cool here?" I asked.

"Yeah, we're good. Where is everyone?" he asked.

"In the parking lot. I'll get them," I said.

I returned with John and Dave, and we all took a seat in the booth. After ordering a round of beers from the jovial waitress, we got down to business.

"Tony, this is John Trahon, my supervisor. This other guy is Dave Donahue. He's an agent from my squad and a native Bostonian. Aside from that, he's an experienced undercover agent. Dave will be our undercover agent for this case. So right now what we need to talk about is the story we give Mello and we would appreciate your input on that topic," I said.

Tony seemed to be sizing up John and Dave while I was doing the talking. Finally, he said, "Nice to meet you guys."

John said, "It's good to meet you, Tony. Dave has told me a lot about you. I'm familiar with what's been going on. I want to thank you for meeting with us and discussing a plan to infiltrate this criminal organization. I know you are putting yourself at risk just being here, and I want to assure you that your safety is our primary concern. We have experience with these types of operations, but there is no getting around the fact that you will be the one at risk if we do not do our job well; therefore, we know our primary job is to keep you safe."

Tony sipped his beer and stared at John. He didn't say anything for a while and seemed to be thinking about John's words.

"That's good to hear, and I'm glad you realize what kind of position I'm in. If we do this thing, my life is in your hands. The guys we are going to be dealing with will kill me if they get a whiff that I'm working with the cops. I'll simply disappear, and they'll act as if nothing has happened," Tony replied.

Dave Donahue spoke up and said, "Tony, I've worked undercover for a long time. I've worked with guys in your position. I'll be with you, by your side. If I feel things are going south, we are out of there. You and I will simply vanish, and that will be the end of it. Nobody has ever gotten hurt on my watch, and I'm not going to let you down."

Tony looked at Dave, John, and then me. He didn't say anything for about thirty seconds but finally smiled.

"I like you guys. Let's talk about how this will work," Tony said.

"Well, that's what we're here for, Tony. We didn't come with any preconceived plan, and I'm anxious to hear from you. What type of scenario will work, in your opinion?" asked John.

"I've given this a lot of thought. First off, I've known Mello practical-ly my whole life. We even did time together. What I'm about to propose may sound really goofy to you, but it will work. As I've been telling Nadolski all along, Mello wants an inside guy in the Loomis vault who's willing to be part of the robbery. He's asked me over and over to find someone. I want Dave Donahue to be that guy," Tony said.

Tony continued, "The way I see this playing out is I'll tell Mello that I was in a bar and ran into my sister's old boyfriend; his name is Carl. We haven't seen each other for years because he moved to California. I'm going to say Carl used to drive the car when I was pulling armed robber-ies for dope money, but he cleaned up and got a real job. I'm going to say we got to talking about our lives and, believe it or not, this kid works for Loomis Fargo! I'll tell Mello that Carl returned to Boston and has a job as a guard in the Boston vault! I'll also tell Mello that after a few meetings with Carl, I confided in him that I'm still doing holdups but on a much bigger scale. I'm with a professional crew now, and we've been casing the Loomis Fargo vault in Easton. I'll tell Mello that our crew has been looking for an inside guy to give up the vault. And guess what? Carl agreed to be that guy. He can arrange a transfer from the Boston to the Easton vault, and he's up for being the inside guy!"

There was silence around the table as Dave looked at John and John looked at me and I looked at Tony.

I cleared my throat. "Uh, Tony, not to be a Debbie Downer, but do you really expect us to believe that lame-assed story will fly with Mello?" I asked.

"Shit yes, it'll fly," exclaimed Tony. "I told you it would sound goofy, and it is, but coming from me it will fly like a hawk! He'll bite on this like a shark on a seal!"

I looked at John and shrugged my shoulders.

"Well, we said the plan was up to you, so if you think this will work, I guess we go with it," I said.

"You're right about one thing: it sounds goofy as shit," John laughed.

"Now assuming Mello bites on this story of yours, what do you think the chances are that he will trust Carl?" Dave Donahue asked.

"I believe he'll trust Carl because I brought Carl forward. The big unknown is whether Mello will deal with Carl directly. It's just as likely as not that Mello will distance himself from Carl, meaning he won't invite him into the group. In that case, Donahue won't be able to record the conversations, so I guess I'm going to be wearing the wire," Tony said as he looked around the table.

"It's a huge ask, Tony, and we won't think worse of you if, in the end, you decide not to do it," John said, looking directly into Tony's face. "Since this is all made-up bullshit to begin with, you can just tell Mello that Carl got cold feet and backed out. At that point, we're back to square one, but that's better than you screwing the pooch and getting caught with a recorder. Now THAT would be melancholy!" We all laughed at the understatement of the year.

"Thanks for the out, John, but hopefully Mello will want to control Carl himself. And if that ends up being the way it goes, I'll be happy as hell, but my gut tells me Mello won't want to have anything to do with Carl," Tony said as he sipped his beer.

"Let's cross that bridge when we come to it," I said. "In the meantime, Tony, you just keep doing what you have been doing. We've got a few hurdles to leap over before this operation gets off the ground. First thing I have to do is contact the parole board again and get permission to use you for this operation. There's no guarantee they'll allow that. If the parole board signs off, we then have a ton of paperwork to do in order to get an undercover assignment approved by Bureau headquarters. They will want a tight rein on this operation since there's a civilian involved, and I don't want a slight blemish on my record because I got you killed," I kidded.

Tony looked at me with a shocked look. "You son of a bitch! You're worried about a fucking blemish on your record if I get killed?" he asked sarcastically.

"Well, a guy doesn't want to jeopardize his chance for advancement," I deadpanned.

"You're all heart, Nadolski! Pay up and let's get out of here," John said as he stood up and slapped the table.

14

GETTING WIRED

QUINCY, MASSACHUSETTS

Fall 1998

I wasted no time getting to work. Dave Donahue, Tony, and I arranged to meet at the Cathay Pacific Restaurant, where we selected a secluded table at the far end of the dining room. Over Chicken Szechuan for three, we devised our first step.

"I'm thinking we need Mello to actually see Dave, aka 'Carl,' so he knows this guy actually exists. How would you recommend we do that, Tony?" I asked.

"The most natural way would be for Dave to bring a car into TRC for some type of work. I could work on the car outside while Dave stands around. I'm sure Mello will see what's going on and want to know what's up since the work wasn't scheduled. Let's do something simple like replacing a radiator hose, which won't take too much time. Maybe Mello will actually walk up and engage in small talk. If so, I'll introduce Dave as Carl, my sister's old boyfriend. If there's conversation, we can play it by ear. Talk about the weather or something like that," Tony said.

"I can arrange for an undercover car. We have plenty of old pieces of shit that need work. The license plates are safe; they trace back to fictitious persons," Dave said.

"Sounds good to me. How about tomorrow afternoon?" I asked.

"Okay, let's plan on 2:00 p.m. If for some reason Mello chooses that time to take a ride, I'll call Nadolski and we can postpone until he gets back," Tony said.

"I'm good with that," Dave said.

The next day Dave and I met at the Bureau garage where a couple undercover cars were stored. We picked out a nondescript blue Ford Taurus.

"Okay, so just pull into the lot and go in. You'll see Mello behind the desk; here's what he looks like," I said as I showed Dave Mello's driver's license picture. "Just ask for Tony. When he comes out, go outside with him and Tony will take it from there. Just stand around looking concerned."

"I think I can handle this," Dave said dryly.

"Okay, okay, don't get your panties in a bunch! I just don't want anything to go wrong. I'm a little nervous," I admitted.

"See you later. In the meantime, suck your thumb," Dave laughed as he started the motor and drove the Taurus out of the garage.

As it turned out, there was nothing to worry about. Dave pulled into TRC, approached Mello behind the desk, and asked for Tony.

Mello looked at Dave and then turned and yelled into the garage, "Romano! Get your skinny ass up here. You got company." He turned back to Dave and said, "He'll be right up."

The rest went like clockwork. Dave stood around as Tony went under the hood and replaced the radiator hose on the Taurus. Mello walked outside and watched for a few minutes before returning to his counter inside. After Tony closed the hood, Dave shook his hand and drove off.

As Tony walked back into the garage, Mello said, "Who's that? Someone special who don't pay?"

"That's Carl; he's an old friend of mine. He used to date my sister. Just needed a radiator hose. Take it out of my pay, you cheap bastard," Tony said, wiping his hands on a rag.

"Don't make a habit of it," Mello said, going back to his newspaper.

Back at the office, Dave filled me in on the encounter. "Everything went smoothly. I saw and spoke to Mello. Like Tony predicted, he came outside to check things out while Tony was under the hood. He seems like a nice grandfatherly type," Dave remarked.

"He carries a shiv in his sock," I said.

The next day I brought John Trahon up to speed in his office and explained, "I want to meet with Assistant US Attorney Rob Richardson now and talk about getting this thing moving. I think now is the time for Tony to have the first recorded conversation with Mello. That will be a make-or-break recording. Either Mello bites, and we roll, or he doesn't, and we shut it down," I said.

"Yeah, I'm betting he bites," John said.

Later that day I called Rob Richardson at his office in the Joe Moakley US Courthouse in South Boston to arrange a 4:00 p.m. meeting there to discuss the investigation.

After exiting the elevator on the fourth floor, I proceeded through a maze of corridors to Rob's office. I entered and sighed. I removed thirty file folders from one of the two guest chairs in Rob's office and took a seat. Now I don't consider myself to be an anal neat freak, but Rob's office was abhorrent. There were files stacked in every corner, on every flat surface, on top of file cabinets, and on all the chairs. He could have had a beautiful view of the harbor if it was possible to see out the window.

After about five minutes, a receptionist stuck her head through the door.

"Hi, Dave, want some coffee?" she asked.

"Thanks, Mary, but I'll pass. There's nowhere to set the cup down," I said.

"Oh, that's a good one! I know, poor Rob! I just can't understand why he lets his office get so messy!" Mary said.

"I can't understand how he can possibly find whatever it is he's working on."

"Oh, I know what you mean! The thing is he knows where every file is. You'll never catch him fumbling through different files to find what he needs. He always goes to the right file the first time. It's incredible!" Mary remarked.

"He must drive his wife crazy," I said.

"It would drive me nuts for sure. He should be back shortly. Enjoy the view!" Mary laughed as she closed the door behind her.

After about fifteen more minutes, Rob bounded through the door. Rob was in his late thirties; about five feet, ten inches tall; and slim with unruly dirty-blond hair. He usually had a half smile on his face that made him look as if someone had just told him a joke. He had his court suit on and removed his jacket as he took his seat.

"Hi, Dave. Sorry for the delay, but Judge Wolf wanted to see me in his chambers and you don't keep Judge Wolf waiting!" Rob explained as he took a seat between the stacks.

"I know you don't if you prize your balls," I laughed.

I looked Rob in the face and explained what happened at TRC the previous day.

"So now Mello has a mental picture of who Carl is and knows he actually exists, right?" asked Rob.

"That's right. So I want to put a recorder on Tony tomorrow and have him tell Mello he found an inside guy for the Loomis job. He'll say the guy is Carl, whom Mello already met. Tony will tell Mello how he ran into Carl recently and found out he works as a Loomis guard, and after a few more meetings, Tony asked Carl if he wanted in on a robbery and of course, Carl wants in!" I said.

Rob rocked back in his chair and clasped his hands behind his head. "I can hardly believe this story is going to fly with Mello," Rob mused.

"I think it will fly because Mello really wants to believe it. So we'll find out one way or the other tomorrow. Watch Mello say something like, 'What the fuck are you talking about? What Loomis thing?'" I laughed. "That would be my luck. Egg on my face."

Rob laughed at that one.

"When are you going to meet Tony tomorrow?" Rob asked.

"Around 4:30 a.m.," I said. "I'm going to use a Nagra recorder instead of the new F-Bird. I love the old, reliable Nagra. It's made in Germany, you know, and Germans make good stuff!"

Rob laughed and said, "They do. Well, I'll be extremely anxious to hear the recording. When do you plan to pick up the recorder?"

"I'll meet Tony in the afternoon. I'll pick it up and have it rerecorded to cassette and then bring it right over here and we can listen to it together, okay?" I asked.

"Agreed; good luck," Rob responded. "Don't knock anything over on the way out."

After returning to the office, I immediately found Neil Cronin and began to fill him in. "Neil, I want to start recording tomorrow. Are you available to help me wire Tony? It's going to be an early start. I want to meet him at 4:30 a.m."

"Yeah, I wouldn't miss it. How about we meet him at Adams Park? It's not too far from TRC but far enough," Neil proposed.

"Sounds good. I'll call you at home if there's a change in plans, okay?" I asked.

"Roger that," Neil said

After I got home from work, I called Tony's apartment. He answered the phone.

"Hello?"

"This is Dave. Tomorrow is D-Day; ready to hit the beach?" I asked.

I was met with a long silence. "What? Speak English," Tony said.

"It's a go for tomorrow. You're meeting Neil and me at 4:30 a.m. tomorrow, and we're going to put a recorder on you. This is it. Do you know where Adams Park is?" I asked.

"Yeah, I used to take my kid there when he was little and I was temporarily out of prison," Tony said.

"Okay, so we'll be waiting. We'll have plenty of time to put the recorder on you and start the tape rolling, but first we'll talk about how to do this thing. I don't want you to worry; it's a piece of cake. We've been planning this conversation for some time so all you have to do is go in and talk to Mello like you do every single morning. Nothing different until you launch into the story about Carl. You won't have to touch any buttons or operate the recorder at all. We'll get it going for you. Are you ready for this?" I asked.

"I think so. I hope so," Tony said after a short pause.

"I know you are. See you at 4:30 a.m. . . . . Bye," I said and hung up the phone.

I told Tony it was a piece of cake, so why couldn't I sleep that night?

The alarm clanged at 3:00 a.m. I punched it off and sprinted to the bathroom before Linda woke up. I was dressed and in my car in a half-hour. It was about a fifty-minute drive to Adams Park, and upon arrival, I saw Neil's car. I pulled up and signaled him to jump in with me. As he slid into the front seat, he said, "How much you want to bet he won't show?"

"Neil, Neil, don't say that!" I complained.

I no sooner had that out of my mouth when another set of headlights entered the park. I immediately recognized Tony's rebuilt Jaguar. He slid up next to my car, and I motioned him to get into the backseat.

The back door opened, and he jumped in. "Jesus Christ, it's fucking cold out here!"

"Hey, hey, don't take the Lord's name in vain!" I admonished him.

"Fuck you," he responded.

"Okay, glad to see you made it. Now we'll get down to business. We've discussed how this will work, but let's go over it again," I said.

"Just before you leave for TRC, we'll put the recorder on you and get it started, but we want to discuss the plan first. You'll go in and have your usual chat about whatever the hell it is you talk about. Let that happen for ten minutes or so. After Mello stops talking for a few seconds, drop the bomb about Carl being willing to join in this escapade. Once you tell him this, just shut up and let him do all the talking from then on. If he asks a question, you can answer, but do not, I repeat DO NOT, talk over him. We want HIS words on the tape, not yours. That is very important to remember. Do you understand?" I asked

"Yeah, I get it. I won't get a chance to talk anyway," Tony said.

"That's good! So after you have the conversation, you can just leave the recorder on, and then at lunch time, I'll meet you at the parking lot in front of the Kmart on Morrissey Boulevard. Let's say at 1:30. I'll be waiting," I said.

"So here it is," Neil said as he pulled the five-inch-by-three-inch recorder with two two-foot cords attached and held it up for Tony to see. "A real beauty, isn't she?" Neil beamed.

Tony's mouth was open.

"What the hell am I supposed to do with that thing?" he exclaimed as he started pushing himself backward into the seat. "I thought you people were supposed to be high tech; that thing is fucking huge! You're not putting that refrigerator on me!"

"Oh yeah, we have this nifty belly band for you to wear under your shirt. You slip the recorder in the small of your back and run the wires over your shoulders. Those are the microphones. Nobody will see it," Neil promised.

"Am I on *Candid Camera*?" Tony looked around furiously for a movie camera.

"Relax, Tony! I admit it's a little bulky, but Mello isn't in the habit of frisking you, is he? We'll tape the microphones in place, and once your shirt is back on, you can't see a thing. We use it all the time, and no one's been killed yet," I assured him. "Come on now, take your shirt off and put this black belly band on."

Tony reluctantly followed orders.

"Good boy. Now Neil is going to tape the microphones to your undershirt and we are going to go live," I said.

"Good Lord . . ." Tony moaned.

"Okay, Neil is going to activate the recorder, and then we have to say a few words so don't interrupt. Oh yeah, I need to mention something first. The recording time on this thing is two hours so you have plenty of time. There is one thing to keep in mind. This is an actual miniature tape recorder with two reels spinning just like a normal reel-to-reel recorder. But what this baby does is record on both sides of the tape. After about an hour, the tape stops for a second while it reverses direction in order to start recording on the other side of the tape. When that happens, there is a slightly audible click that might be detectible in a very quiet environment. Just keep that in mind," I warned him.

"Right. Then the next click I hear will be Mello pulling the hammer back on the revolver pointed at my head!" Tony complained.

"You really are a funny guy; I do like your sense of humor!" I said.

"Okay, going live now," Neil said as he activated the Nagra recorder.

"Are you ready, Tony?" I asked.

"I'm ready," Tony replied.

With that, Tony left the car, reentered his Jaguar, started the engine, and drove off.

"Whew, why am I so goddamn nervous, Neil?" I asked.

"Because the whole case rides on this first conversation," he said

"Yeah, see you back at the office," I said.

Back at the office, I busied myself reviewing administrative paperwork. I couldn't help but feel guilty. Tony was out there alone, and if anything went wrong, it was on me. I kept telling myself it was going to be all right. Tony had prepared himself for this day, and it was going to go like every other day in the past year. He knew how to deal with Mello, and ultimately, it was up to him to get it done.

John Trahon walked in around 7:00 a.m. I joined him in his office, closed the door, and sat down.

"Okay, he wasn't exactly thrilled when he saw how big the Nagra was. By the time he left for TRC, I think he was feeling better about it, but I just hope he holds it together," I said.

John had his hands folded on his desk and was looking right at me. "Well, he's prepared, and I'm confident it will go smoothly. When are you meeting him?"

"We're meeting at 1:30 p.m. at the Kmart parking lot on Morrissey Boulevard. I'll retrieve the Nagra and come right back here to have the original tape entered into evidence after we copy it onto a cassette. After that I plan to shoot right over to the US Attorney's office and listen to it with Rob Richardson," I said.

"Okay, sounds good. I'm anxious as hell so let me know how the recording goes," John said.

"Roger that," I replied.

The morning seemed to last for an eternity. I kept looking at the clock and was amazed to see only five minutes had passed since the last time I looked. The time to meet Tony finally arrived, and at 1:15 p.m., I pulled into the Kmart parking lot and found a spot away from other cars. Time continued to drag by as I anxiously scanned the lot for any sign of Tony's car. Ten minutes, fifteen minutes, twenty minutes passed, and I started to get panicky. I thought about going to TRC and looking for his car when suddenly I saw the familiar Jaguar pull into the lot. Thank God!

Tony popped out of his car and jumped into the front seat with me. "Here, take this fucking thing, will you?" Tony said as he threw the Nagra in my lap.

"You took it off yourself?" I asked.

"Yeah, so sue me. I couldn't stand wearing it, so after our talk I went into the john and pulled it off. I stashed it under the seat in my car," Tony said.

"Well, okay. So how did it go? Any problems?" I asked

"No, I'm still alive as you can see. I think you're going to like what you hear; however, if you don't mind, I would prefer you listen to it and tell me, rather than having me tell you. I'm mentally drained right now and need some downtime," Tony said.

"Okay, that's cool. Did he seem suspicious about anything?" I asked.

"You'll have to listen to it and tell me what you think, but I didn't get the impression he was suspicious. He didn't act like he was. I think he bit hard," Tony said.

I put my head back on the headrest and expelled a sigh of relief.

"Fine, it sounds like you did a good job. I'll get this processed and listen to it. I'll call you tonight," I said.

"Okay, I got to get something to eat and get back. I'm glad this is over," Tony said as he opened the car door to leave.

I hoped it wasn't over but, rather, was just getting started.

I rushed back to the office and went directly to the tech shop. I grabbed an electronic surveillance technician and asked that she expedite the rerecording of the reel-to-reel tape to cassette.

"Sure, Dave, this will only take a few minutes. We'll mark and store the original as evidence. Just fill out the submission form for me please, and I'll be back with a couple copies of the tape," Michelle said as she walked into a back room with the Nagra.

I rushed back to the squad area and stuck my head into John's office. "I've got the cassettes; I'm going to head over to the US Attorney's office now," I informed him.

He flashed a thumbs up.

I stopped by Neil's desk. "Yo, I've got the cassettes and I'm heading over to Rob's office. You coming?" I asked.

"Hell yes, let's go!" Neil exclaimed as he jumped up and grabbed his jacket.

On the drive over, Neil quizzed me about what Tony said.

"Well, he did say we would like it. Understandably he was mentally exhausted, so I didn't press him for details. He went into the bathroom and took the recorder off after the conversation with Mello," I informed Neil.

"Huh, that was unexpected," Neil said.

"Yeah, but I understand. It probably felt like it was burning a hole in his back!" I said.

After parking the car in the potholed, dirt parking lot next to the gleaming new courthouse, we shot up to the US Attorney's office. We found Rob sitting at his cluttered desk reading a file. He looked up and smiled.

"Got it?" he asked.

"We got it," I said.

"Okay then! As they say, let's roll tape!" Rob enthusiastically exclaimed.

The tape started with the introduction we recorded when Tony was in the backseat of my car. The next conversation was with Mello as Tony walked into TRC. They spoke about events in the newspaper. Mello also expounded upon his theories regarding the Gardner Museum robbery for about ten minutes. Tony only made a few short comments during this portion of the tape. Eventually we heard Tony say:

"Listen, Mello, remember when you were talking about that Loomis score and you thought we needed an inside guy to pull it off?"

"Yeah, what about it?" Mello asked.

"I got a guy on the inside, but this thing is too big for me to do," Tony said.

"Well, it ain't for me!" Mello exclaimed. "Who is this guy?"

"You met him already. It's Carl, the guy whose radiator hose I fixed outside, remember?" Tony said.

"Yeah, your sister's old boyfriend, right?" asked Mello.

"That's right. Turns out he's a guard at that facility and he's willing to take part in a robbery. Can you believe it? He used to drive my getaway car when I was doing stickups. Luckily for us he cleaned up his act and got a job, but he's a degenerate gambler and has been thinking about a robbery. He just hasn't got the connections to get it done right. I told him we'll take care of that. He knows I'm with a professional crew," Tony said.

"This is fucking perfect! Listen, can this guy stand up? There will be a lot of pressure after the robbery because the cops always figure it's an inside job and everyone inside will be interrogated and asked to take a polygraph test. Can your guy hold up? I worry he might crack. He's got to tell the cops that he's not going to take a polygraph because his lawyer told him not to. Another thing is, me and you got to keep our jobs here at TRC. Quitting would look too suspicious. Anybody who goes in with us has to be careful about spending money afterward. If somebody starts going crazy, he's gotta be clipped," Mello said.

"Yeah, my guy will hold up; don't worry about that. He won't do nothing stupid," Tony said.

"Good. We're gonna need some guys for this. I know who I want for this job. We need some heavy armament too. What about trucks? Loomis has unmarked vans that they use; are they parked inside there?" Mello asked.

"Yeah, he told me they got about four of them inside. He also said they have tens of millions in the vault!" Tony said.

"Good, we take the fucking trucks and stuff 'em with cash. That's how we get away. Those vans got nothing written on them; nobody can tell who owns them. Who's the guy Carl works with in the vault?" Mello asked.

"Listen to this. Carl has one other guy with him on Sundays. They've already agreed that if the place was robbed, neither one is going to pull an alarm or do anything to stop it. They're going to lay down. No one wants a bullet to the head," Tony said.

"I know they got cameras all over the outside and motion detectors. Those have to be dismantled," Mello said.

"He'll take care of that," Tony said.

"Perfect! Here's another thing. Carl is your buddy, not mine. I'm never going to see him or talk to him. All connection between him and us is through you, Tony. If he goes south and pukes the story to the cops, the only one he can finger is you. That's the way it has to be," Mello said.

"Yeah, sure, I get it. I'm bringing him in so I'm responsible for him," Tony said.

"Exactly! Okay, this is great news. Now we don't talk about this during the workday here. We can talk in the morning or at night, that's it," Mello said.

"Okay, I'm getting to work on that brake job now," Tony said.

End of tape.

Rob, Neil, and I looked at each other and broke out in high fives. This tape could not have gone better! Tony did a fantastic job.

"Mello can kiss the entrapment defense good-bye! Once he heard there was an inside guy, he took complete command. This tape is pure gold! We got us a big case, boys," Rob gushed.

Rob decided he needed a meeting with Tony.

"Rob, I know you like having an excuse to work late since you hate to go home, so why don't I bring Tony by tomorrow after he gets off work? Or would you rather meet him someplace like a restaurant?" I asked.

"Who's buying?" asked Rob.

"FBI," I responded.

"In that case Momma Mia's in Cambridge, 6:30 p.m.," Rob said.

That evening I called Tony at home.

"Hello," Tony said.

"You alone?" I asked.

"Not exactly," he said, which meant his girlfriend was there.

"Okay. Go to Momma Mia's Restaurant in Cambridge tomorrow at 6:30 p.m. I'm buying dinner. We're meeting Rob Richardson from the US Attorney's office. You did great today. Okay?"

"Is that an Indian place? I hate Indian food," Tony said.

"You've got to take your comedy act on the road. See you at 6:30 p.m. tomorrow," I said and hung up.

I made reservations for three at Momma Mia's Italian Restaurant. I arrived twenty minutes early and was given a table in the corner. Rob walked in next, and Tony walked in ten minutes late.

I signaled Tony to join us.

"Tony, this is Rob Richardson. I've told you about him. I was just telling him how you always arrive early for meetings," I said.

"You gotta pick Cambridge? There's nowhere to park!" he complained.

"There's plenty of parking when you've got an FBI parking pass," I said.

"Tony, it's a pleasure meeting you," Rob extended his hand with a smile and Tony sheepishly accepted.

Rob continued, "Dave and I listened to the work you did yesterday, and I have to say I'm very impressed with your performance! You followed Dave's instructions to the letter, and the result was fantastic. Based upon what you did yesterday, we are on very solid legal footing to continue with our investigation, congratulations!"

Tony was taken aback by Rob's praise. It wasn't something he was used to hearing, especially coming from a government attorney.

"Thanks" was all he could muster.

"Now we've got to talk about what to do going forward," I said.

"That's right. Based upon what was said yesterday, we are at a crossroads. You can probably guess what I mean?" asked Rob.

Before Tony could answer, the waitress walked up to take our dinner order.

"What are you gentlemen having tonight?" she asked politely.

I said, "Well, I'm having linguine with white clam sauce and my friend here [pointing to Tony] will have Indian curried lamb."

The waitress looked at me strangely. "Uhhh, sir, this is an Italian restaurant," she said.

Tony quickly interjected, "Don't listen to my father; he's senile. Chicken Marsala please."

Rob ordered spaghetti, and as the waitress walked away, we broke into laughter. At least Rob and I did.

"Okay, so now we have to decide if we are going forward with the mission," I said.

I addressed Tony directly. "Based on what we heard, Carl is out of the picture and you're in. You've got to carry the ball, meaning you're going to get really familiar with the Nagra recorder. I've always said the choice is yours to make. Originally you said you would do it, but that was then, and this is now. We need to know you are still committed to this case, and if so, we need to discuss what we are doing going forward."

Tony looked away from me and seemed to be studying his water glass. "I wish that was vodka," he said.

I looked at Rob. He had his poker face on.

Finally, Tony looked up and said, "I agreed to it, and that's what I'm prepared to do."

He was nodding his head as he said it and making direct eye contact with Rob and me.

"Well, we are very happy to hear that. Based on what I heard yesterday, I believe you were born for this type of work," Rob said happily.

"Salute!" We raised our glasses.

The rest of the evening we talked about our families and personal lives. With the main question answered, we enjoyed ourselves and put the undercover case in the backseat for the night.

The following Monday, I arrived at work ready to plan out the rest of the undercover operation. I met with John Trahon and informed him that Tony was willing to go forward, and since Mello was refusing to meet with Carl, Dave Donahue would not be recording any conversations.

"So Tony is wearing the wire then?" John asked.

"That's what he agreed to, so that's how it's going to play out. I confirmed it with him, and AUSA Rob Richardson is up to speed as well. We still need Dave Donahue in an undercover capacity. We may need him down the line to be seen at the vault in uniform, so Mello is assured he's for real," I said.

"Yeah, let's meet with Loomis Fargo Security as soon as possible to inform them of what's happening here," John said.

"I'll grab Dave and do that today," I said.

After meeting with John, I hustled down to a small windowless office in a secure area of the FBI space. It was occupied by two women who were referred to as Electronic Surveillance Support Staff. They listened to recorded conversations and transcribed them into written format for the agents.

"Hi, Ginny. I've got a new case for you," I said.

"Great, Dave, always looking for more work!" Ginny replied. Ginny was a petite woman, midforties, with short dark hair; she had an easygoing disposition and appeared to enjoy her job.

"Our first recorded conversation was last week, and I need a transcribed copy. There will be more to come," I said.

"Well, you've come to the right spot. I hope it's an interesting one. Trish and I have been bored to death with an endless white-collar case that's putting us to sleep," she said.

"I've listened to this one already, and I think you'll be happy with it. It's a planned robbery of the Loomis Fargo vault facility in Easton, Massachusetts. The cooperating witness, who is recording the conversation, is a guy by the name of Anthony Romano. He'll be talking to a second person by the name of Carmello Merlino. Anthony will be referring to Merlino as 'Mello,' which is his nickname. You may have to listen close to some of it as Mello is a little hard to understand sometimes. There's a lot of mob guy talk going on here with references you may have difficulty deciphering. Just do your best."

Ginny looked over her shoulder at Trish, who had her back to us and was wearing headphones. She leaned in and whispered, "Don't tell Trish about this one. She'll want to steal it from me!"

I laughed. "Got it."

After dropping off the tape, I hooked up with Dave Donahue in the squad area.

"Dave, my man! We got us a case!" I said.

"Really, so I'm wearing a wire?" Dave asked.

"Unfortunately not. Mello refused to meet with you, so Tony has to do all the recording," I said.

"Shit! I was counting on it," Dave complained.

"There's still a role for you. Mello wants Tony to provide some inside information about the facility. Going forward he may want to see you at the location, so he's assured you really exist," I said.

"Well, half a loaf is better than none," Dave sighed.

"Right, buddy, so what I want to do first thing is get together with Loomis Security, and I'd like you to go with me," I said.

"Sure, when?" Dave asked.

"Today. We need an accurate description of the inside layout of the facility. I don't think this is something we can fake because Mello may be testing Tony. Mello may already know what the inside of the facility looks like, so if we come up with an inaccurate description, it wouldn't be good," I said.

"Makes sense," Dave responded.

"I'm going to get an appointment with someone in charge over there," I said.

"Okay, standing by," Dave said.

I was able to quickly get in touch with George Coleman, regional security chief at Loomis Fargo Armored Car Company, and arrange a meeting at his office for 1:00 p.m. that day. At 12:30 p.m., Dave and I drove over to the corporate offices north of Boston in Wakefield, Massachusetts, and after identifying ourselves, we were ushered into Mr. Coleman's office.

George Coleman was a big, burly, no-nonsense guy with a short crew-cut, who wore a concerned expression on his face and a nicely tailored suit on the rest of him.

"Nice to meet you fellows, I think," George said.

"Thank you for meeting with us, Mr. Coleman; this is a matter of some urgency," I said.

"I was afraid of that. Have a seat and please call me George."

"First off, George, let me assure you the Loomis Fargo Armored Car Company is not in any imminent danger of being robbed. What we are here to discuss, however, is a robbery of your Easton vault that is in the planning stage right now. We know this because we have an informant in the middle of it, and we are recording his conversations with a man by the name of Carmello Merlino. This may be a lot to take in, but here's the story," I said.

After sitting listening to our plan for ten minutes, George sat back and wiped his forehead with a handkerchief.

"Jesus Christ! You said it was a lot to absorb, and that's an understatement! But I'll tell you what, I have the authority to make this call and I have respect for the FBI. I know you people are thorough and careful, and I trust you will control this. You can count on the cooperation of Loomis Fargo," he said.

I smiled broadly and looked at Dave, who was also grinning.

"Thank you, sir, we will not drop the ball on this. Which leads us to the next thing. Carmello Merlino has already tasked Tony to contact Carl and obtain from him an accurate description of the inside of the vault facility. This could be a test to see if Carl is the real deal. Merlino may already know what the facility looks like on the inside, maybe not. We just don't know. I'd like to provide Merlino an accurate description of the vault facility. That would put his mind at rest. Can you provide that for us today?" I asked.

"Yes, I can. There is a sally port entrance that allows a person to be buzzed in. The person, once identified, is buzzed through a second door into a hallway that leads to the control room on the right and also to the main garage area. The garage area has two bay doors that allow trucks to enter and exit. The control room is always manned by two employees, neither of which are allowed to exit the facility while on shift. The back of the facility contains a locked vault where the currency is stored until transported. There is a locker room for employees that contains a bathroom and shower. That's all there is. Let me draw a rough sketch for you," George said.

I accepted the sketch and then stood up. I extended my hand to George and said, "Thank you for putting your trust in the FBI. I assure you that you are making the correct decision by allowing us to complete this investigation. Agent Donahue or I will be in touch with you going forward and will keep you briefed on every development."

"Thanks for that, Dave. I have higher-ups who will be very interested in how this is playing out. The more you can tell us the better," George said.

"I understand; same in my shop as well!" I replied.

I met Tony in a secluded parking lot on the edge of Dorchester late on a Monday night. I signaled him to jump in my car.

"So, what's up, chief?" Tony asked.

"I met with the head guy at Loomis and briefed him about what's being planned for his vault facility," I said.

"I'll bet he was thrilled," Tony said.

"Not sure. He just kept moaning and hitting his head on the desk," I joked. "Anyway, they are on board, and I have an accurate drawing of the inside of the Loomis vault." I gave the drawing to Tony. "Now, you can give this to Mello tomorrow. Of course, you will say it came from Carl."

"I hope it's accurate," Tony said.

"I told Mr. Coleman it needed to be accurate because Mello specifically asked for it and we aren't sure one way or the other if this is some kind of test," I said.

"I wouldn't put it past Mello to test me like that. He's stayed alive this long by being careful," Tony said.

I then reached into the backseat and pulled the Nagra recorder up and handed it to Tony.

"Going forward I want you to handle the recorder. You can put it on, turn it on just before arriving at TRC, then turn it off when you guys are done talking in the morning. Think you can handle that?" I asked.

"I can tear apart and rebuild a carburetor; I think I can deal with this!" Tony exclaimed.

"Okay. Every evening after you do a recording, we'll meet or you can call me and let me know what was discussed. When it gets toward the end of the tape, we'll meet, and I'll take your recorder and give you a new one. Got it?" I asked.

"Got it, chief."

"Call me tomorrow evening and let me know how it went and what you guys talked about. I'm anxious to hear what Mello says when you tell him about the inside layout of the vault facility," I said.

"Cool. See ya," Tony replied as he let himself out of the car.

Tony called me at home the day after he picked up the recorder.

"Hi, chief. Sorry to say something went wrong with the recorder and a half-hour conversation was erased," Tony said.

I couldn't believe my ears! "What happened?!" I demanded to know.

"Ha, gotcha!" Tony laughed into the phone.

"Real funny, asshole!" I said.

Tony continued, "Actually it went very well. Mello liked the details of the inside of the Loomis building. It didn't seem like a test to me, but who knows? Anyway, you'll hear him talking about how many guys it will take and more random thoughts about the robbery. He talked about recruiting his nephew Tony Merlino. Tony is on parole for armed robbery though, and that small fact has Mello a little concerned about using that particular nephew. He's got more criminal nephews he can use for this."

"I'll bet he does," I replied.

"So tomorrow he won't be at work; he sold his house in West Roxbury, and there's some legal stuff to do. The next time we talk should be Thursday morning. I've got plenty of tape left so no need to swap recorders yet," Tony advised.

Tony was starting to sound comfortable in his role now. Maybe making the decision was the hardest part for him. Whatever the reason, I liked the way this was going.

"All right, amigo. Let's meet at the same spot, same time Thursday night, and I'll swap out the recorder. I've got a lady at the office anxiously waiting to transcribe chapter 2. She thinks it'll make a great movie," I said.

"Robert De Niro for my part," Tony said.

"I was thinking Steve Buscemi for your part," I said and hung up.

Thursday night Tony and I met at the usual spot. He jumped into my car and handed me the tape recorder.

"All good. No problems," Tony reported. "So do you like working on Sundays?" he asked me.

"Not particularly, it's football season," I said.

"The Patriots suck. Anyway, Mello and I are going for a ride to Easton. He wants to show me the facility and cruise the area," Tony said.

"Noooo shit!" I exclaimed.

"Yes, sir," Tony responded.

"We're going too then," I announced. "I'm putting the squad on this. We'll put a transmitter on you, and I want you to wear a recorder of course. With the transmitter, we can hear you in real time, but the recorder is necessary as well," I said.

"He wants me to pick him up at the Comfort Inn in Dedham around 9:00 a.m. He and his wife are staying there. They sold their house in West Roxbury and bought another one in Quincy, but they have to stay in the hotel for a week before they move in," Tony said.

"Okay, I know where that is. On Elm Street about a half mile east of the hotel is an abandoned industrial area. There's a large building on the property. Meet me behind that building at 8:30 a.m. I'll have a transmitter that we can conceal on you or in your car. Are you doing the driving?" I asked.

"Yeah, I'm driving," Tony said.

"Good, the transmitter has about a half-mile range, so once you guys are on the road, we'll do a loose surveillance behind you. This is good because we never have to get close. I presume Mello is surveillance conscious for the most part?" I asked.

"Yeah, he's always looking for cops when he's in a car," Tony said.

"Okay, so wear a loose-fitting flannel shirt and a jacket. Any questions?" I asked.

"Nope."

"Good. See you Sunday."

Now, since it was Friday night and this ride was to take place on Sunday morning, I had to work fast to get a surveillance organized. First, I called John Trahon.

"John, sorry to bother you on a Friday night, but I just met with Tony, and he told me Mello wants to go check out the Loomis vault facility together on Sunday morning. I need our squad to conduct a surveillance, and I also need an agent from the tech squad to meet me in Dedham at 8:30 a.m. on Sunday with a transmitter and Nagra," I said.

"This is great! Where are you going to meet?" he asked.

"Mello sold his house in West Roxbury and bought a place in Quincy. Currently he's staying at the Comfort Inn in Dedham, so that's where Tony is supposed to pick him up at 9:00 a.m., Sunday. Do you know about that abandoned industrial area on Elm Street east of the hotel? There's a large building on the property. We're meeting behind the building at 8:30 a.m.," I said.

"Yeah, I know that building. We staged there once before for a surveillance, didn't we?" John asked.

"Yeah, that's why I thought of it. Everyone should be familiar with it," I said.

"Okay, round up three more guys, and I'll get ahold of the tech squad supervisor," John said.

"Will do. I'll touch base with you tomorrow," I said.

I made some calls and recruited Dave Donahue, Larry Travaglia, and Gary Cacace. Despite it being a Sunday morning surveillance, they were all excited to join in and agreed to meet at the industrial area no later than 8:30 a.m.

At 8:00 a.m., I was situated behind the abandoned building on Elm Street waiting for the rest of the group to arrive. It was a perfect morning. The weather was clear, and it was around forty degrees outside. One by one the agents checked in. Everyone maintained radio discipline and stayed off the air until we were gathered behind the building. At that time, I made sure everyone was transmitting in the private mode that prevented our transmissions from being overheard by someone with a police scanner. Ted Baker of the tech squad was there with the recorder and transmitter.

"Hey, Ted, sorry to drag you out here on a Sunday morning, but thanks for doing this for us," I said.

"No problem, Dave. My supervisor called me and filled me in on this case. Sounds really interesting!" Ted remarked.

"So far, it's been very interesting, and I hope it stays that way. We're meeting my informant in about fifteen minutes. We need to get him set up with a recorder and a transmitter. He'll be picking up Carmello Merlino at the Dedham Comfort Inn up the road. They'll be taking a ride to Easton. We need to maintain a loose surveillance, and I'm hoping to be able to hear the conversation in their car," I said.

"Okay, I've got the equipment for that," replied Ted.

At 8:30 a.m. on the dot, Tony rolled into the parking lot and drove around to the back of the building. He was driving his spare car, a four-door 1990 brown Mercury Sable. It looked like shit, but I was sure it was mechanically sound. I motioned him to join the group.

"Everyone, this is the famous Anthony Romano. He'll be going into the belly of the beast today, so we have to do our best to keep him safe," I said.

Tony had a sheepish look on his face as each of the men walked up, introduced themselves, and shook his hand.

"So, Tony, this is agent Ted Baker of the technical squad. He has the recorder for you. He also brought a transmitter that will transmit the conversation from your car to our car radios," I said.

"Nice to meet you, Tony. Now I need you to take your jacket and shirt off so I can fit you with the body recorder," Ted said.

Tony did as he was told and was quickly wired up.

"Tony, we are using the latest technology today. It's a completely digital recorder, no tape, no noise whatsoever; it's called an F-Bird. Tony, next I want to find the best place to conceal the voice transmitter in your car. I believe we will get the clearest conversation if the transmitter isn't on your body," explained Ted.

With that, Ted went into Tony's car and started feeling around under the driver's-side seat.

"Okay, good. Tony, the transmitter is about the size of a pager and has a two-foot wire. The stereo microphone is at the end of the wire. I'm going to turn on the transmitter and tape the microphone to the bottom front of your seat. It's not visible to the passenger and is in a good spot to catch all conversation. Do us all a big favor and don't turn on your car radio," Ted instructed.

"Understood," said Tony.

"So now, get into your car and start counting for me," Ted said.

Tony did as he was told and started counting. Ted went to his car and switched his Bureau radio to channel 7. Suddenly Tony's counting came through the radio speakers loud and clear.

"You can stop now, Tony. We have a strong signal, and you are coming in loud and clear," Ted announced. "Last thing we will do is have Dave Nadolski put the preamble on the recorder then you can be on your way."

"Tony, we will be behind you, but since we have the transmitter, we'll be farther back and out of sight. When you make a turn, try to articulate something identifiable that we can use to get your specific position. If we get too far behind, we may lose the signal. You don't need to be obvious; just give us a clue every now and then. Above all, don't worry about anything; the cavalry is right behind you. Good luck," I said.

We all got into our vehicles and switched to channel 7 to listen to the transmitter. Each agent also carried a handheld radio with which we communicated with one another on a different channel.

As Tony left the parking lot, I could hear his car shifting through the gears. Thankfully he remembered to leave his car radio off. After about three minutes, I heard Tony's turn signal, and the car slowed to a stop. A door opened, and I heard Mello get into the car.

"You're almost late, jackass," Mello said.

"Fuck you, Mello," Tony replied.

Things were going splendidly!

"My old lady is buggin' the shit outta me. She wants to get out of this fucking hotel. Can't blame her. There's not enough room to fart in there," Mello said.

"Uh-huh. Where to, boss?" Tony asked.

"Go south on the expressway, but don't fucking speed," we heard Mello say.

After about three silent minutes, Mello said, "Look at this."

"Jesus Christ, is that a gun in your pants?" Tony exclaimed.

"Well, it ain't my dick!" Mello chuckled. "Never know when it might be needed so better safe than sorry."

"Man, I'm on parole. That could be really bad if we get pulled over," Tony complained.

"Well, don't get pulled over!" Mello barked. "Slow down; you're takin' the next exit."

"Isn't this Washington Street, the exit for Stonehill College?" Tony asked, for the benefit of the FBI agents behind him.

"Yeah, about three miles down is Bristol Drive. That's the street with the vault. It's a gray buildin' on the left; we can see it from this road. When you come up to a 99 Restaurant, slow down a little because it's right after that," Mello said.

As the restaurant came into view, Tony began to slow.

"See it, right there." Mello pointed to the vault building. "God damn!"

Tony saw a nondescript, windowless, one-story, gray cinderblock structure with an oversized garage door, a pedestrian entrance door next to the garage door, and a couple of cars parked in the driveway in front of the garage door. It appeared to be one of several plain-looking warehouse-style structures on a side street running off of Washington Street.

They drove past without slowing down and continued down Washington Street. The entrance to Stonehill College was on the right. As they got to the end of Washington Street, Mello directed Tony to make a right turn.

"That was perfect! You know exactly which building it is now. I've been running this thing through my mind. We're going to do it on a Sunday, real early. I never seen shit happening here on Sunday. Find out from your guy if there is any activity on Sunday. I'll bet there ain't. Hell, there's only two cars in the driveway. I'll bet your guy is in there right now. Did you see his car?" Mello asked.

"No, he isn't working today," Tony said.

"Okay, continue down this street for a while; I'm looking for something," Mello said.

"What?" Tony asked.

"A good place to dump the guards' bodies," Mello said.

Long pause. "What the FUCK are you talking about, Mello?" Tony screamed.

"Take it easy, prick! I'm not serious! At least not about killing them. We do need to dump them someplace where they won't be found for a little while. Turn left here," Mello directed.

"Jesus Christ, Mello, I never know when you're serious or joking," Tony complained.

"Robbery is one thing; killin' is another. But if somebody don't hold up though, he's gotta go! For the safety of the rest of us, right? That includes your buddy." Mello was looking directly at Tony.

Tony squirmed in his seat.

"Stop up here; now go down this dirt path on the left, toward the power lines over there," Mello instructed.

They drove down a dirt path for about a quarter mile.

"Okay, stop. Perfect," Mello said as he got out of the car.

Tony put the car in park and got out with Mello.

"This is where we dump them, bound and gagged, not dead! You fuckin' sissy."

Tony was really starting to think Mello had some sinister plans for the guards. Shit, maybe for him too. More money for the rest of them and fewer people to squeal.

"All right, I've seen enough; let's get back," Mello ordered.

Mello was unusually quiet on the way back to the hotel. He looked out of the window and seemed to be deep in thought. Tony worried that Mello wasn't telling him everything that was on his mind, which could be a serious problem.

Twenty minutes later, Tony pulled into the parking lot of the Comfort Inn. Mello opened his door and got out. "See you at work tomorrow," he said as he closed the car door and walked toward his room.

Tony now spoke out loud for the benefit of the agents following him.

"I hope you guys heard that conversation with Mello. We found a place to dump the guards after the robbery. I got the funny feeling he's actually thinking about killing them," Tony said nervously.

Tony pulled into the parking lot behind the abandoned building on Elm Street and was surprised to see the agents standing outside of their cars. *How the hell did they beat me back?* Tony wondered.

As Tony cruised up, I got out of my car and greeted him.

"So, how'd it go?" I asked him.

"What do you mean 'how'd it go'? You heard it all, didn't you?" Tony asked.

I cleared my throat. "Uh, well, not exactly."

"What are you talking about?" Tony asked.

"Unfortunately, we lost contact with you about five minutes into the surveillance. The transmitter shit the bed. We didn't want to take the chance of trying to follow you closer, so we just came back here and waited for you to get back," I confessed.

"Oh my God! The son of a bitch was carrying a gun! You really didn't hear us?" Tony asked again.

"Really, but no problem because we have the recorder, so we'll just listen to that," I assured him.

"Good because we drove right past the armored car company and then Mello took me into a secluded area. He said that was where he was dumping the guards' bodies! When I blew a gasket, he then said he was kidding. But I don't think he was kidding," Tony exclaimed.

"Well, that'll be great evidence. I'm going to have the conversation downloaded and transcribed first thing tomorrow," I said.

At that point, Ted Baker took the F-Bird recorder from Tony.

"Good thing you were wearing this device, Tony; otherwise this whole exercise would be wasted," Ted said.

"Okay, my friend, go back to using the Nagra tape recorder tomorrow, and I'll call you after work. Good job today," I said to Tony as I patted him on the back.

The next morning, I got a call from Ted Baker shortly after I walked into the office.

"Dave, come down to the tech room, will you?" Ted asked me.

"Sure, on the way," I said.

As I walked into the tech room, I saw Ted musing over the F-Bird.

"I don't know how to tell you this, but the F-Bird stopped recording a few minutes after we put it in the car. It must have somehow gotten interference from the electrical system in his car. We don't have anything on the recorder. I'm sorry," Ted said glumly.

I was shocked! "So you're telling me the transmitter and the recorder both failed? Are you sure about that? Check it again?" I said.

"I've checked it over and over. There's nothing. Unfortunately, this isn't the first time we've had a problem with the F-Bird, but we thought we had it straightened out. Apparently not," Ted confessed.

"Mother of God!" I said as I slumped into a chair. "Yesterday was a total waste!"

Later that evening, I wasn't exactly looking forward to talking with Tony, but I reached him at his apartment after work.

"Hey, anything happen today?" I asked Tony.

"Nah, not really. Mello came in late, so we didn't get a chance to talk about anything. He made some phone calls, but I'm not sure what that was all about. How was the recording?" Tony asked.

"Well, about that. I have some bad news," I said.

Silence.

"What happened?" Tony asked cautiously.

I decided to just spill it. "Well, the transmitter isn't the only piece of equipment that failed yesterday. The F-Bird stopped working, and we didn't record any of the conversation you had with Mello."

More silence.

"Are you shitting me?!" Tony finally asked incredulously.

"Unfortunately, I am not. Obviously, it was good that you did the drive by yesterday. That shows us Mello is really serious about this," I lamely replied.

"You're the FBI; your equipment isn't supposed to fail! This doesn't give me a warm and fuzzy feeling at all!" Tony yelled into the phone.

"I know, I know. We aren't supposed to fail at this, and all I can say is I'm sorry about it. Luckily it doesn't impact the case. Technical problems do pop up from time to time, and we are getting fantastic evidence from your recordings at TRC. Going forward, we stick with the Nagra. It's a proven workhorse, so we no longer rely on whizbang techno crap," I said, trying to sound reassuring.

"Yeah, sure. Talk to you tomorrow," Tony said abruptly as he hung up the phone.

15

BEST PANCAKES IN TOWN

DORCHESTER, MASSACHUSETTS

Early the next morning, Tony, wearing his trusted Nagra tape recorder, opened the door to TRC and started to step in when an attractive young woman in skintight jeans brushed past him on the way out.

"Hi, cutie!" she said.

Tony turned and looked at her as she sauntered down the sidewalk snapping her bubble gum. As Tony stepped in, he observed Mello fastening up his pants.

"Best twenty bucks I've ever spent. Want me to get her back for you?" Mello asked.

"Uhhh, no. Mello, you're a degenerate," Tony said.

"Well, I'm in a pretty good mood now. Listen, I've been giving this job a lot of thought. I've decided to contact David and Stevie. I want them in on this thing," Mello said.

Tony recognized Mello was referring to his two favorite partners in crime, David Turner and Stephen Rossetti.

"Sounds good, Mello. They're a couple of serious players. I imagine they'd be all in for this," Tony replied.

"I'm gonna call them today and set up a meeting somewhere. I think this sketch you gave me of the vault will go a long way to convince them. They are pretty cautious, but they got huge balls and are perfect for a hit like this," Mello said.

Tony was disturbed by Mello's use of the word "hit" but didn't let on. He was becoming more convinced that Mello wasn't leveling with him about this whole operation. For one thing, Mello was well aware that Tony had never participated in anything like this and so he really had no idea how Tony might react after everything was over. Additionally, Mello didn't like loose ends, and Carl and the second vault guard working with Carl were total unknowns. Mello made it sound as if Carl would be accepted into the crew and trusted since he was a friend of Tony's, but alarm bells were going off in Tony's brain. Mello was not the type of guy to rely on others if there was the slightest possibility those people could fold when the pressure was on. Tony knew not to accept Mello's enthusiasm at face value. He had seen what Mello had done to other prisoners whom he suspected of being unreliable within the prison walls, and they never saw it coming. The more Tony thought about this, the more he believed Mello wasn't going to leave any loose ends. Tony was beginning to see this clearly now. Carl, the other guard, and Tony himself were not going to live to spend any money if this crime was actually carried out.

Later that evening, Tony called me at home.

"Hey, chief, I got some news for you," Tony said when I answered the phone.

"What's that?" I asked.

"Mello wants to meet with Turner and Rossetti to talk about joining the crew. I've got the feeling he's ready to meet as soon as they can, so it could be tomorrow sometime. The best I can do is talk with Mello tomorrow morning to see what he's doing. I'll contact you the minute I know so you can put a surveillance on the meeting," Tony said.

"Hey, that's great news, and you're right: we definitely want that meeting covered! I'll get into the office early, and you can give me a call as soon as you have any details. I'll reserve a surveillance team to cover the meeting, wherever it takes place. Good work!" I said.

"Just make sure these guys aren't made. If Mello suspects anything, I might not live through the day," Tony said.

"Being a little dramatic, aren't we?" I asked.

"No, I don't think so. I hate the way this whole thing is shaping up. Turner and Rossetti are careful killers, just like Mello. They don't know me or trust me, so if your people get spotted by these guys, they won't let it show. Their next step would be to shut it down and eliminate all loose ends. I'm a big loose end," Tony replied seriously.

After a pause, I responded, "I see your point, and I understand your concerns. In fact, I agree with you 100 percent. Covering this meeting would be important to the case, but I will personally direct the surveillance and immediately shut it down if I suspect anything is going wrong. I believe they will meet in a public place. If I know beforehand where that is, we can have the coverage in place when they arrive. All we are going to do is document that they are meeting together. I think that's the safest thing to do."

"Okay, you know more about this than I do. I'll call you tomorrow as soon as I have anything to report. Be ready to move; it could happen fast. Good night."

"Good night, and good job," I said as I hung up the phone.

Stephen Rossetti and David Turner were protégés of Mello. They were a criminal team who liked to work together. Rossetti was a forty-two-year-old "armored car guy" from East Boston who enjoyed getting off by sticking a gun in someone's face and watching him crap his pants. He wasn't a "made" man like his uncle Mark, but he was a mob associate when it suited him. Rossetti didn't appreciate the structure of Mafia life; he wanted to be his own man. He did allow himself one close partner in crime, David Turner.

Turner was thirty-four years old, with California-surfer good looks, and he couldn't have been more different than Rossetti in most ways. He was big and blond and gregarious. His girlfriend was an outrageously sexy bikini model. Turner had been a good high school student, athletic and popular. He grew up in the Boston suburb of Braintree. He was a successful businessman who owned a fleet of dump trucks that were earning him a lot of cash hauling dirt from Boston's massive public works project known locally as the "Big Dig." The problem with Turner was, like Rossetti, he had a dark side.

During the early 1990s, it's believed, Turner and an associate, Charlie Pappas, heard about a Boston-area businessman that kept large sums of money in his home. The businessman couldn't afford to put all his cash in the bank as that would leave a paper trail. The word on the street was that Turner and Pappas broke into the house and Turner pistol-whipped the businessman and threatened his wife. Without too much effort, they got what they came for and left, but not before Turner told the unhappy couple that if they went to the cops, they were dead. Turner made a real impression on the couple, so they just licked their wounds and stayed quiet. Pappas, on the other hand, was later arrested for a large drug sale and was looking at serious prison time. He asked the cops if they were interested in solving a home invasion in exchange for a pass. A deal was stuck, and Pappas agreed to testify against Turner. Word of Pappas's betrayal reached Turner, and three days before Pappas was scheduled to testify, two masked men barged into his kitchen and shot him eight times. Pappas's girlfriend was in the room and witnessed the killing. The home invasion case against Turner was eventually dropped—the only witness was dead.

I immediately called the supervisor of the surveillance squad at home and informed him of the situation. I requested and received a six-agent surveillance team to be on standby in Dorchester first thing in the morning. I didn't sleep well that night and remember constantly waking up and checking the digital clock; I didn't want to oversleep and get to the office late. Finally, at 4:00 a.m., I just got dressed and drove to the office where I dozed beside my phone until the other agents started filing in.

Dave Donahue sat down at the desk next to mine.

"Why are you here?" he asked.

I filled him in on my conversation with Tony the previous night and the surveillance team I arranged for that day.

"Okay, if you're going out on it, so am I. I want to see this," Dave said.

"Fine with me. All I want to do is have a loose surveillance in the area of the meeting, wherever that is. I want to confirm that Mello, Turner, and Rossetti meet together, and I'd like to get some pictures if possible. I'd like to verify what they are driving as well. We need that information and photo evidence. After that, we let them go and we melt away. Under no circumstances do I want to do anything that might get us noticed. The only person who will know about this meeting besides Mello, Turner, and Rossetti is Tony. If they sense anything unusual, Mello will know who to 'talk' to," I said.

"I get it. Bad news for Tony," Dave confirmed.

At 11:15 a.m., my phone rang. It was Tony. He was whispering.

"Listen, Dave, I gotta be quick. Mello just got off the phone with Turner. He's meeting Turner and Rossetti at Linda Mae's restaurant. He's leaving in about fifteen minutes." With that message delivered, Tony hung up.

"Donahue, let's go. It's Linda Mae's!" I shouted.

We grabbed our jackets and ran to the parking garage below our building. As soon as we cleared the garage onto Congress Street, I grabbed the Bureau radio and called the surveillance team. We were communicating in the private mode so no one outside the Boston office of the FBI could overhear our conversation. Burt O'Connor, the team leader, came up immediately, and I filled him in.

"Burt, get your team to Linda Mae's on Morrissey Boulevard. Our targets will be meeting there in about fifteen minutes; sorry about the short notice. Look for a brown, banged-up T-Bird. Carmello Merlino will be driving it. He's described as five feet, nine inches tall; medium to heavy build; wearing mechanics clothing; and he's partially bald and in his early sixties. He's meeting David Turner and Stephen Rossetti, who will probably be arriving individually. Turner is in his early thirties and has blond hair. Rossetti has black hair and is a little older than Turner. Unfortunately, I don't know what they are driving, but we know they are all meeting together in the restaurant. Get someone into the restaurant ASAP. If possible, I want an agent inside and at a table eating a meal when they walk in. I want to know when they get there and when they leave. I don't want photos inside the restaurant, but if we could get a photo of them leaving together, that would be good. I want their cars photographed and get the license plates. Above all, and this is *very important*, this is a discreet surveillance. Do not move close to these guys. Use telephoto lenses from as far back as possible. Do not follow them away from the restaurant. These guys are very surveillance conscious. Got all that? Any questions?" I asked.

"No problem, Dave. I understand completely. We will be very cautious. I'll keep you informed as the situation unfolds. Will you be in the area?" Burt asked.

"Yes, I'll be in the area with Dave Donahue. We're staying out of sight, but afterward I'd like to speak with the agent who you have on the inside of the restaurant," I explained.

"Got it." With that, Burt signed off.

Dave and I parked in the lot of a bowling alley approximately a quarter mile away from Linda Mae's. We monitored the surveillance squad frequency on our radio. To my surprise, I heard our surveillance airplane come over the radio. Bob Lawson was keeping an eye on Linda Mae's from eight hundred feet in the air. Dave and I both looked for the plane but were never able to find it.

"I love our eye in the sky!" I said to Dave.

I called Burt on the radio. "Thanks for the angel, Burt, nice touch," I commented.

"We are here to please, my friend," Burt responded with a laugh. "By the way, no sign of anyone yet, but we have Marianne inside the restaurant. Wow, those pancakes look good!"

"Sounds like they have this covered like a blanket," I told Dave.

"They are good," he agreed.

Approximately ten minutes passed when the radio crackled. "This is Tango 3. Subject one just parked and entered the restaurant."

Subject one was Merlino. One down, two to go.

Five minutes later another message: "This is Tango 6. Subjects two and three have parked and are entering together. They arrived in separate cars. Photos taken."

Very soon after that a whispered female voice came over the air. "All three are sitting together by the window."

I looked at Dave Donahue and smiled. "Bingo!" I said.

The meeting lasted about forty-five minutes, after which all three men rose together and left the restaurant. They returned to their cars and left the parking lot in different directions.

I called for Burt to meet me in the bowling alley with Marianne.

Dave and I grabbed a table in the restaurant and ordered Cokes. Burt and Marianne entered together and joined us.

"How were the pancakes, Marianne?" I asked.

"Dave, they're always good at Linda Mae's, especially when the Bureau is paying for them!" she replied with a laugh.

"So what did it look like to you, Marianne?" I asked.

"Well, I wasn't close enough to hear anything but the older guy, Merlino, did most of the talking. The blond guy said very little but listened closely, I could tell that. The other guy with the black hair did a lot of talking, and I saw them all nodding their heads from time to time. I saw Merlino show them a piece of paper, which they looked at very closely. It seemed to me that whatever was on that paper was of interest to them because the blond guy looked at it for a couple minutes straight. I didn't want to draw any attention to myself, so I left before they did. They never looked my way at all as far as I could tell," Marianne reported.

"Thanks, Marianne, that was very helpful. I like the idea of a woman alone doing the inside work on this surveillance. These guys would be expecting a man if they were looking for cops," I said.

Burt continued the debriefing. "Just before we joined you here, I checked in with the airplane. Bob saw them all go to their cars and leave in different directions. He stuck with Merlino who returned to TRC Auto Electric on Dorchester Boulevard; then Bob returned to the airport. He got photos from the air."

"Those will come in handy. What about ground photos of the subjects and their cars?" I asked.

"We were able to stay back, and while they were inside, we got good photos of the cars and their license plates. Just before they left the restaurant, I had the team disperse. I stayed behind and got good telephoto shots of your subjects together in a group. I noted the cars each of them drove away in. I have all that and will get a full report to you along with the developed photos ASAP," Burt assured me.

"Thank you, Burt, and please pass my thanks to your team. The airplane was an extra touch I didn't expect but really appreciated," I said.

Burt laughed. "It's what we do, my friend! I'll send you the photos from our orbiting space satellite too as soon as they are beamed down!"

Tony called me later that evening.

"Dave, were you able to get the meeting covered?" he asked.

"Yeah, very discreet but thorough. We saw everyone at Linda Mae's and got photos of them together and the cars they were driving. We had a female agent inside before they walked in, and she saw them interact together. She couldn't hear anything but did see Mello showing Turner and Rossetti the sketch of the vault facility. They appeared very interested. Did Mello give you any feedback after he returned to the garage?" I asked.

"He sure did. He said Turner and Rossetti are on board. They loved the sketch and said they would be ready to do this as soon as it can be arranged. They had a lot of questions but apparently liked Mello's answers. Mello was in a very good mood when he got back from that meeting. He further decided he wants to have his nephew Billy Merlino in on this as well," Tony replied.

"What's Billy's story?" I asked.

"He's Mello's sister's kid. Not a kid exactly since he's in his thirties, but he's been a construction laborer off and on his whole life. Mostly off. He did time for drug distribution and worked for Mello in his drug business. He's never done anything like this job before and never been arrested for anything violent. He definitely will not be the brains of this operation, and frankly, I don't know why Mello thinks he's a good fit for this job. Anyway, if Billy agrees, then I think we have our whole team," Tony said.

"Okay, we are making solid progress. Keep up the good work!" I said.

"Dave, listen, something else has come up. Mello started doing some planning, and he gave me marching orders. He wants me to locate and steal a van for the job. His idea is to have everyone meet at TRC the morning of the robbery. We'll be ready with disguises and guns. He wants us to pile into the van and drive to Loomis where we will do the robbery. Mello knows there are white unmarked Loomis vans inside the vault facility, so after the robbery, he wants to put the guards in the stolen van, then abandon the stolen van and guards at that location we found in Easton by the high-tension wires. Cash from the vault will be stuffed into the two Loomis vans. So, basically, I have to come up with a stolen van. I don't think you want me to really steal one, do you?" Tony asked.

"Wow, I guess we are really making solid progress, damn! You're right; I don't want you to steal a van. I'll find one for you. We've got a contact at an insurance company, and I might be able to get one from them. You can tell Mello you stole it, and we'll even stash it somewhere so he can see it. Just tell him you are going to start looking for a good van to grab," I said. "Any more news?"

"Actually, yes. At the Linda Mae's meeting, Mello told Turner and Rossetti about the inside guy you recruited, and they want to do a dry run to test the plan," Tony said.

"So what's the plan?" I asked.

"Mello said on the day of the robbery they want Carl to come out of the vault facility and go to his car at a particular time. He's supposed to tell the other guard he wants to get a newspaper from his car. When Carl comes out to his car, we roll up and grab him. Remember I told Mello that Carl said he has an agreement with the other guard that if the facility was ever robbed, they would cooperate fully with the robbers and not trigger any alarms. We got to have Dave Donahue in the facility for the dry run.

That way everyone will see Dave in his role as Carl the guard. It should put them all at ease."

"I love it! Let's plan on next Sunday," I said.

"Okay, that's a good day and gives us a few days to prepare. I'll let Mello know," Tony said.

"In the meantime, I'll see about getting a van to use. Man, I got to tell you, this is going pretty smooth; you are doing a fantastic job!" I said.

"Thanks," Tony replied and hung up.

I was in the office at 7:00 a.m. the next day waiting in my cubicle for Dave Donahue and John Trahon to arrive. They both came into the squad area at 8:00 a.m.

"Guys, grab some coffee. We've got to talk in John's office," I said.

"Is it about the Loomis case?" John asked.

"You bet your ass!" I said with a huge grin.

Five minutes later, we were huddled in John's office. I told them about my conversation with Tony the night before. They both looked at one another, and Dave said, "Damn, this thing is really going to happen!"

John said, "We've got some quick work to do. Donahue, do you have a guard uniform yet?"

"Not yet, boss, but I can get one from George Coleman quick enough. I'll call him as soon as we are done here and tell him I need to be in the vault this Sunday and that I need a uniform right away," Dave said.

"Good. Nadolski, on Sunday, you and I are going to be in the area doing a loose surveillance," John ordered.

"Okay, I like that idea. It's got to be very low key. Later tonight I'll talk to Tony and let him know it's a go," I said. "I've got one more issue to discuss, John. Mello wants Tony to steal a van to be used for the robbery. I need to provide one for him and was thinking of borrowing one from our insurance company contact."

John went into his Rolodex and copied a number on a piece of paper.

"Here, call this guy. Tell him what you need. He's helped in the past; should be no big deal," John said.

Back at my desk, I dialed the number John gave me.

"This is Rick Hamilton; how can I help you?"

"Rick, this is Special Agent Dave Nadolski from the Boston FBI office. I got your name and number from John Trahon," I said.

"Okay, how can I help the Boston FBI today?" Rick asked.

"Well, Rick, we are running an undercover operation; it's a pretty big deal, and I was hoping you could help us. Our operation calls for a stolen van. I'm looking for a van that I can pop the ignition on to make it look as if it's been stolen. We would need to use it for a couple weeks or so. Do you have anything like that by any chance?" I asked.

"Probably do, Dave. I might even be able to come up with something that's already got the ignition punched. How would that work for you?" Rick asked.

"That would probably work just great!" I responded.

"We have a storage lot on Center Street in Woburn. Our inventory is over there, and if you want to meet me on Friday, I'll can see what we can come up with," he said.

"Sure, Rick. I know the location. How about 1:00 p.m.?" I asked.

"Perfect, see you then. I'll meet you at the gate."

"Great, see you there!"

Later that evening, I called Tony at his apartment.

"Hey, can you meet me at 12:30 p.m. this Friday at our Bureau garage in Everett? I'm meeting with an insurance guy who is loaning us a van. They have all their repos parked in a lot on Center Street in Woburn. You can pick whichever one you want. You can leave your car at the garage and ride with me," I said.

"Actually, that would be a good day to do it. I'll tell Mello I'm heading out at noon to scout for a van to steal. He'll be happy to let me go do that. What's John Trahon think about Sunday?" Tony asked.

"Oh man! He is stoked about this and so am I! He and I are going to be in the area doing a very loose surveillance. Nobody else will be around," I said.

"Are you sure that's a good idea?" Tony asked.

"Yeah. What if for some reason Mello and his merry band of killers decide to skip the dress rehearsal and go for it? We've got to be there. If something like that goes down, get the hell out of there because bullets will be flying. Donahue will be wearing a concealed bulletproof vest and have his handgun in an ankle holster. We don't have any real reason to suspect they would stray from the original plan. A daylight robbery like that would be suicide," I said.

"I hadn't really thought about that, but it is a remote possibility, I guess. If you see me jump out of the car and run, you'll know the plan has changed," Tony grimly responded.

"Don't forget to zigzag!" I laughed.

16

"STEALING" A VAN

WOBURN, MASSACHUSETTS

Friday, January 22, 1999

Friday at 12:30 p.m. Tony pulled into the parking lot of the FBI garage located north of Boston.

"Hi, buddy. Ready to steal a van?" I asked as Tony folded himself into the front seat of my car.

"Sure, why not? You can be the lookout," he said.

"Ha, ha. Buckle up; it's the law, you know," I said.

"So this guy we're meeting is just going to give us a van to play with?" Tony asked.

"Yep. Commonwealth Insurance Company is a good corporate citizen who wants to do everything they can to advance the cause of justice. Just like you, actually," I said.

Tony let out a snort. "Just drive the car; it's getting deep in here!"

We pulled up to the gate of the storage lot and met a middle-aged man with short gray hair and glasses, wearing a blue blazer, gray slacks, and a huge smile.

As we were getting out of the car, the man walked straight up to Tony and grabbed his tattooed hand. "Nice to meet you, Agent Nadolski. I'm Rick Hamilton," he said.

"Nice try, but the agent is the guy over there with the suit and badge," Tony said, pointing to me.

Rick looked stricken. "Oh, of course, of course. Sorry for the mix-up. So who are you exactly?" Rick asked.

"I'm the car thief," Tony said.

"Now that you mention it, you do look more like a car thief," Rick laughed.

"Rick, this is my specialist, Tony," I said. "Tony is going to help us select a suitable van for the case we are investigating. You sure have a lot of vehicles here. You must have an acre of land at least."

"Yep, just under an acre and pretty crammed as you can see," Rich responded.

The vehicles were parked in rows with an access lane between the rows.

"I can just wait here until you find the one you want. Like I said when we first talked, some of them have punched ignitions already, but if you need to punch it yourself, that's okay. Most of these vehicles have ignition keys in them as well," Rick offered.

"Thanks, Rick, really kind of you. We'll find something, I'm sure," I said.

Tony and I started walking around. We focused on vans, which there seemed to be a lot of. Tony was in his element: crawling in and out of various vehicles, checking the ignition, starting the motor, opening the hood, and poking around the engine compartment. I followed along and just let him do his thing.

Finally, he called me over to a blue Ford van. It appeared to be in good shape. He had the hood up and the driver's-side door open.

"I like this one. It's in pretty good condition and has only 35,000 miles on it. The storage area is clean and roomy, and the tires look decent. I'm going to drive it around a little," Tony said as he closed the hood and jumped behind the wheel.

The van started up after a few tries. The motor was a little loud at first but evened out after thirty seconds. Tony pulled into the access lane and started toward the gate. At the open gate, he put the van in reverse and then forward again. He hit the street and took off. I walked up to Rick Hamilton, who was watching the van disappear down the street.

"He does know the van has no license plates, right?" Rick asked.

"Yeah, he doesn't care. He can outrun any cop," I said.

Rick slowly turned his head and stared at me. "Can I see your identification again please?" he asked.

I was just pulling my credentials out when Tony roared up the street and screeched to a halt five feet from where I was standing. He jumped out of the van with a huge smile. "We'll buy it!" he proclaimed.

After signing a bunch of paperwork for Rick, I thanked him again for his help. Then I slapped a couple undercover license plates on the van and told Tony to follow me back to the garage.

Once back at the garage, I had Tony park it in a bay with a hoist and looked around for a mechanic.

"Hey, Mickey, can you come here a minute please?" I called out.

Mickey, one of our professional mechanics, stepped from beneath a Bureau car that he was working on and wiped his hands on a clean rag as he approached.

"What can I do for you, Dave?" he asked.

"This is Tony. He's part of an undercover operation we're running. He's a mechanic, and we are using this van in the operation. We need to make it look like it was stolen, so Tony is going to punch out the ignition and hot-wire it. First, I need to put it on a hoist so he can look underneath. Can you help me with that?" I asked.

"Sure thing, Dave; glad to meet you, Tony," Mickey said as he shook Tony's hand.

"Let's give her a ride," Tony said.

Mickey put the car in the air, and he and Tony worked together inspecting everything they could see from under the van, then lowered it and buried themselves into the engine compartment. Eventually Mickey handed Tony a large screwdriver, which he used to pop the ignition. Tony then concentrated on the exposed wiring for about five seconds before the engine started.

"Smooth work, Tony! You've done this before, haven't you?" Mickey said with a huge grin.

"Once or twice," Tony responded.

"Well, okay then. Mickey, we need to park this inside where it won't be seen, and I think a tech agent will need to make some modifications as well. If all goes according to plan, it won't be taking up space here for very long," I said.

"Okeydokey. Just park it over in the corner out of the way," Mickey said.

After the van was safely parked in its spot, I said good-bye to Mickey and walked Tony to his car.

"So now you can tell Mello you found a van to steal and give him whatever bullshit story you want. This Sunday, Dave will be inside and we'll do the rehearsal. Let me know exactly when this is going to happen, how this is going to happen, and who is going to be there, okay?" I said.

"Got it. Mello will probably want to do it in the morning but not too early since we are just doing a dress rehearsal. I'm telling Mello that Carl is working the day shift so we can do it any time before 3:00 p.m. I'm going to have that conversation as soon as I get back to TRC. I'll call you tonight with the details," Tony said.

I was restless and on edge all evening waiting to hear from Tony. I was beginning to think something was wrong when the phone rang. "Hi, Dave, this is Jimmy from the office. I have Tony on the line for you."

"Put him through please," I said.

"So what's the good word?" I asked immediately.

"Well, Mello loved that I located a van, and he wants to do the dry run Sunday at 11:00 a.m. He told me to tell Carl that we will be approaching the location of the vault at that time, and we want to see him come out, go to his car, and return inside with a newspaper. One more thing, give this phone number to Donahue: 471-1677. That's Mello's pager number, and if there are any problems, Carl is supposed to dial in 9999. That way we will know Carl can't come out for some reason and we will leave the area," Tony said.

"Got it. Who will be participating in this dry run?" I asked.

"The whole crew. Mello, me, Billy Merlino, Turner, and Rossetti. I'll be driving my car with Mello and Billy, but Turner and Rossetti will be in their own car. They operate as a team. In fact, we aren't even going to see them. We aren't meeting with them before or after the dry run," Tony explained.

"Cautious bastards, aren't they?" I asked.

"Big time. This show is primarily for their benefit. If it doesn't go well, they're out," Tony said.

"I would be too, if I were them," I said. "Okay, so here's the deal. Like I told you before, John and I are doing a loose surveillance. We'll be hidden somewhere in the area with a view of the vault facility. I'd like to be able to see Donahue come out. Normally I'd put a transmitter on you so John and I can keep track of what's being said in the car, but we're not doing that. We know where you are going and we'll be able to spot you when you're in the area, so your body recorder is enough and it's safer that way. Less chance of something going wrong. I know the cars Turner and Rossetti were driving when they met at Linda Mae's restaurant, so we'll be on the lookout for those as well. I'm going to assume you're driving again, but if not, no big deal. If Mello wants to drive, that's okay. I'll spot his car. I think John and I will be in the 99 Restaurant parking lot if there are enough cars in the parking lot to hide among. It's a good spot because we can view the vault from there and also observe cars driving by. After the dry run, meet John and me in the Kmart lot. I want to get the recorder from you and find out how everything went. Any questions?" I asked.

"No. See you at Kmart," Tony said.

"Good luck," I said as I hung up the phone.

My next two calls were to Donahue and John Trahon. I briefed John on my conversation with Tony and arranged to pick him up at his house at 9:30 a.m., Sunday. Dave Donahue said he would be in the vault and would exit the vault at exactly 11:00 a.m. Sunday morning. Dave also agreed to contact George Coleman from Loomis to inform him of the Sunday dry run and make arrangements for Dave to be at the vault.

Everything seemed to be in place, and there wasn't anything to do except wait for Sunday.

17

THE DRY RUN

EASTON, MASSACHUSETTS

Sunday, January 24, 1999

At 9:30 a.m. sharp, I stopped in front of John Trahon's house and sat waiting with the car running. Two minutes later, John popped out the front door and opened the passenger-side door.

"You ready?" I asked as John slid into the passenger seat.

"Ready as I'll ever be. Did you bring the vests, jackets, and MP5s?" John asked, referring to our body armor, blue FBI raid jackets, and assault rifles.

"They're all in the backseat. MP5s are unloaded, but we each have two thirty-round magazines. I've got two pair of the high-powered binoculars as well," I said as I pulled from the curb.

"Well, that should do the trick. If not, I don't know what will," John sighed.

"Yeah, I'm glad we took this precaution, but I'm 99 percent certain this is going to go off without a problem. There's been no indication that this is anything but a dry run," I said.

"So Donahue is all set inside, right?" John asked.

"He is. He parked his car just outside the front door, and it's the same car he was driving when he met Mello at TRC. George Coleman is inside the vault with Donahue. He insisted on being there today so he arrived at 6:00 a.m. and pulled his car inside so it wouldn't be seen. Donahue's car is in the parking lot. George has suspended any activity at the vault today, so the stage is set," I said.

"Good, I would have done the same thing Coleman did. Can't be too careful, and if the shit hits the fan, he needs to be there," John replied.

I really liked working with John and admired his management style. When I first transferred to the Boston Division from New York City, John was an agent on the Bank Robbery Task Force. After many years in the Boston FBI office, he was promoted to supervisory rank and was awarded the Bank Robbery Task Force squad to supervise. John worked as a street agent in New York City and eventually managed a transfer to his hometown of Boston.

Being a supervisor on the task force was a unique position. Of all the squads in the office, the task force had the most life-and-death decisions to make. If you didn't have the knowledge, temperament, and ability to lead in stressful situations, you had no business calling the shots on our squad. Given the nature of the cases handled by our squad, an indecisive or incompetent supervisor put agent and cop lives at risk. Everyone had complete faith in John.

After John and I were on the road for ten minutes, he instructed me to pull over in an abandoned parking lot.

"Let's gear up here," John said.

We retrieved our body armor, consisting of bulletproof plates designed to cover our upper body front and back, then slipped them on and secured them with Velcro straps. Next, we removed the MP5 assault rifles and loaded one thirty-shot magazine into each. We deliberately did not load a bullet from the magazine into the rifles. That step would only be taken when it was clear we would need the guns. Until that step was taken, the rifles were no more dangerous than clubs. We placed the rifles into the backseat and continued on toward Easton.

While I was picking up John Trahon at his house, Tony was pulling into the parking lot of TRC. He discreetly checked to make sure the concealed tape recorder was operating, then slipped it back into the small of his back. He noticed Mello's car was already parked in the lot along with Billy Merlino's car.

"Hey, you old fart!" Tony called as he walked through the front door of TRC. Mello and Billy were in the front office talking.

"Who you calling an old fart? I can still knock your ass to the moon!" Mello responded.

"Calm down, calm down, you'll have a stroke and we'll all be out of business!" Tony said as he covered his face.

"Listen up, pretty boy. Let's get in your car and start heading toward Easton. Is everything all set with your boy?" Mello asked.

"He's good to go, Mello. Ready to show his face in the parking lot at 11:00 a.m. on the dot. What about Turner and Rossetti?" Tony asked.

"They do their own thing. I told them what was happening, and they said they would be in the area somewhere. I don't know where and don't care," Mello said as the three men slid into Tony's car.

En route to the vault, Mello immediately started talking about a plan.

"If this thing goes smoothly today, I'm thinking we do this job sooner rather than later. The more time we wait, the better chance for something to go wrong. We definitely want to do it on a Sunday. We're gonna travel to Easton in the van Tony stole. Once we see Carl in the parking lot, we rush him and force him inside. We'll immediately tie up both guards and blindfold them. While we are doing that, Tony brings the van into the building. We'll have that van inside along with two unmarked Loomis vans. We load the Loomis vans with as much cash as we can stuff in and put the two hog-tied guards in the stolen van. We're gonna be in the building no more than nine minutes. If the phone rings while we are inside, we let Carl answer it. He'll act like everything is fine and won't panic like the other guard might do. Tony, you're going to drive the van to the spot we located by the high-tension wires. You'll dump the stolen van with the guards blindfolded and tied up inside. I'll be right behind you in one of the unmarked Loomis vans, so once you dump the van, you jump in with me and we screw," Mello said, emphatically.

"What happens after the robbery?" Tony asked.

"We're heading straight back to TRC and hiding the Loomis vans inside. We'll dump all the cash, which I think will be at least twenty million. I'll stay behind with Turner. You and Billy will get rid of the Loomis vans. Tony, I want you to find a good place to dump the vans. Rossetti will follow you in his car and pick you up. It's got to be a secluded spot because we don't want anyone to see you or Rossetti's car. Got it?" Mello asked.

"Yeah, I got it. I already have a good spot in mind," Tony said.

"So Rossetti will bring you both back to TRC. Me and Turner will have divided the money into duffle bags by then. When you get back to TRC, all our cars will be inside where we'll load them with cash. Everyone has to have a place to hide their haul. If anyone is caught with this cash, we're all fucked. If anyone spends a lot of money after the robbery, he's gonna be clipped. It's gotta be that way for the rest of us," Mello warned.

As he was driving the car toward Easton, Tony was pondering Mello's plan. Conveniently, he had Tony driving the stolen van with the two guards to the dump spot by the high-tension wires. All three of them would be in a secluded spot together. Tony was sure Mello wasn't intending to leave the guards alive, but why did he specify Tony would drive the stolen van? His alarm bells, honed by years in prison, were clanging in his head. Mello wouldn't tolerate loose ends, and Tony was becoming more convinced that he was a loose end.

As John and I approached the Loomis facility, we began to look for a discreet spot to watch the parking lot where Donahue's car was parked.

"John, let's pull into the parking lot for the 99 Restaurant and check that out," I suggested.

"Good idea," John said.

As I pulled in, we both observed it was fairly crowded. That was a good thing.

"Dave, pull up to that spot over there," John directed.

It was an open parking spot with other vehicles on either side. It was almost in the center of the parking lot, so it provided us good cover. Best of all, it afforded a view of the Loomis parking lot approximately five hundred yards in front of us. We could see Donahue's car in the lot. I reached into the backseat and brought the binoculars out.

"Damn, this is perfect!" I exclaimed.

"Yeah, we can see Donahue's car clearly," John said.

The time was 10:50 a.m., ten minutes from showtime.

We were careful not to be obvious with the binoculars. One of us would briefly train the binoculars on Donahue's car while the other kept a lookout for anyone walking near our car.

At 10:57 a.m., I was using the binoculars when I saw something that I didn't expect.

"God damn!" I said.

"What?" asked John.

I quickly lowered my binoculars.

"See that bronze Chevy Tahoe three rows ahead of us?"

"Yeah, what about it?" John asked.

"That's the car Turner drove to the Linda Mae's restaurant meeting," I said.

"God damn!" John said.

"It's facing the Loomis parking lot. I can't see inside due to the tinted windows, but I've got to believe Turner and Rossetti are in there right now," I said.

"Yeah," John agreed, "they aren't here for the breakfast buffet. Let's lock and load."

I reached back for the rifles. I handed one to John and kept the other one for myself. We quickly chambered a round and put the safeties on. One quick finger motion would make the rifles ready for firing. The selector switch allowed for a single shot or a three-round burst. I left mine on single shot for now.

At 11:00 a.m. exactly, we observed Dave Donahue exit the vault facility and walk to his car. Dave took his time getting into his car and finally emerged with a folded newspaper. He slowly walked back toward the building and reentered the door he came out of.

"Thank God! No fireworks today!" I exclaimed.

"Look, the Tahoe is on the move," John warned.

We watched as the Tahoe backed out of its parking spot and headed through the rows of parked cars. We could see the brake lights come on as it stopped at the end of the driveway and then turned right, taking it away from the vault facility and toward the expressway.

"There's someone in the front passenger seat," I announced.

"So they're both in the car. Good stuff!" John proclaimed.

Since we didn't know where Tony's car was, we decided to stay put for a while before heading out ourselves.

"Well, this case has just gone into high gear," John said.

An hour later, we were at the prearranged Kmart meeting location when Tony pulled up and parked next to us. He got out of his car and jumped into the backseat of our car.

"Hey, guys, we saw Donahue come out. . . . What the hell is this?" Tony asked, referring to the rifle cases and bulletproof vests in the backseat.

"Life insurance policy. Did you turn off the recorder yet?" I asked.

"Yeah sure, here it is." Tony handed me the Nagra. "It's got some great stuff!" he exclaimed proudly.

"Like what?" I asked.

"Well, when we were driving to Easton, Mello laid out the whole plan for the day of the robbery. It's all there on the tape! He talked about how we were gonna rush Donahue and make the other guard let us in. Then he discussed tying up both guards and putting them in the stolen van after one of them opened the vault. Meanwhile, we stuff as much cash as we could into the two unmarked Loomis vans. Then I'm going to drive the stolen van out to the dump site and leave the van and the two guards tied up inside. I jump in with Mello for the ride to TRC. By the way, I really got the feeling Mello is planning to kill both the guards and probably me too. He isn't going to want to share any money with 'Carl.' I don't think Mello trusts him, and I'm not too sure he believes I'll hold up either," Tony said.

I looked at John.

"I presume he didn't actually say anything about killing the guards?" I asked Tony.

"Nah, of course not. He knows I'd go bullshit!" Tony said.

"Too bad," John said.

"Really," I replied.

"What do you mean?" Tony asked.

"With those comments on tape, we could lock him up tomorrow," I said.

"Oh, well. I guess we'll just have to wait and lock them all up," John commented.

I said, "Hey, by the way, you guys weren't alone out there. We saw Turner's Tahoe with two people inside, parked in the 99 Restaurant lot. They definitely observed Donahue come out and go to the car. I gotta believe this thing is going to happen fast now."

John turned in his seat to look Tony directly in the face.

"You sure you're ready for this, Tony? It's not too late to shut it down if you've got second thoughts. Things are going to happen fast, and you have to be on board 100 percent from here on out. You've got to do your part all the way to the end and then leave town. You have to testify in court and that won't be easy. You may never come back to Boston since you'll have a target on your back," John said.

Tony looked from John to me, then back to John.

"Don't sugarcoat it, John; just give it to me straight," Tony deadpanned.

I couldn't help but laugh, which caused John to crack up and Tony to reply with a huge grin.

"Don't worry, John. I'm in all the way," Tony said reassuringly.

18

A WOLF IN SHEEP'S CLOTHING

Monday, January 25, 1999

Dave Donahue and I met in John's office first thing Monday morning, seated in leather chairs in front of John, who was sitting behind his desk. John had a pretty good office. It had a window view of Congress Street below and the hideous Boston City Hall across the street. The "new" city hall, built in the 1960s, looked like a concrete bunker. Not only were the exterior walls made of concrete, the interior walls were as well! Real cozy. I often wondered how the mayor hung pictures in his office, with a jackhammer?

John had no such problem since our building had drywall. He decorated in typical FBI style. Bookcases along the back wall, a credenza against the side wall with a radio, and some family photos. On his desk, he had a statue of a 1930s G-Man wearing a suit and a fedora hat and cradling a Thompson submachine gun, aka "Tommy Gun," under his arm. This was a present from his New York squad after he earned his transfer to Boston.

"Well, boys, yesterday went very well. I believe we got a great tape recording, and our surveillance confirmed Turner and Rossetti are involved. You played your role perfectly, Dave," John said, looking at Dave Donahue.

"Thanks, boss. I was very relieved to get back inside the vault without having a gun at my head. George Coleman was great as well. He's very happy with the way this is being handled by the FBI," Dave said.

"So, Dave, you will speak with Tony later today, right?" John said to me.

"Yes, we expect Merlino will be hot to get going with this robbery, and chances are he has already reached out to Turner, so I believe they will have a date in mind very soon. I've already listened to the tape from yesterday, and it's exactly as Tony said. Merlino is heard planning the robbery and going into detail. When I talk with Tony later, I hope to hear Turner and Rossetti are satisfied and ready to go," I said.

"Okay, let's wait for that confirmation. In the meantime, I'll meet with ASAC Bill Chase and fill him in. He and the SAC are very interested in this case and are asking for frequent updates. This is going to be a full-court press, and we are going to need a lot of help from other squads," John said.

I arrived home well after dark, as usual. Dinner was waiting for me, but the family had eaten much earlier, and the kids were doing homework. After dinner, I received a call from the office.

"Hi, Dave. I've got Tony on the line," the caller informed me.

"Put him through please," I said

"Hey," Tony said.

"What's the story?" I asked.

"Turner stopped by today. He and Mello talked for about a half-hour in the parking lot," Tony said. "After Turner left, Mello came back in and pulled me aside. He was beaming. Turner and Rossetti were satisfied with the dry run yesterday and are ready to join in," Tony explained.

"That's great! What's the plan?" I asked.

"There's going to be a face-to-face meeting between Mello, me, Turner, and Rossetti. They want to do this meeting on Thursday night. They're talking about meeting at Bickford's restaurant on Gallivan Boulevard near Morrissey Boulevard. We're going to make final plans and set a date for the robbery," Tony said.

This is what I was waiting for!

"Okay, this is HUGE! We are going to cover the meeting and record everything! Excellent work!" I said. "Keep me informed of all the details. In the meantime, I'm getting the surveillance squad on board for Thursday night and C-6 as well. This is the first and maybe only time we'll have everyone in one place before the robbery. The recording will be critical."

"Okay, but make sure everyone is really careful. Turner and Rossetti are sneaky bastards and constantly looking around for surveillance. If they sniff anything, they probably won't show it, but they'll shut it down and kill me as well. If my body is found in a ditch with two holes through my hat, I'll haunt you forever!" Tony warned.

"Don't be so goddamn melodramatic! We know our business. Have we gotten you killed yet?" I asked.

"Just once," he reminded me.

"Okay, one little minor slipup that almost got you decapitated. I'm fairly certain that won't happen again," I said.

"I'll call you with the details when I have them, and kiss my ass!" Tony said as he hung up.

I was glad to see he didn't seem too nervous.

First thing the next morning I met with John and Dave Donahue.

"Tony called last night and informed me Turner and Rossetti are in!" I said.

"Beautiful!" John said as Dave slapped me on the shoulder.

"There's more news. Turner and Rossetti called for a meeting with Merlino and Tony for Thursday night at the Bickford's restaurant on Gallivan Boulevard. They want to talk details," I announced.

"No shit? This is it! We get them all on tape planning this robbery!" John exclaimed.

"Rob Richardson is going to love this. It's like a mob swearing-in ceremony!" I said.

"Okay, all of C-6 will be in the area, and I'm getting the surveillance squad to cover this as well," John said.

"The only thing that may cause us a problem Thursday night is the weather. It's supposed to snow, big time," I said.

"Well, that could work in our favor actually. It should make it more difficult for Merlino's crew to spot surveillance vehicles," Dave Donahue said.

"Yeah, but it'll knock out the plane and driving will be miserable. We'll just have to see how it goes and play it by ear a little bit," I said.

After the meeting with John and Dave, I called AUSA Rob Richardson and filled him in on the Thursday night meeting.

"This is the big recording we've been waiting for! Everyone in one spot planning and scheming. You've got to pull out all the stops to get high-quality recordings of the meeting," he said enthusiastically.

"I know, Rob. I'll be meeting with the tech guys later to figure out how to wire Tony, so we get everything clearly on tape. My thinking is multiple recorders and a transmitter so we can hear what's happening in real time. Since it's colder than Siberia, we can have Tony wear a bulky jacket that will conceal the equipment. It would be great if we could somehow steer the group to a particular table that's wired for sound in the restaurant, but I doubt that's feasible," I said.

"I don't know. Maybe a table with a sign on it that reads: 'Reserved for the Merlino Gang'; we can have a velvet rope around it," Rob deadpanned.

"I like the way you think! WINNING!" I laughed.

After the call to Rob, I hustled down to the tech squad and met with Ted Baker.

"Ted, we've got a big meeting on the Merlino case this Thursday night, and we need foolproof, high-quality recordings. The whole gang is coming together at Bickford's restaurant on Gallivan Boulevard, and this may be the only chance we get to record the gang together talking about the robbery. There will be at least four participants, maybe five. I'm going to ask for the surveillance squad to have someone inside taking pictures. They have all the hidden camera stuff to get that done, but the gold will be found in the audio recordings," I said.

"Yeah, of course. Pictures are good, but tapes are a lot better. I have some equipment that will do the job for you. First off, look at this," Ted said as he walked over to a closet and removed a dark-blue jean jacket with a white lamb's wool lining.

"What do you think?" he asked as he tried it on.

"You look like the Marlboro man, very macho," I said.

"Right you are! But that's not the best part. This beauty is prewired with microphones for a Nagra recorder and a transmitter with a hundred-yard range!" he proudly exclaimed.

"I hope the transmitter is more reliable than the one we put into Tony's car," I warned.

"Oh yeah! We dumped that piece of crap. This one works! We've used this jacket a number of times, and it's produced excellent results. I love it," Ted said with a huge smile on his face.

"Okay, the style is perfect for something Tony would wear, and the size looks good as well. I like the fact that we can receive the conversation over the Bureau radios. That way I'll record from the cars as well," I replied

"Also, the Nagra recorder has a four-hour range so no worry about running out of tape before the meeting is over," Ted said.

"Yeah, that's real important. It wouldn't look too good if that happened," I agreed.

"I'll set you up with recorders for your cars so you can record the conversation coming over the radio from the transmitter in the jacket. Come back Thursday morning and I'll have it all ready for you," Ted said.

"You're the best, my man," I said as I walked out.

The next conversation was with Burt O'Connor of the surveillance squad.

"I'm going to need a full-court press on Thursday evening. It's the Merlino case again, and I need pictures inside the restaurant and surveillance help before and after the meeting," I said.

"Oh man, we are committed to an organized crime case that day and it will last into the night. The best I can do is get you someone with a concealed camera inside the restaurant. I'm sorry," Burt apologized.

I wasn't happy to hear this news, but honestly, my C-6 agents were all very qualified surveillance drivers, so it wasn't a fatal blow.

"No sweat, Burt; I understand. Have your cameraman contact me, and I'll brief him," I said.

"It'll probably be a camera woman, agent Patricia Clawson. We have a camera concealed in a shoulder purse that's excellent for this situation. She can be standing somewhere as if waiting for a table while actually taking photos of the group. She can even walk past for close-ups if the situation calls for that type of coverage," Burt said.

"That sounds great to me! Have Patricia call me Thursday during the day. If she can have a concealed radio transmitter and earpiece, that would be very helpful. I'd like to warn her when they are approaching the restaurant, and I'd like her to be able to contact us as well," I said.

"All standard-issue equipment, Dave. She'll be wired for sound!" Burt assured me.

Wednesday, January 27, 1999

After work on Wednesday, I put in a call to Tony at his apartment. He picked up right away.

"Can you talk, amigo?" I asked.

"Yeah, she's not here. She's at her mom's place this evening," Tony said.

"Good. Tomorrow is going to be a huge day for us, and I wanted to go over the plan with you tonight. We won't have much time to talk tomorrow. First off, any clue as to when you are meeting tomorrow?" I asked.

"Yeah, we are shooting for 7:30 p.m. Rossetti and Turner want to meet at the Boston Bowl bowling alley on Morrissey Boulevard first, then go over to the restaurant," Tony said.

"Why do you think they want to meet at the bowling alley first?" I asked.

"I don't know for sure, but that's what Mello said this afternoon. If you ask me, it's just a routine Rossetti and Turner like to follow. They're hinky as hell, which reminds me: I hope your guys are going to be real discreet," Tony emphasized.

"We will be, believe me. Now I want to talk about what we will be doing tomorrow. It's supposed to be snowing pretty hard starting around 5:00 p.m. The way I see it, that's good for us because the snow will provide us cover. Turner and Rossetti's visibility will be limited. It'll be dark and traffic will be bad, so it will be tough for them to do countersurveillance. This all works in our favor. I'm going to meet you at the park down the block from your apartment at 7:15 p.m. sharp. I'm going to have a new jacket for you to wear. It's perfect for you; you'll look really cool!" I said.

There was silence on the other end of the line.

"I hope it isn't a straitjacket. Then again, maybe that's what I should be wearing," Tony deadpanned.

"Ha, that's really funny! Actually, it's a denim jacket with lamb wool lining. Perfect for the weather tomorrow. It's prewired with a four-hour Nagra and a transmitter. All this stuff is sewn into the lining of the jacket, and the miniature microphones are all concealed. You're gonna *love* it! Just don't let anyone try it on," I said.

"What's the transmitter for?" Tony asked.

"I know we had a bad experience with the last transmitter we tried, but this one is state of the art and battle tested. It's going to work, guaranteed," I assured him. "Also, it allows me and my team to listen in live to make sure there are no issues that may require our intervention. Of course, that won't happen; but we will also be able to record the conversation in our cars as a back up to the Nagra. I assume you'll be driving, but if not, we won't miss a beat since you'll be wearing the transmitter," I said.

"All right. How many agents will be out there?" Tony asked.

"Around ten, in five cars," I said.

"Wow, that's a lot of agents," Tony said.

"I think it's a good number. Enough but not too many. So meet me tomorrow at 7:15 p.m. sharp. Call the office or call my beeper anytime if you need to reach me tomorrow or if you need to leave a message. The communications people know what to do. Good night and God speed, John Glenn," I said as I hung up.

The next morning, I met Ted Baker in the tech shop.

"Here's the jacket, Dave, loaded up and ready to go," Ted said as he handed me Tony's new denim jacket.

Ted showed me how to activate the Nagra and the transmitter concealed in the lining of the jacket.

"We have the four stereo microphones sewn into the collar. They are very discreet," he said.

"Yeah, they sure are. I can't feel a thing," I said as I squeezed the collar of the jacket.

"They are also very durable, but tell Tony to try to face whoever he's recording as that will provide the best reception. When he's in the restaurant, I'm sure the microphones will do fine recording everyone at the table," Ted said.

"Well, that's the goal for sure. I'll have this jacket back to you first thing tomorrow morning, and you can remove the Nagra. I'm not touching it," I said.

"Good idea. See you tomorrow and good luck!" Ted said as I left the shop.

At 1:00 p.m., I received a call from agent Patricia Clawson.

"Hi, Dave, this is Pat. I'm checking in to make sure everything is a go for tonight," she said.

"Hi, Pat. Everything is still a go. They should be arriving at the restaurant around 8:00 p.m. Did Burt give you photos of the subjects yet?" I asked.

"He did. They are good quality; I shouldn't have any trouble finding them," she said.

"There will be a fourth person in the group, wearing a blue denim jacket with a white lamb's wool lining. He's about five feet, nine inches, black hair, and skinny. That's our informant. All four men should be sitting together at a table. We need photos of them in the restaurant, so I'll let you play it by ear. I don't expect them to be looking for a surveillance by the time they get to the restaurant, but be cautious just the same. Get a few good shots, then disappear. I'll recover the film from Burt tomorrow. When you exit the restaurant, please call me on the Bureau radio. We will be in private mode, and my call sign is Victor 6. I just want to make sure all went well inside," I instructed Patricia.

"Sure thing, Dave; should be a piece of cake! I'll reach out for you when I leave the restaurant. Good luck tonight," Patricia said.

John called a squad meeting for 2:00 p.m. The agents participating in the surveillance were just filing into the squad area.

"Okay, everyone, tonight is a big night for the Loomis case. As you all know, we are covering a meeting between Carmello Merlino, David Turner, Stephen Rossetti, and Dave Nadolski's informant Tony Romano. You've all received photos of the subjects and the cars they are expected to be driving tonight. Romano will be wearing a blue denim jacket. The jacket will have a Nagra and a transmitter sewn into the lining. You will be monitoring channel six on your car radios in order to pick up the transmitter in Tony's jacket, so make sure you also have portable radios to communicate with one another. Make sure the radios are all coded! That is extremely important. God knows what kind of radio-monitoring devices Turner and Rossetti have. They are cautious guys, and if they suspect any surveillance, it will go very badly for Romano. Probably not tonight but they will absolutely take him out. Dave Nadolski is running the show, so I'll let him take it from here," John said.

"Thanks, John, especially for the warning to have the radios coded and to make sure we are discreet at all times. Turner, Rossetti, and Merlino are badasses. They may or may not be armed, but they are definitely dangerous. You are all familiar with their criminal histories, so you know what I'm talking about," I warned the group. "It's starting to snow a little already, and by this evening, we are looking at significant accumulation. I believe that is good for us since we don't have to be particularly close to these guys. The transmitter has a half-mile range, and Tony will be riding with Merlino most likely. We can keep track of them by listening in to the conversation in his car. Additionally, we already know they plan to eat at Bickford's restaurant on Gallivan Boulevard. Pat Clawson, from the surveillance squad, will be inside the restaurant to get pictures of them sitting together. She has a camera concealed in a purse so she's getting some shots, then leaving, quick and dirty. We'll probably see her come out.

"We already know that Tony and Merlino are supposed to meet Turner and Rossetti at the Boston Bowl bowling alley on Morrissey Boulevard. As you know, that is about a half mile from the Bickford's restaurant. Turner and Rossetti set the meeting spot, so there must be a reason for that particular location. It has a good-sized parking lot and it's wide open. They'll probably arrive early to look for surveillance. The last time I saw them together they were in Turner's bronze Tahoe. I have no idea what they will be in tonight, but look for both cars belonging to them. If you spot them, let everyone know and give them a wide berth.

"I've handed out the car assignments. I'm riding with John Trahon in my car. Larry Travaglia is with Gary Cacace. Dave Donahue is with Peg Cronin; Rob Carrol is with Neil Cronin, who agreed to help us out. I'm meeting Tony at 7:15 p.m. and getting him set up. I'll find out if there have been any last-minute changes to the plan and pass that information on if there are any. Otherwise, just be in the area of Bickford's by 8:00 p.m. We should all be tuned in to Tony's transmitter and recording the conversations we are listening to. Use your handheld radios for car-to-car communications, and above all, remember to code your radios before you leave the garage today," I said as a final instruction.

The squad broke up and busied themselves with final preparations for the surveillance. I waited by the phone until 6:30 p.m. in case Tony needed to get in touch with me. Luckily the phone never rang. At 6:40 p.m., I stuck my head into John's office.

"John, I'm going into the garage to code the radios. How about meeting me down there in about ten minutes?" I asked.

"See you there, Dave," John replied.

At 6:50 p.m., John met me in the garage, and we headed out to Dorchester in my car. The weather was worsening. The streets were becoming snow covered and slippery, so the drive took a few more minutes than normal. At 7:10 p.m., we arrived at the park where we planned to meet Tony, and at 7:15 p.m., on the dot, Tony pulled up in his car. He pulled alongside us and jumped into the backseat.

"You're late!" John chided Tony.

"I am not. Dave said to be here at 7:15 p.m.; its 7:15 p.m. on the nose! Right, Dave?" Tony protested.

"Hey, if the boss says you're late, then you're late," I said.

"But that's not right!" Tony blurted out.

John and I both cracked up.

"Relax, just a little pre-game ball busting," I assured Tony. "Okay, joke time is over. Take your jacket off and leave it here in the car. Put that denim jacket on."

"Hmm, nice material! Can I keep it?" he asked.

"If you come through tonight, you can be buried in it for all I care," John remarked.

I climbed into the backseat with Tony, activated the transmitter, and tested it. Loud and clear coming through the Bureau radio.

"Okay, perfect! So where are you meeting Mello?" I asked.

"He wants me to meet him at the bowling alley. We'll wait there for Turner and Rossetti," Tony replied.

"Okay, we have cars in the area, but only John and I will be in the vicinity of the bowling alley. We will set up in a position to view the parking lot but not too close. We will be able to hear your conversation with Mello, so we will know what's going on. We'll keep a loose surveillance on you tonight and listen to everything that's being said, even in the restaurant. After everything is over with, meet me back here, and I'll take the jacket back. Any questions?" I asked.

"Do I get overtime pay?" Tony asked.

"No," I said.

The snow was really coming down by this time. I got on the radio and told the rest of the squad that the bird had flown the coop, meaning Tony was on the move and all units could now listen to his transmissions when he got within range of their vehicles.

I headed for the area of the bowling alley. I found a good vantage point in the parking lot of a Ford car dealership next to the bowling alley. I parked the car among others in the lot, turned off the motor, and let snow accumulate on my car in order to better blend in. We were monitoring Tony and could hear him driving. He arrived at the bowling alley and advised that Mello had not yet arrived.

After ten minutes of silence, Tony said, "There's a car approaching me. It's Mello."

The next thing we heard was a car door opening and Mello's voice saying, "I didn't count on this fucking snowstorm!"

"You should watch the news once in a while," Tony responded.

Mello was heard getting into Tony's car. "Did those other pricks show up yet?" he asked.

"Haven't seen anyone," Tony replied.

"They'll be here. This snow is slowing everything down. How'd you get away from your sweetheart?" Mello asked.

"Just told her I had a business meeting, not sure she bought it," Tony said.

"Why would she buy it? You're a fucking mechanic, not a banker," Mello said.

"Well, soon enough I'll have more goddamn money than any banker!" Tony exclaimed.

"You got that right, kid!" Mello said.

After a few more minutes of small talk, Mello said, "Hey, these guys are running late. Go inside and see if they're waiting in the bar."

John and I heard the car door open and snow crunching as Tony walked through the parking lot. He was heard opening the door and entering the bowling alley. Loud voices and crashing bowling pins were heard over the air. Once inside, he said for our benefit, "I'm in the bowling alley looking for Turner and Rossetti. They're late, and I'm checking to see if they're in here."

We could hear the din of the bowling alley activity as Tony walked around. After a few minutes, we heard him exit the bowling alley and crunch back to his car. We overheard the car door open and Mello ask, "Are they in there?"

"I couldn't find them if they are," Tony said as he reentered the car and closed the door.

Just as Mello was beginning to start bitching, Tony was overheard saying, "Hey, someone is pulling up beside us."

We heard a car door open and a male voice say, "You guys ready to get something to eat?"

"Turner, you asshole, we've been waiting twenty minutes for you guys. What the fuck?" Mello said.

Turner replied, "Mello, relax. We just wanted to make sure the coast was clear, so we sat up in that Ford dealership and kept an eye on the parking lot for a while. Can't be too careful you know. Shit, you taught me that!"

"All right, goddamn it, let's get over to the restaurant," Mello barked.

We heard Tony start the car and put it in gear.

I looked at John. "They were sitting in the Ford dealership?" I asked incredulously.

"With this snowstorm, they could have been parked next to us!" John said.

I picked up the radio microphone. "All units, this is Victor 6. All four subjects have left the bowling alley and are headed to the Bickford's right now. There are two vehicles. You should be able to monitor conversation in the primary vehicle," I said.

I received a series of microphone clicks. A common method of communicating acknowledgment of a message without actually saying anything is to depress the microphone key a couple times resulting in a clicking sound on the receiving end. That wordlessly acknowledges that your message was heard and understood.

The time was now 8:20 p.m., so I quickly relayed a radio voice message to agent Patricia Clawson that the subjects were en route and should be arriving soon. She responded with several microphone clicks.

"John, I feel pretty good about things, up to this point at least. Shit, we could have been blown out of the water in that car dealership. Thank God for the snowstorm!" I remarked.

"No lie. The transmitter is working very well so no need to get too close to the action," John suggested.

We listened as Tony and Mello were driving to the Bickford's restaurant. We heard them arrive and park the car. We heard them get out of the car and join up with Turner and Rossetti outside the restaurant. We clearly heard them go inside, and the noise inside the restaurant suddenly muffled the transmitter slightly. We did hear Mello ask for a table for four and overheard an employee say, "Follow me please."

We overheard the employee seating the group at a booth.

The recording went well for several minutes. We heard the voices of Merlino, Turner, and Rossetti, but suddenly those voices faded out and we found ourselves listening to the conversation of a totally different group of people. These people were not related to our group, and they seemed to be other patrons of the restaurant.

I turned to John. "What that hell is this?" I asked incredulously.

"I have no idea!" he said.

Since Pat Clawson was in the restaurant and on our radio frequency, I called out for her. She responded with a click on the radio microphone, signaling she was standing by.

"Pat, do you have the group under surveillance?" I asked.

She responded with one click meaning "yes."

"Pat, we cannot hear the conversation the group is having. The conversation we are hearing is from some other group of people. Can you determine what's going on?" I asked.

Pat clicked once meaning she understood.

Several minutes passed before we heard Pat's voice over the air. "Victor 6, I'm out of the restaurant now. I've obtained good photos for you. Regarding your question about the conversation in the restaurant, I was able to observe that Tony removed his jacket and laid it across the back of his booth. What I believe you are listening to is the conversations of the patrons in the booth next to your subjects, I'm sorry to say."

"Holy shit!" John exclaimed.

"Thanks, Pat; I really appreciate your input. We had no idea what was going on," I said.

"Can I do anything else for you?" Pat asked.

"No, good job and thank you," I said.

"Oh my God! If they talk about their plan while sitting in that booth, we won't be able to hear any of it, nor will we get good recordings!" I said to John.

"This could be a real waste of time, not to mention a really big lost opportunity," John said.

I felt like shit. There was no way to fix this. It's not like I could walk in and say, "Excuse me, guys, I need to adjust Tony's jacket. We aren't picking up your conversation."

"John, this whole thing is going down the tubes!" I complained.

Pat Clawson came on the air again, "Victor 6, I went back into the restaurant. Your group is getting ready to leave. I observed that three uniformed Boston police officers were just seated next to your group. I believe that may have prompted your group to get out of there."

WHAT? A last-minute, out-of-the-blue, Hail Mary reception?

"Thank you, Pat! This is very helpful information," I quickly responded.

I called out to the rest of the team.

"All units, this is Victor 6. The subjects are on the move, getting ready to leave the restaurant. We believe they may have been interrupted by the arrival of several Boston police officers. Stay alert."

Suddenly I heard Tony's voice loud and clear.

"Let's get into my car and talk," I overheard him say.

"All units, it sounds like the group is heading for Tony's car, parked in the Bickford's restaurant. Stand by and keep monitoring. This meeting may not be over just yet," I said.

I received a series of clicks in response to my transmission. The team understood.

We heard muffled voices and the sound of car doors opening and closing. The next voice we heard, loud and clear, was Merlino's.

"Let's get out of this parking lot. Go across the street to the drugstore over there. The lot is empty, and we can talk without a bunch of people around," he said.

"All units, in case you didn't hear, all the subjects are in Tony's car and heading for the drugstore parking lot across the street. If you are in that lot, leave NOW!" I said emphatically.

I heard many clicks over the radio.

The weather was really bad at this point. It was snowing like crazy, and there weren't many cars on the road or in the parking lots of closed businesses such as the drugstore. We had to give Tony a wide berth but still maintain the ability to monitor his transmitter. Luckily, since he left the restaurant, the transmitter was working very well and we were able to hear the conversation in his car.

"Pull up over here," Mello ordered.

"In the drugstore parking lot?" I overheard Tony say.

"Yeah, dumbass. What do you think I meant?" Mello said.

"Okay, okay. What's your problem?" Tony asked.

"I can't believe those fucking cops decided to sit down next to us is all! Can you imagine talking about the biggest heist in Boston history with three cops within earshot?" Mello complained.

"I think we need to write a letter to the owners of that restaurant telling them we will never frequent their establishment again!" Stephen Rossetti said dramatically.

Everyone burst out laughing.

Rossetti went on to say, "Me and David watched your dry run last Sunday, and we like what we saw. Your guy Carl came out on time, got the newspaper out of his car, and walked back in. It went like clockwork, and me and David are happy with it."

"Hey, I told you Tony had this worked out, didn't I?" Mello asked.

"Yeah, I got to admit I had my doubts, but so far so good," Turner remarked.

"This isn't the first time I've done something like this. I got some great equipment for this job. I've got scanners, walkie-talkies, rubber masks, and all the hardware we need—including rifles, handguns, and, get this, a military hand grenade! If any cops get on our tail when we're getting away, I'll toss that son of a bitch and end our troubles! BOOM," Rossetti said laughing.

That caused a round of applause from the merry band of killers.

Rossetti continued, "I've been involved in a few capers like this already. I've got masks of all kinds, rubber masks, ski masks, a Nixon mask, a plastic hockey mask; you name it, I got it. The thing to remember is be ready to do something nuts when the time comes. I've had to ram a few cop cars in my day in order to get away. I'm one crazy son of a bitch behind the wheel when I need to be. I'll drive on the sidewalk, against one-way streets! I'll do whatever it takes to get away and leave nothing but destroyed cars in my wake, believe me!"

"I took down an armored car in Brockton. I had the guards on the ground and the truck opened in about one fucking minute! That was a good payday, but nothing like this one is gonna be," Merlino said.

"Look, I know the law; I know how investigations are done. We need to give the inside guy a defense so it doesn't look like an inside job, but most importantly, if the cops come in while we're there, I'm going to take them down, pure and simple," Rossetti said.

"I feel nice about this, real nice!" Turner remarked.

I looked at John. "This is unbelievable stuff! Man, am I glad they came out to the car to talk. Thank you, Boston PD!" I exclaimed.

"Larry, are you hearing this conversation in the car?" I asked.

Travaglia responded, "I'm recording every word."

Beautiful! Just beautiful!

Mello assumed control again and asked what day they should schedule the robbery for. The consensus among the group was to plan for Sunday, February 7.

During all this planning and posturing, Tony did exactly what we told him to do: kept his mouth shut.

The conversation continued for another twenty minutes. Every word in that car was being recorded. These guys were digging themselves in deeper and deeper. We had plenty of evidence now and I was beginning to hope the party would break up soon, and happily it did.

"Okay, Tony, drive us back to Bickford's; I want to get home while I still can. I don't have snow tires on my car," Merlino said.

"All units, this is Victor 6. The party is breaking up; you can all start to leave now. Make sure to do it discreetly," I said. Numerous clicks came in over the radio.

We overheard Tony stopping in the Bickford's restaurant and everyone exiting his car. After he started driving away, he came over the air: "I'm on the way back to the park. I'll see you there."

Tony was waiting in the park for us. After we pulled in, he quickly jumped in the backseat.

"Oh my God, that was intense! I almost crapped when I realized my microphones were pointing in the wrong direction inside the restaurant. Was your agent in there? I never saw anyone," Tony said.

"Okay, hold on a second. I need to stop the recording," I said.

After shutting off the recorder and transmitter, I had Tony remove the jacket. I gave him his own jacket back.

"Yeah, our agent was there, keeping us informed," I said.

"Those cops were a real stroke of luck! After you guys left the restaurant, we were able to copy the conversation in your car. It came in loud and clear," John said.

"Were you guys in the area for that?" Tony asked.

"Of course. We could see you and hear you. You were covered like a blanket. A snow blanket to be precise!" I laughed.

"Well, I don't know where you were and nobody else was suspicious, so thanks for that!" Tony said.

"It's what we do," John said.

"Hey, did you hear about the hand grenade Rossetti is bringing?" Tony asked.

"Yeah, that should add about twenty years to their sentence," John remarked.

"So, I'm going in to TRC tomorrow. I've still got my regular Nagra, and I've got a feeling that things are gonna get rolling quickly now. I'm sure Mello will have me brief Carl that it's a go for Sunday, February 7. I don't know if we'll have any more meetings before that day, but I'll call you tomorrow and fill you in on everything I find out," Tony said.

"Dude, you did a beautiful job today. I couldn't have asked for anything more out of you. Congratulations!" I said as I shook Tony's hand.

He broke into a wide grin. "Talk to you tomorrow," he said as he bolted out of the backseat and into the blinding snowstorm.

BOSTON FBI OFFICE

Thursday, January 28, 1999

I met Ted Baker in the tech shop at 8:00 a.m. sharp.

"Ted, here's your jacket back; it worked great, my man! We recorded some very solid conversation. It started in Bickford's restaurant, but with all the noise in there, the audio sucked. Luckily, three Boston cops took a table right next to Merlino and his crew, so they decided to make a hasty retreat. They went out to Tony's car and drove to a secluded parking lot where they talked and talked. It was a beautiful thing to listen to!" I exclaimed.

"That's great to hear. I imagine you need the cassette tapes of this conversation ASAP," Ted said.

"I'd love to have them quickly. I want to sit down with AUSA Rob Richardson and play this for him today," I said.

"Okay, then give me an hour. I'll have them ready for you," Ted said.

True to his word, the cassette copies of the previous day's recordings were ready in one hour. I took one copy and walked directly to the transcription office.

"Ginny, here's the latest on the Merlino case. You're gonna love this one!" I promised.

"Excellent, I can't wait! Hey, Trish, we got another Merlino tape," Ginny called out.

Trish Auger removed her headphones and turned to face Ginny. "I want it now!"

"No way, you had the last one!" Ginny protested.

"You're hallucinating; it's my turn!" Trish claimed.

I walked away laughing as the argument between them grew louder. Back at my desk, I put in a call to Rob Richardson.

"Rob, we got an excellent recording last night. I want to come by and listen to it with you. We need an hour, so what's your availability?" I asked.

"Oh man, this will be the highlight of my day! Pop in here around 10:00 a.m., and I'll spend as much time as we need. Looking forward to it," Rob exclaimed.

Just as I was getting ready to head to the US Attorney's office, my desk phone rang. It was Tony.

"I gotta be quick," he said. "Mello said we are definitely going for Sunday, February 7. He talked to Turner this morning, and they don't want to wait any longer than that. He wants Carl to be ready to do it. Turner and Rossetti will supply all the gear we need including the firearms. He also asked about the van and where it was located. I told him I've been moving it around so as not to let it sit in any one place for too long. He liked that idea and said it had to be in TRC the day before the robbery. He also mentioned he wants all hands on deck to prepare at TRC on Saturday night before the robbery. He wants us to go over the plan one last time and bring our gear for inspection."

"Tony, this is awesome news! This thing will be over with soon. Keep up the good work, my friend." With that, I hung up the phone.

I walked into Rob Richardson's office with a copy of the recording from the night before. The chairs were clear of files, and I could actually see out of the window behind his desk.

"Damn, I didn't know you had a great view of the Boston Harbor!" I remarked.

"It is pretty sweet, isn't it?" Rob responded.

"Where are all your files? I asked.

"Well, it's kind of embarrassing actually. My wife made a surprise visit a few days ago and blew her stack. I had to find someplace other than my office for all those files. Luckily there was a spare storeroom available, so I grabbed it. It took me all day to move that stuff, and now I have to walk down the corridor every time I want one! I should have kept my office door locked and pretended I wasn't here," he said.

"That's what I'd do," I agreed. "Let's roll tape."

We listened from the time Mello got into Tony's car until I took the jacket back from Tony after the meeting. Rob took notes through the whole recording. I didn't forewarn him about the glitch inside Bickford's when Tony took his jacket off. He suddenly got a little concerned when he listened to that part.

"Stop the tape," Rob said. "Who are those people?"

"What people?" I asked.

"Those strangers talking about their kids! That's who!" Rob exclaimed.

"Oh, those people. Yeah, I don't know who they are actually. Keep listening," I said.

He looked at me for a few seconds, then restarted the tape.

After five minutes of this, he said, "You better have something more than this crap!"

"Why? I like the story about the little soccer player," I said with a smirk.

It was at this point that we heard the guys leaving the booth and the audio quality suddenly improving.

"Where are they going?" he asked.

"You'll see," I said.

Finally, Rob lightened up when he heard Merlino instructing everyone to get into Tony's car.

"Ha, ha, this is the good part!" I said.

After listening to the whole conversation in the car, I stopped the tape.

"So what do you think now?" I asked.

"This is explosive! They buried themselves! I particularly appreciate that Tony sat quietly and didn't interrupt at all." Rob beamed.

"Yeah, he's a smart guy," I said.

"Those cops saved the day. What a hoot! Were you guys in the area?" Rob asked.

"Yeah, we were. We had a transmitter on Tony plus the recorder. Since it was snowing so hard, it wasn't difficult for us to hide. Our cars and their car became snow covered. They didn't see a thing. I also had a female surveillance agent inside the restaurant. She really blended in and got good photos with a hidden camera. She was our eyes and ears inside the restaurant and warned us when they were coming out. It really went like clockwork, I'm happy to say," I said, beaming.

"I've got to play this for my boss; he won't believe it," Rob said.

"Yeah, Tim should like it," I remarked. "One other thing: Tony informed me today that Mello wants to definitely go on Sunday, February 7. He told Tony to get 'Carl' ready to do his part inside the vault. That gives me time to plan the takedown. This is going to be a real Cecil B. DeMille production. One for the books!"

"Who's playing me in the movie?" Rob asked.

"George Clooney, for sure," I said.

19

TONY'S NEW DIGS

LOWELL, MASSACHUSETTS

Friday, January 29, 1999

Since it looked like this case was going to come to a conclusion in just over a week, I had to start preparing for after the arrest. Tony would need to move out of his apartment the day of the arrest and go into a safe location. When word spread among Mello's associates that Tony was working for the FBI, they would most likely come looking for him. The reasoning being, with Tony out of the way, a critical witness against Mello and his gang would be gone. David Turner had already profited from the death of a witness against him, so obviously it could happen in this case as well.

I started looking for an extended-stay hotel near Boston. I found one in the city of Lowell that worked just fine. It was a newer establishment close to I-495 and one that I could easily get to. It had two bedrooms, a living room area, and a kitchen. It was a perfect hideout for Tony and his girlfriend, Patricia.

Patricia was another challenge. She and Tony lived together in a furnished apartment in Boston. She was African American and a former bookkeeper for TRC Auto Electric, which is where Tony met her. She had no idea what Tony was involved in and would have to be brought into the loop sooner rather than later. Tony was hoping she would agree to stick with him when he was eventually moved out of state; however, she had her mother in Boston, so it was up in the air whether she would go along with the prospect of moving.

On Saturday, Tony's regular day off, I picked him up at the park down the street from his apartment. I decided to show him the place I had picked out for him to stay in.

I met Tony at 10:00 a.m. He climbed into my car after shaking the snow off his jacket.

"Man, its fucking cold out here," he said.

"Yeah, it is. Maybe in a few months you'll be in a much more agreeable climate. So anything new from Mello?" I asked.

"Well, he's definitely decided we are going to meet next Saturday, the day before the robbery, to go over everything. I told him 'Carl' was all ready for Sunday and just waiting to hear what time it was going to go down," Tony said.

"Great. Listen, I've been thinking about Patricia. Do you definitely want her to go with you when you leave the state?" I asked.

"Yeah, but she doesn't know anything yet, and I'm not sure how she'll react to this whole situation once I tell her. She has noticed a change in me and has been real curious about the nighttime meetings," Tony said.

"I agree; she's a gamble. There are three ways we can handle this actually. First, we can just level with her. Tell her the whole truth later this week but allow enough time for her to adjust to the idea before the arrest takes place and you have to disappear. She can go with you to the safe house. After the arrest, she will have time to adjust to the move. If she wants to back out, then you go alone," I said.

"Second option, we just have you disappear after the robbery, and I'll visit her to say you are involved in a huge case and must leave the state and that you will call to confirm what I just told her. I can also offer her the chance to join you if that's what you both want," I said.

"What's the third option?" Tony asked

"The third option is to cut ties, disappear, and forget about her," I said.

"I can't just leave her. I really want to tell her what's going on before Sunday and let her decide to stay or leave. I really hope she sticks with me; we've been getting along really well, and I think there's a future for us," Tony said.

"Fair enough. How about I stop by to see you and meet her next Friday night? I'll identify myself and explain that you have been working with me on a huge case and you will have to go into hiding after the conclusion of the investigation, which will be very soon. I don't want her to have any details about the case until after the arrest so that's about all I'll be able to say. I will tell her she is welcome to join you if she wants to, but if not, she may never see you again," I explained.

Tony looked out the window. After a minute, he turned and said, "I like the first option. Let's level with her," Tony said.

"Sounds good. Make sure she's in the apartment on Friday night, and I'll stop by around 7:00 p.m.," I said.

"This part sucks," Tony said as he turned to look out the window again.

"Anything else bothering you?" I asked.

"Actually, yeah. I've been giving this a lot of thought. Don't get pissed, but I don't want to record the meeting at TRC on Saturday night and I don't want any agents doing surveillance outside," Tony said as he looked straight out the windshield.

I looked at him. "Why the hell not?" I asked.

"I'm freaked out about this meeting! I've got a bad feeling, and I know Turner and Rossetti will be looking hard at any cars on the street. I know you guys are good, but the street will literally be empty of cars. If they see anything at all suspicious, they'll be after me. If they find a wire, I'm dead! I will NOT make it out of that place alive! I haven't asked for much, but you've got to go with me on this. I've grown up in prison and managed to survive because I've listened to my instincts," Tony was looking directly in my eyes and his gaze was intense.

"Aren't you perhaps overreacting a little? By the way, if they find a wire, won't they assume we'll come busting in like the cavalry?" I asked.

"Nope, they'll slit my throat and go out the back door, never to be seen again. That's how they've managed to stay alive, eliminating witnesses. You've got to go along with me on this. I'll only feel safe if I know I'm doing this my way. If I don't feel safe, I won't be calm enough to pull this off, and that's not going to end well!" Tony pleaded.

Now, deciding to purposely not record a significant meeting such as this could potentially be costly in court. It might raise a lot of questions for the jury. They may ask why this particular meeting wasn't recorded, when all the others were. I had to weigh that possibility against the reality that Tony may come apart under the pressure of wearing a wire for this final meeting. I could sense he was serious, and I had to ask myself if I had the right to demand he do something he was so against. I decided to suffer the potential legal consequences and let him do what he felt was best.

"I'm certainly nervous about letting you go into the lion's den without cover, but ultimately I have to trust your judgment. It's true you've managed to stay alive in prison based upon doing what you feel is best for you, so I believe it's more important that you're comfortable. I don't want to blow this in the end, and I certainly don't want to be responsible for something terrible happening to you. The minute you get home after the meeting I need you to call me. I have to interview you about everything that was said and everything that happened there. That's not as good as a recording, but it'll have to suffice. I believe I can justify doing it that way," I agreed, reluctantly.

Tony literally sighed and slumped into the passenger seat. I noticed he was actually starting to perspire. He wiped his forehead and looked at me.

"Thanks" was all he said.

We arrived at the hotel, and as I pulled into the parking lot, Tony seemed to perk up.

"This place looks nice. It's new!" he said.

"Yeah, let's see your new living situation," I said.

We parked the car and entered the upscale lobby and passed the reception desk. "Hi, Mr. Nelson!" the attractive female employee behind the desk called out.

"Hi, Sheila! Beautiful day!" I responded as we walked to the elevator.

Once on the elevator, Tony asked, "Who's Mr. Nelson?"

"That would be me," I said.

I reached for my wallet and pulled out a valid Massachusetts driver's license and a couple credit cards in the name of David Nelson. I showed them to Tony.

"What the fuck?" he said.

"I guess you don't know me as well as you thought. Here we are, fourth floor!" I announced.

He was still staring at me as I opened the door to suite 410.

"What do you think?" I asked.

"Holy shit! This is beautiful!" Tony said, amazed at the spacious living room, huge television, upscale furniture. He inspected the kitchen.

"A dishwasher, microwave, stove, full-sized refrigerator, dishes, kitchen table—the works!" he exclaimed.

"Check out the bedrooms," I said.

We looked at the master first.

"King-size bed—and look at this huge closet! Look at this attached bathroom! Unbelievable!" Tony said in amazement.

"There's a guest bedroom as well in case Patricia gets pissed at you," I said.

"Man! Look at that balcony with a view of the river!" Tony exclaimed. "This is mine? Really?"

"For as long as you need it," I said. "By the way, you'll also get an allowance for food, gas, and regular expenses. You'll be out of a job, so your new job will be staying alive and preparing for trial. Actually, you'll only be here until we can arrange to have you transferred out of state, but we'll set you up wherever you land. Eventually you'll need to get a job and earn your way, but the US government is here to help until you're on your feet," I explained.

Tony dropped into a swivel chair and spun around and around.

"Did I ever tell you I think you guys run a first-class operation?" he asked.

20

TEAM HUDDLE

FBI, BOSTON DIVISION

Thursday, February 4, 1999

At 8:50 a.m., members of squad C-6, members of the SWAT team, members of the surveillance squad and technical services squad, and other agents recruited for the takedown started filing into the conference room and pouring themselves coffee from the Dunkin' Donuts one-gallon containers on a folding table at the side of the room. Folding chairs were set up in four rows of ten across. Another folding table located in the middle of the room provided a platform for a slide projector loaded with pictures that was aimed at a large white projection screen behind another table located at the front of the room.

At precisely 9:00 a.m., ASAC Bill Chase called the room to order.

"Ladies and gentlemen, please take seats; the briefing is about to begin."

John Trahon and I took seats in the front row, facing Bill.

"Thank you for your attendance here today. As you are all aware, we anticipate the conclusion of an undercover operation early Sunday morning. All of you will be taking part in the arrest of the subjects involved and seizure of evidence. The subjects may be heavily armed at the time of the arrests, and most significantly, we expect one of the suspects will be in possession of a live military hand grenade. We further expect the group to have rifles and handguns. They may be wearing body armor as well," Bill announced.

A groan went up, and the agents started talking among themselves.

"Okay, hold up please!" Bill called out.

"We are here to discuss the arrest plan; therefore, case agent Dave Nadolski will fill you in on the details. Dave, you have the floor," Bill said directly to me.

I rose and faced the assembled agents.

"Okay, everyone, we are going to earn our overtime this Sunday," I said to the group.

"Or get blown up!" someone yelled from the back of the room.

"Well, that's a possibility too, but hopefully we can prevent that from happening," I replied.

"As a lot of you are already aware, this case involves a cooperating witness. The cooperator is my informant Tony Romano. The other players are Carmello Merlino, David Turner, Stephen Rossetti, and William Merlino," I said.

I projected mug shots of all four subjects onto the screen, then displayed the photos taken by surveillance agents from the Linda Mae's restaurant meeting and the surveillance photos from inside the Bickford's restaurant.

"I've made copies of these photos for everyone along with their individual rap sheets. Displayed on the screen now are the cars associated with these guys. You'll find that information in your packages as well," I said.

After I explained the scenario to the assembled agents, I observed one agent raise his hand.

"Sounds kind of far-fetched, Dave," a voice asserted from the back.

"I agree. The key to this, however, is my informant Tony Romano. He's a close associate of Carmello Merlino. It was Merlino's idea to locate a guard who could be coopted. Merlino tasked Romano with finding an employee inside Loomis who would get himself posted to the vault for the sole purpose of facilitating the robbery. Romano worked on this for a year and finally found that person, and he's right here in this room. Will the Loomis guard please stand up?" I called out.

Heads started turning, looking around the room. After about twenty seconds, Dave Donahue stood up and removed the jacket he was wearing to reveal the uniform shirt of a Loomis Fargo guard.

"Donahue, you dog!" one agent called out.

"I never trusted you, Donahue; now I know why!" another agent yelled.

Everyone else was laughing and hooting.

"Come on, people! What's wrong with a little side job?" Donahue asked the crowd.

"Anyway, needless to say, the robbery is not going to take place, and Dave Donahue has perfectly played his role as the crooked vault guard. Thank you, Dave!" I said.

Dave performed a dramatic bow and sat back down.

"So here's the deal," I began. "The surveillance squads have been given the home addresses of David Turner, Stephen Rossetti, Carmello Merlino, and Billy Merlino. On the morning of the robbery, surveillance agents will position themselves near those locations and will follow them to TRC. We are fairly certain the guns, grenade, and all the rest of the equipment will be with either Turner or Rossetti. Other agents will discreetly position themselves in the streets near TRC. The SWAT team will be around the corner from TRC. As the gang comes together at TRC, the plan is for the SWAT team to pick them off individually, or collectively, after they park in the lot and start walking to the front door. The agents following the subjects will call out when their target gets close to TRC in order to allow the SWAT team to position themselves to make the quick arrests. As each subject is arrested, they will be swiftly removed from the scene by our SWAT guys, quickly searched, and then turned over to other agents for transport to the office. Piece of cake, right?" I asked.

"Yeah, what could possibly go wrong?" someone yelled from the middle of the pack.

"Not much, hopefully. Your individual assignments are in the packets you received. Please review them today. You have today and tomorrow to drive around the streets surrounding TRC Auto Electric to familiarize yourselves with the layout there. The surveillance agents should physically locate the addresses of Rossetti, Turner, Carmello Merlino, and Billy Merlino so you aren't doing that for the first time on Sunday morning," I informed the group.

"Any questions?" I asked.

Hands went up immediately.

I called on agent Sheryl McGowan.

"Dave, you mentioned the four subjects, but what will Tony Romano be doing on Sunday morning?"

"Great question, Sheryl; thanks for bringing that up. Tony will be doing the setup. Tony will drive to TRC before everyone else arrives. He's going to park his car in the parking lot and enter the building, where he will turn on the lights. After doing that, he will join Bill Chase, John Trahon, and me in the command car. Seeing Tony's car in the lot and the lights on inside TRC should put the rest of the gang at ease as they pull into the parking lot. They will be allowed to park their own car and walk toward the building. The front door will be locked so they will have no way to get inside, and when they try and fail to open the door, they will be momentarily confused and focused on getting the door open. Our SWAT team will move in and scoop them. We will repeat this process for each of the subjects as they pull into the parking lot. Every time we grab one of the gang, there will be one more parked car in the lot for the rest of them to see as they pull up. Having the lights on and several cars in the lot will make the scene very convincing," I explained.

"Dave, this idea of a hand grenade and multiple firearms has me a little concerned," an agent in the back of the room called out.

"Me as well. We need to assume they will at least be carrying the handguns as they arrive. We don't know exactly where the hand grenade will be, but I'm certain it will be with Rossetti or Turner. Most likely Rossetti since he was the one who claimed to be in possession of it. The thing about Rossetti is he already bragged about how he'll do anything necessary to get away if it comes to that, so when the SWAT team jumps him, they have to do a fast and thorough takedown. But then, that's what the SWAT team does for a living," I said.

"There will be another meeting of the gang before Sunday. It's planned for Saturday night at TRC. Tony has been told to have the stolen van at TRC by Saturday, and I'm sure Merlino wants to check it out before relying on it for this job," I said.

Supervisor Mike Hannigan spoke up: "Speaking of the so-called stolen van the gang is planning to use, that van has actually been supplied to us by an insurance company. The ignition has been punched to make it appear stolen, and it has undercover license plates that trace to a fictitious owner. We've taken another precaution as well. We've installed a kill switch on the engine in the unlikely event things go south and the gang attempts to flee in the vehicle. They won't get out of the parking lot."

"Thanks for mentioning that, Mike, just another security precaution in case we need it," I said.

"Okay, if there are no more questions, let's wrap this up; we have an early day Sunday. Those of us who will be assigned to the area around TRC will meet at 4:30 a.m. in the parking lot of the Universalist Church across the street from Adams Park in Dorchester. Your supervisors will be notified of any last-minute changes to the plan if necessary. I'll take this opportunity now to thank each and every one of you for your support with this operation. Don't forget: these guys are experienced and very dangerous. Expect the unexpected Sunday, and please remember to code your radios before going out. No radio transmissions in the clear! Rossetti and Turner are bringing scanners, so if even one conversation is intercepted, the whole operation could be compromised," I warned the group.

As the group was filing out, I stopped Bill Chase and John Trahon at the front of the room. "Guys, a couple things have come up, and I need to talk to you both. Can we meet in your office, Bill?" I asked.

They both looked at me. "Anything serious, Dave?" Bill asked.

"Nothing we can't handle," I said.

Once back at Bill's office, he advised his secretary not to put any calls through. We occupied a seating area in the corner of his office.

"Okay, I've had a conversation with Tony about what happens after the takedown. His live-in girlfriend could be a problem. So far, she's in the dark about this whole thing but becoming very suspicious of Tony's nighttime activities lately," I explained.

Bill looked grim. "I knew she'd be a problem. Why can't he just dump her and move on?" he asked.

"Because that would be too simple! Actually, from what he told me about her, I have to say she's been a good influence. If he's left alone to wallow in the aftermath of this thing, who knows where that will lead? After all, while he's doing well right now, he's going to need someone after it's all over. He is a recovering drug addict, and quite honestly, I don't want to be his live-in babysitter. The press will be all over this story. His friends and family may go against him, and after the excitement wears off, he could slide," I said.

John, stroking his chin, began, "You've got a good point, Dave. The trial will be at least a year away. He needs to keep it together, and having someone with him could be very helpful for his state of mind. I say go ahead and meet with both of them. You'll be able to judge where this is heading with her. Let them stay together if that's what they both want."

Bill said, "Okay, let's do it that way. You can't give her any details about the arrest. After Sunday, it won't matter."

"Thanks, guys. I believe we are making the best decision," I said, "but we've got another issue as well. Remember when I told you about the final meeting at TRC before the robbery and you said we needed to cover it?" I asked Bill.

"Yeah, what about it?" Bill asked looking directly at me.

"I told Tony about that, and he freaked out. He's been getting pretty edgy as we close in on Sunday. In fact, real edgy. Don't worry: he's good to go on Sunday—that's no problem, of course—but Saturday night is a problem. Tony doesn't have faith we will be able to put a surveillance team in the street without Turner and Rossetti seeing them. I've got to admit those guys are cautious as cats, and I believe they will check for surveillance just like they did before the Bickford's restaurant meeting. This time we won't have a snowstorm for cover, and the streets around TRC are usually bare at night. I have to agree having a team out there would be dangerous," I said.

Bill looked at John, then back at me. "I don't like the idea of not having backup available," he said.

"Exactly what I told him, and his response made sense. Tony said he would be much calmer during the Saturday meeting if he knew there was no reason to worry about agents in the street blowing this thing for him. He feels the tension is going to be high enough, and he is fully equipped to handle whatever comes up inside without FBI help. He will be calmer and able to play his role if he has less to worry about," I said.

"Well, at least he'll have the recorder on him, and not having to wear a transmitter may make him more comfortable. I can see where if he suddenly acts edgy during this final meeting, Turner and Rossetti are going to wonder about him, and that would be bad," John said.

"Well, that leads me to the second thing. Tony doesn't want to wear a recorder either," I said.

"What?! He has to!" Bill shouted.

"This is nuts!" John agreed. "We can't have gaps in coverage. There will be no record of what was said in there!"

"Hear me out, please. I've thought about this, and do we really need the conversation recorded on Saturday? After all, the next day is D-Day.

We have all these other recordings already. These guys are toast on a conspiracy charge. On Sunday, when we collect the guns, grenade, masks, scanners, disguises, and God knows what else, they will be dead in the water. We really do not need to put Tony through the stress of making a final recording. He's in a fragile state of mind right now and needs to feel he can get through the Saturday meeting without being discovered. That recorder will be burning a hole in his back! If Rossetti or Turner sense his nervousness—and they will—they'll search Tony. He won't come out of that meeting alive, and Turner, Rossetti, and the Merlinos will be in the wind. Believe me when I say Tony will be much more relaxed, normal, and safer without any transmitter or recorder on him. They can strip him naked and he'll come out of it just fine. Besides, he's survived prison and everything that goes on there by listening to his instincts. He will not wear a recorder or a transmitter, and he doesn't want anyone surveilling the meeting, including me. We really don't have a choice if we want to wrap this up," I said seriously.

"The US Attorney's office isn't going to like this," Bill muttered.

"I agree, Bill, but we are at the one-yard line and we've got to get into the end zone! That's all that matters now," I exclaimed.

John was looking at the ceiling and stroking his neck; I could tell he was deep in thought. Bill was sitting in his chair drumming his fingers on the table while looking at the floor.

After about thirty seconds of this, John said, "I agree with Dave. At this point, we need to wrap this up. If the issue comes up in court, we can truthfully say Romano was so anxious for this to end he just couldn't take the stress of another recording session. Dave can interview him on the phone as soon as the meeting ends and write a report."

Bill cleared his throat. "Okay, the guy has been through enough already. I can see where he's reaching the breaking point; I would be too. If he won't do it, he won't do it. That's it. Tell him okay, Dave. He's on his own tomorrow. The last thing we want is to be responsible for something bad happening to our informant. These things never go exactly as planned anyway. Any other surprises?" Bill asked looking me in the face.

"Nope" was my reply.

After dinner, I put in a call to Tony at his apartment. He picked up right away.

"Can you talk?" I asked.

"Yeah, go ahead," Tony said.

"Good. I had a talk with Bill and John; they've agreed to let me talk with you and Patricia tomorrow night. Can you arrange for her to be available?" I asked.

"Yeah, no problem. How'd the big meeting go today?" Tony asked.

"Very well. This thing is going to go like clockwork. Everything is all set. It's going to be a big show!" I said.

"I hope there's no fireworks at the end," Tony said.

"Ha, you're funny!" I exclaimed.

"Listen, the final planning session is definitely set for Saturday night at 7:00 p.m. at TRC. Everyone will be there. Mello wants the van by then. Is it ready?" Tony asked.

"All set. Let's do this. Can we meet at 4:00 p.m. Friday? I'll take you out to the garage in Everett, and you can get the van. You can park it at your apartment so it's ready to go for Saturday. I'll meet with you and Patricia after that. Don't say a word to her about this before I meet her. Agreed?" I asked.

"Sure, sure. I feel a lot better knowing I can level with Patricia. That's one less thing to worry about," Tony sighed.

"Yeah, I have a feeling you're going to need someone once this is all over with on Sunday. Your life will change, and you'll need someone to support you. One other thing you should like: Bill Chase and John have agreed to let you go to TRC Saturday night without any FBI surveillance in the street and without a transmitter or recorder. No wires at all. I've got to say it was kind of a hard sell, but they eventually agreed that you've done enough dangerous work and it would be best for you to have the peace of mind that you won't die. I will need you to call me immediately after the planning session Saturday. I need to do a detailed report," I finished, hearing Tony let out a sigh of relief on the other end of the phone.

"Get some sleep tonight and meet me at the park down from your apartment at 4:00 p.m. tomorrow, okay?" I asked.

"See you then. I'll page you if I need to talk to you before we meet," Tony said.

"Roger that," I concluded.

21

WILL SHE STAY OR WILL SHE GO?

FBI GARAGE, OUTSIDE BOSTON

Friday, February 5, 1999

Friday was a day to tie up any loose ends before the big show on Sunday. Logistical details were worked out. I had individual meetings with the SWAT team leaders to discuss their operational plans. We'd worked together in the past during bank robberies, so we had a good relationship and I was confident they were prepared. I also talked with the surveillance supervisor, who assured me the gang would be discreetly covered by ground teams and aircraft as well, as they made their way from their homes to TRC on Sunday morning. At 3:50 p.m., I was waiting for Tony, who arrived at 4:00 p.m. exactly and jumped into the front seat with me.

"Jesus Christ, I'll be glad when this is all over with!" Tony exclaimed as I pulled onto the road.

"Getting stressful?" I asked.

"Shit, yes!" Tony barked.

"By Sunday afternoon, it'll all be a crazy memory. Hey, I know! Want some heroin to take the edge off?" I asked as I reached into my pants pocket. "Oh crap, sorry. I'm out of heroin. All I have is a Tootsie Roll. Here, you can have it."

"You are a dick, Nadolski!" Tony laughed.

"So I've been told," I replied.

"Mello was peppering me with questions today. He's getting hyper about this. He wanted to make sure Carl was ready to go. He told me at least five times to have the van at TRC for the meeting at 7:00 p.m. It's going to be a full dress rehearsal. He wants the guns, masks, scanners, jumpsuits, everything for the meeting. He wants to go over the van to make sure it's all set for Sunday. He wants everyone to be at TRC by 6:00 a.m. Sunday. He told me to tell Carl to leave the vault and go to his car at exactly 8:00 a.m. on Sunday. That's when we will roll up and grab him. I told him to relax, Carl is all set, and everything will go fine. In fact, I told him Carl thinks there's going to be a lot more cash in the vault than normal. The trucks have been doing more pickups this week. He's literally salivating!" Tony said.

I looked over at Tony.

"I think you're finally getting the hang of this undercover stuff. That was a very nice touch, appealing to his greed that way!" I said.

We arrived at the Everett garage at 4:45 p.m. I pulled in and found a mechanic.

"Hey, Jimmy, we're taking that van over there," I called out.

"Good, we need the parking space. Just got some new Bureau cars in, and they need the lights and radios installed," Jimmy responded.

Tony jumped out of my car and walked directly over to the van. He climbed in and had it started within fifteen seconds. I let him drive out first, and I followed him back to Boston.

TONY AND PATRICIA'S APARTMENT, DORCHESTER, MASSACHUSETTS

Tony parked the van in the parking lot of his apartment complex. I let him get in my car, and I drove to where his car was parked.

"So do you think Patricia is home now?" I asked.

"She is. I saw her car in the lot," Tony replied.

"How do you want to play this?" I asked.

"Just walk in with me. I'll introduce you, and then you can take over from there," Tony said.

I could tell his mood was dramatically better.

"Lead the way," I said.

We entered the back door of the apartment building and walked up to the second floor. Tony stopped at the third door on the right and put in his key. He opened the door and called out, "Lucy, it's Ricky. I'm home!"

A very attractive woman—about five feet, eight inches; early thirties; with a slim build and wearing tight blue jeans—walked from the kitchen wiping her hands on a small towel.

"Oh, Tony didn't tell me we were having a guest this evening. I'm Patricia," she said with a smile as she extended her hand.

"It's a pleasure to meet you, Patricia. My name is Dave Nadolski," I said with a smile while lightly shaking her extended hand.

"Uhhh, Patricia, this isn't exactly a social meeting," Tony said nervously.

"Are you a parole officer, Mr. Nadolski?" Patricia asked.

"I am not. I'm an FBI agent," I said, taking my FBI credentials out of my sport coat and displaying them for her.

"FBI! Tony, what's this about? Are you in trouble?" she asked, obviously concerned.

"Tony is definitely not in trouble, Patricia, quite the opposite in fact. He is working with me on a very serious criminal case. May we sit down so I can explain?" I asked.

Patricia was visibly stunned. Her mouth was open, and she looked at me, then Tony, then back at me.

"Uhhh, yeah, please take a seat," she gulped.

"Patricia, what I'm about to tell you is strictly confidential. Can I have your word that you will not tell anyone else what I am about to discuss with you?" I asked.

"Uhhh, sure?" Patricia said nervously.

"I've known Tony for several years. He helped me with a case involving stolen artifacts from the John Quincy Adams Library. They were extremely valuable books, and more importantly they were part of our national heritage. He called me out of the blue from Concord prison to offer his help. I visited him there, and he identified the person who stole those books. There was nothing in it for him, but his information did lead to the arrest of the person responsible and the return of the books. We kept in touch while he was still incarcerated. Eventually he was paroled," I said.

"Ohhh, okay," Patricia said with a puzzled look on her face.

"He's been doing some work at night for me on a new case, which he wasn't able to talk to you about," I said.

Patricia looked directly at Tony. "Is that what you've been up to? I was beginning to think you had another girl on the hook! But I like this explanation better."

Tony reached over and took Patricia's hand. "No other girl, honey, just you," Tony assured her.

"I can assure you of that as well," I said.

"Wow, I guess that explains a lot. What kind of work are you doing, Tony?" Patricia asked.

I interjected. "Very important work, Patricia. I can't, and Tony can't, divulge the details just yet. I can say this is going to be over sooner rather than later, which brings me to why I'm here tonight. When this investigation is over, Tony will have to leave the state, permanently. He will never be able to return to Boston as his life will be in danger here," I confided.

Patricia was shocked, and it showed.

"You have to leave and never come back? What?" Patricia was incredulous.

"I do," Tony confirmed.

"But you're on parole here. You can't just walk away from that!" Patricia declared.

"He's not walking away from his parole obligation. I've arranged for it to be transferred to another state," I said.

She looked at me, surprised. "You can do that?"

"Yes," I said.

Patricia looked directly at Tony and asked, "But what about me?"

I interjected again. "Patricia, what would you like to see happen?"

Patricia looked at me now. "Can I go with him?"

A smile covered Tony's face. "I was hoping you would ask that, honey," he said softly, still holding her hand.

"Really?" she asked, looking at Tony.

"Yes, really," Tony said.

Patricia started to cry and laid her head on Tony's shoulder.

"Oh Lordy, this is a lot to process!" Patricia exclaimed.

"I am certainly aware of that, Patricia, and you'll have plenty of time to let it sink in. This move to another state won't happen for a while. In the meantime, Tony will be relocated to a very nice apartment in the Boston area. There is plenty of room for you as well if you choose to accompany him. Unfortunately, there are restrictions. You cannot divulge to anyone where you are staying. Of course, you are free to come and go as you please and to visit your mom and friends but under no circumstances are you allowed to divulge where you and Tony are staying. I've got to become official now and warn you that if you do divulge his location, to anyone, I will have to charge you with a serious federal crime. Do you understand that?" I asked seriously.

"Wow! Okay, I get it," she said.

"Like I said, this local move is going to happen fairly quickly for Tony, but you have time to think things over and decide if you want to make this big change in your life. You are under no obligation to do anything, other than protect Tony's life by remaining silent. You can stay here or you can choose to accompany Tony. Tony cannot tell you where he is at until, and unless, you decide to join him. You can talk on the phone as much as you like until then."

"Honey, I really hope you decide to join me, but I totally understand if you decide not to. It's a huge ask on my part," Tony said, looking directly into Patricia's worried face.

"Patricia, please do not question Tony about this investigation. That is for your own protection as much as it is his. Before too long, your questions will be answered. This case is going to make a huge splash in the press, at which time everything will be revealed. What we have to guard against is tipping off the people involved in this criminal plot before we bring it down. If that were to happen, the FBI would have to ask tough questions. We will direct those questions at anyone who had knowledge of the details of this case. If you know nothing, you have nothing to divulge and will not be suspect. If you do get details out of him, he could be put in danger and you could be under suspicion. Does that make sense?" I asked.

"Yes, it does, Mr. Nadolski," she replied.

"Do you agree not to ask questions?" I asked.

"Yes, I do," Patricia affirmed.

"Remember, you will not be in the dark for long. We still have some work to do, but very soon this will all be over. At that time, you can ask him whatever you want to," I said, smiling at Patricia.

"Thank you, Mr. Nadolski." Patricia returned the smile.

"Okay, I'm going to go now. After I leave you two can talk, but remember: he cannot divulge details just yet and you've agreed not to press him," I said.

"I understand, Mr. Nadolski, but I need to know one thing. Is Tony in danger?" she asked.

I struggled with the answer to that question. If I said no and something bad did happen at the Saturday meeting, she would be very upset and rightly so. So I played it as close as possible.

"This investigation has its dangerous elements. Luckily Tony's survival skills, honed in prison, have served him well in this case. He is in no danger as of today, and that is because Tony knows how to handle himself and has done so perfectly. The people he is involved with are the same type of people he was in prison with and has dealt with for years. At this time, and I truly believe for the remainder of this investigation, he will remain safe. The FBI has put all its resources toward keeping him safe as well, and we are a big gang with a long reach. I hope this answer to your question gives you comfort. You are the only person in the world who knows as much as I told you today, and it needs to stay that way for a short while. I realize you have a million questions, and once I walk out the door, you'll think of a million more," I said.

I reached into my jacket pocket and removed my business cards. I pulled one out and held it out to Patricia.

"This is how you can reach me anytime night or day. If you need to talk, I am available for you. If you decide to stay with Tony after this is over, I will chaperone you through that process. I may not be able to answer all your questions now, but I will never lie to you about anything. You have a very big decision to make, and you can take as much time as you need to make that decision. There is no rush to decide anything yet," I said as I held Patricia's hand in both of mine and smiled. She smiled back, and I took that as a good sign.

"Tony, I've got to talk with you outside for a few minutes," I said.

"Good night, Patricia," I said as I turned toward the door.

"Good night, Mr. Nadolski," Patricia replied.

Outside, we stood by my car. "That seemed to go well, wouldn't you say?" I asked.

"Yeah, except for the part where you threatened to put her in prison," Tony laughed.

"Ohhh, come on, women's prison? Piece of cake!" I said.

"Not for her; she's been there already once. Killed a guy," Tony smirked.

I stood up straight and looked intently at him. "Are you shitting me?"

"Nope. Down south. It was domestic violence, on the guy's part. She ended it the only way she could, permanently," Tony said.

"Holy crap! Give me her full name and date of birth; I've got to check this out. I gotta say, though, she seems nice, otherwise!" I said.

"Yeah, but don't piss her off," Tony assured me.

"Thanks for the warning," I replied seriously.

22

FINDING A STEADY RHYTHM

GROTON, MASSACHUSETTS

Saturday, February 6, 1999

Saturday morning, I woke up with a wicked stress headache. After a quick shower, I met Linda downstairs in the kitchen.

"Coffee ready yet?" I asked.

"Can't you smell it?" Linda asked.

"Oh yeah. Smells good," I said.

"Tough night last night? You were thrashing around and muttering stuff," Linda said as she sipped from her coffee cup. The kids were in the next room watching Saturday morning cartoons.

"I guess. I don't even remember having a dream. I do have a throbbing headache though. Well, tomorrow will be a big day. It's going to start early and end late. Nothing to do today except wait. I can't go anywhere tonight. Tony is going into the lion's den, and I've got to debrief him after it's all over. We were supposed to cover him, but he refused. No recorder, no transmitter, no surveillance. He's afraid of a couple guys in the gang. They don't seem to trust him, and he sure as hell doesn't trust them. He thinks they may strip-search him or something, looking for a wire. Consequently, we're in the dark, and I don't like it one bit," I said.

"Couldn't you have installed microphones in TRC like they do in the movies?" Linda asked.

"Actually, it would have been possible if I had more time, but he sprung this on me too late for that. He's really keyed up, imagining all kinds of bad stuff. He needs this to end more than I do, and I need this pretty badly," I said. "Hey, do you mind if I go for a run?"

"A run? You're a treadmill guy," Linda observed.

"Yeah, I want to do the railroad trail and then the Groton School woods," I said.

"Knock yourself out. Not literally." She smirked, taking a sip of her coffee.

Our property bordered an abandoned railroad bed that had been converted into a "rail trail" for runners, bicyclists, horseback riding, anything nonmotorized. It was dirt with large puddles that needed to be carefully navigated. If I stayed on the trail, it would lead directly into downtown Groton in one direction or downtown Ayer, Massachusetts, in the opposite direction. I chose to head toward Groton. I really hated running on pavement. My shin splints from the Academy days would come back if I ran on a hard surface; therefore the softer dirt surface was much easier for me to handle.

The trail was empty as I headed toward the center of town at a slow, steady pace. I had to continually look back for Lady, our miniature Collie. If she was out and saw me leave, she would follow me. Luckily, I got away clean.

After about a half mile, I got into a steady rhythm and let my mind wander. I went over my mental checklist for that night's TRC meeting. *How many things could go wrong?* I wondered. *A lot*, I concluded. I chose not to dwell on it. It was pretty much out of my hands and in Tony's hands now, but I couldn't help but think he was not prepared well enough. He sure as hell wasn't covered well enough. I had to keep reminding myself that he was a big boy. He had faced similar situations in the past and came through all right. He was a survivor. The trouble was I put him in this particular spot and I didn't know how I would live with myself if, God forbid, the lions ate him.

Was I good enough to manage this case? Maybe I should have remained a Sterling Heights cop. A big fish in a small pond as opposed to a small fish in a big pond. I told myself the entire FBI was working together to make this case. In reality, it was all on my shoulders alone. I started it and I owned it, good or bad.

I made my left turn onto the narrow trail winding through the Groton School woods. The terrain was a little more dangerous here, and I had to slow down considerably. Numerous trees were gnawed off two feet above the ground by beavers who built huge lodges in the ponds and dams to block streams. I passed areas where the brush was crushed down and hoofprints from deer were visible. I decided to stop running and walk the rest of the way. I was in the middle of the woods. My pager was at home since it wouldn't do me any good here anyway and I'd probably lose it. It could be beeping; Linda and the kids could be looking for me. I decided not to worry about it. I needed a vacation. I wished I was in Disney World. Nothing bad happens in the Magic Kingdom; everyone is happy.

I broke out of the woods at the edge of an old cornfield. I could see my house a quarter mile away. The lights were on in the kitchen; wispy white smoke was coming out of the chimney. I stopped and took it all in.

I am one very lucky man, I finally concluded. *I have the best family in the world. I have a job that five thousand applicants failed to qualify for, and I am on the verge of the biggest bust of my professional career. Okay, pull up your big-boy pants; stop feeling sorry for yourself and worrying about everything. It's time to get to work.*

23

ON EDGE

Saturday, February 6, 8:00 p.m.

It was late on Saturday, February 6, 1999, and the mood in TRC Auto Electric was just that, electric. The windows in the bay doors were covered with blackout shades, but the bright fluorescent lights were on inside.

Billy dropped his load of gigantic, hockey-style duffle bags on the grimy concrete floor in the main bay. A red Ford F-150 pickup truck had its hood up, and engine parts were scattered on a wooden workbench; however, the focus tonight was on another vehicle, a blue Ford van. All the doors of the van were open, and a portable work light was illuminating the bare interior. The heat was off in the garage, and the temperature was a cool forty-five degrees.

As uninviting as the main floor of TRC was, the building had a particularly disturbing dungeon-like cellar accessed by a narrow stairway hidden behind the main bay. It was rumored that the cellar was used for several interrogations that ended badly for the interviewees.

"Hey, boys, want to see some of the hardware?" asked Rossetti.

With that, he opened two green Army duffel bags and removed a semiauto rifle, three semiauto handguns, masks, jumpsuits, scanners, plastic flex ties, bulletproof vests, gloves, and lots of ammo.

"You guys are going to like this. I saved the best for last," he said.

Rossetti then reached in and slowly removed a green, cylindrical cardboard box. He carefully slid the top of the box open and gently removed a dull-green metal object the size of a baseball. It had a distinctive pressure release arm with a large metal ring attached to it.

"Is that what I think it is?" asked Billy.

"Fucking right, dude. Behold an M67 fragmentation grenade. What I have here is a handful of pure whoop-ass, compliments of Uncle Mark," laughed Rossetti. "I told you guys, if any mother-fucking cop tries to stop us on the way out, I'm going to pull over, get out, then let fly!" he proclaimed, adding, "This bad boy should keep the rest of those pricks busy picking up the pieces while we disappear."

Turner grinned and looked happy. "I love having a spectacular backup plan," he said.

Tony Romano was uncomfortable around these guys and looked like it. He'd known Mello and Billy Merlino his whole life, but Turner and Rossetti were new to him. Tony had never done anything with the dynamic duo before and didn't like or trust them one bit. He was even concerned that he was now expendable in their eyes. Tony had made this score possible by providing the key element—he had recruited the inside guy. Tony had also "stolen" the blue van being prepared for their trip to the vault tomorrow; however, all he was needed for in the execution of the plan was to drive and stuff cash in the bags.

"Hey, Tony, wanna play catch with my little baseball?" asked Rossetti with a sly grin. "Me and David want to see what kind of stuff you've got."

Tony hated this prick. "No thanks, fellas. I'm going to leave the athletics to you guys and focus on driving the van tomorrow," he replied. "I don't want to intrude on your specialty. You could get jealous."

"No chance, hotshot. In fact, let's me and you have a chat over here," Rossetti said, indicating a dark corner away from the group, who were busy sorting and packing their gear. Rossetti put his right arm around Tony's shoulder and led him away.

"We've never really talked, just you and me, and I need to ask you a few questions. First off, how is it you were so lucky as to run into Carl the way you did and then convince him to join our little party?" Rossetti asked. "That was a real happy coincidence, huh?"

Tony started to feel dizzy. He didn't like where this was heading, and he certainly didn't like the way Rossetti was using his left hand to touch his chest. He might just be emphasizing a point, or he could be looking for a wire. He didn't even notice how Rossetti was maneuvering him closer to the cellar stairs.

Tony stared into Rossetti's dead eyes and started to panic because he was having a hard time thinking of an answer that would satisfy this fucking ape. His mouth was suddenly bone dry.

My God, he thought, *this son of a bitch knows what's up and he's going to kill me right here and now!*

"Look, Rossetti, I don't know what the fuck you're thinking, but whatever it is, you're wrong! You think I'm wearing a wire or something? You don't trust ME? I don't trust YOU!" shouted Tony in a heated exchange.

"Hey, what the hell's going on over there?" Mello yelled. He dropped the bag he was working on and stormed over to Rossetti and Tony.

"This son of a bitch thinks I'm wired. I think he's wired," Tony said.

"Stevie, leave him alone. He's cool," Mello said.

"Mello, want me to get naked?" Tony yelled.

Turner and Billy Merlino were standing staring at the drama unfolding.

"That's okay; now cut the shit. We're in this together, and I trust all of you guys. Tomorrow is going to be the biggest day of our lives; we'll be rich beyond our wildest dreams, and we're going to make history! Don't let nerves get the best of you now. We've got to focus on the prize and keep our shit together," Mello responded, taking command of the situation.

Tony walked over to the van and stood behind it. He was glaring at Rossetti. "I'll wipe down the van. I probably got prints on it," he said.

With that, he put on cotton gloves and grabbed a rag. He climbed into the van and started wiping down the exposed surfaces.

Mello walked over to Rossetti and Turner. "Okay, guys, pack all your gear and get it out of here. I want to see you back here at 6:30 a.m. sharp. We'll gear up here and head out. Get going," Mello ordered.

Turner and Rossetti wordlessly did as they were told and left the building.

"Billy, you can take off—6:30 a.m. sharp tomorrow. Don't be late," Mello warned him.

"Okay, boss. See you tomorrow," Billy responded as he left the building.

Mello walked over to the van where Tony was busy wiping and said, "You about done in there? I want to get home."

"Yeah, I'm done," Tony replied. "Sorry about that little dustup, Mello, but Rossetti was really getting on my nerves."

"It happens just before a big score. Nerves. I know two guys who went at it with knives the night before a bank heist. Don't worry about it," he laughed. "Let's go. I want you to be here at 6:00 a.m. to open up and turn the lights on. I want to see your car in the parking lot when I get here. Got that?"

"No problem, I'll be here. It's not like I'm going to get any sleep anyway." Tony grinned.

"Okay, get the hell out of here. I'll lock up," Mello said.

Tony walked out to his car and got in. As he started the engine, he suddenly felt nauseous. He managed to get out of the parking lot and onto a side street before he opened his car door and barfed his dinner into the street.

GROTON, MASSACHUSETTS

My phone rang at 9:30 p.m.

"Hello," I said.

"Dave, this is the office. Tony is on the line for you," the operator said.

"Put him through please," I said.

"Dave?" Tony asked.

"Of course, who'd you expect, the Easter bunny?" I joked.

I heard a sigh on the other end.

"Is there a problem?" I asked.

"Almost, but everything is cool now. We're good to go for tomorrow."

"What happened?" I asked seriously.

Tony went on to report the evening activities, including the dustup with Rossetti. I recorded every word for my report. I didn't say anything until he was through talking.

"Son of a bitch! I'm glad you talked me into letting you go in without a wire. I love the way you handled it," I said.

"Yeah, I spent a lot more time in prison than that prick did. I resorted to my 'training' to shut him down. It worked like a charm I'm happy to say!" Tony laughed.

"Yeah, act crazier than the other guy!" I commented.

"How do you feel?" I asked.

"I'm ready to go tomorrow. My part is over, and the stage is set. I'm actually going to get some sleep tonight," Tony said.

"Okay, make sure to be at the church tomorrow by 5:30 a.m. Look for my car. There may be a crowd of people by that time, but I'll keep an eye out for you. Good job tonight. It's almost over," I said as I hung up.

24

HAMMER TIME

TRC AUTO ELECTRIC, DORCHESTER, MASSACHUSETTS

Sunday, February 7, 5:00 a.m.

As I pulled my car into the church parking lot, the sight that greeted me was pretty impressive. There were about ten Boston police cars, motors running and exhaust smoke curling into the frigid air. I also spotted several unmarked cars that I knew to be FBI. I spotted Bill Chase's black Mercury Marquis and walked over after parking my car. Bill was behind the wheel and John Trahon was in the front seat, so I climbed in behind John.

"Good morning, Vietnam! What's with all the cops?" I asked.

"I called them in for security, in case things don't go as planned," Bill said.

"Well, you'll be happy to know everything went well last night at least. There was one little blip when Rossetti basically accused Tony of being a snitch," I said.

"What?!" Bill and John said in unison as they turned to look at me.

"Yeah, Tony went ballistic on him and Mello had to calm them down. Tony offered to get naked to show he wasn't wearing a wire. Mello just put an end to the issue and sided with Tony. Tony resorted to prison tactics by accusing the accuser and it worked," I said with a chuckle.

"Jeez. Good thinking. I guess it was a good idea to let him work solo last night," John said.

"Yeah, he handled it," I said.

"We've been monitoring the surveillance crews. They're set up around the guys' houses waiting for movement. Nothing yet. The aircraft is up as well and waiting to join in as soon as things get going," Bill said.

"How about the SWAT team?" I asked.

"Well, we have several and they are en route. Should be here shortly. Look for their black SUVs," Bill said.

No sooner had Bill made that declaration when three blacked-out Tahoes entered the parking lot. Four black-clad figures exited each vehicle. We left Bill's car and joined the team.

"Nadolski, where's the coffee?" SWAT team leader Bob Callen asked.

"Hey, Bobby 'C Note'! Glad you could make it!" I exclaimed as I shook his hand. Bobby's day job was on the Organized Crime squad, so I gave him the mob nickname of "C Note."

"So you guys will be positioned near TRC," Bill said, "and you need to monitor the surveillance squads as they follow the subjects into the area. Once you hear a subject is in the parking lot and away from his car, you pounce and scoop him. Take him up Dorchester Avenue to the corner of Linden and Freeport where you will hand him off to C-6 agents who will be standing by there. They'll transport the prisoners to the office for booking. After the handoff, return to the area around TRC. Bobby, you can direct your team."

"Got it, boss," Bobby Callen said. He then met with his team and gave them their individual assignments.

C-6 agents left their cars and walked over to where we were standing. John Trahon met with them to make sure they were prepared to do their part.

I looked to the driveway of the parking lot to see Tony's car entering. I signaled him to park next to Bill. As he got out of his car, I walked up and shook his hand.

"Almost over now!" I said to him in greeting.

"Yeah, I wish it was over already," Tony said. I could tell he was pretty jittery.

"Did you get any sleep?" I asked.

"Enough" was his reply.

"Come on, let's get in the back of Bill's car. It's freezing out here," I said.

Bill and John had already resumed their seats in the front. Tony and I shared the backseat.

John reached back and shook Tony's hand. "Good to see you, Tony. This is Bill Chase, Assistant Special Agent in Charge of the Boston FBI office," John said.

"Hi, Tony. I've heard a lot about you," Bill said, looking into the rearview mirror.

"Good, I hope," Tony said with a grin.

"For the most part. I heard you had a little excitement at TRC last night," Bill said.

"Yeah, I'm glad that's over. That Rossetti character scares the shit outta me," Tony exclaimed.

"Dave told us how you handled yourself. Quick thinking on your part, Tony," Bill said.

Tony cracked a slight grin and seemed to calm down some. "Yeah, I had to deal with a few guys like him in prison. You never back down unless you want to be someone's bitch," he said.

Suddenly the car radio came alive. "Yankee 6 to all units. Subject number one is in his car and leaving his residence."

"Okay, showtime.," I said. "Tony, get in your car and head over to TRC. Merlino is moving. We'll follow and pick you up as soon as you open up TRC and turn on the lights."

Tony quickly got out of the backseat and jumped into his car. We followed as he left the parking lot and headed directly to TRC several blocks away. Upon arriving at TRC, Tony parked his car in the parking lot, jumped out, and unlocked the front door of the garage. He disappeared, and lights started popping on inside the business. Less than one minute later, Tony exited, locked the door from the outside, and ran to Bill's car.

After Tony was in the backseat, Bill pulled out and drove several blocks south on Dorchester Avenue, then pulled onto a side street where we stopped and monitored the radio.

"Yankee 6 to all units, subject number one is approximately one mile from the target location" was announced over the radio.

Bob Callen came on the air. "SWAT teams are ready."

Tony started fidgeting in the backseat. He was craning his neck to see around Bill. Suddenly he practically shouted, "He just went by! That was his T-Bird!"

"Yankee 6 to all units, subject number one is parking his car in the lot. He's wearing a gray shirt and dungarees."

Bob Callen was on the air immediately. "We see him."

After approximately two minutes, there was another transmission. "Yankee 6 to all units, subject number one is in custody and out of the area. His car is still in the parking lot."

"HOLY SHIT!" Tony screamed. In the command car, we shared high fives all around; Tony was literally bouncing.

The next transmission was from a C-6 unit, Gary Cacace, "Subject one en route to the office for processing. No weapons recovered."

"Sounds like the mother lode of weaponry is with Rossetti. That's probably good," I said.

No sooner had I said that when another surveillance unit came over the air.

"Yankee 4 to all units, subject number two has left his residence and is heading toward the target location."

"That's Billy Merlino. He should be here in five minutes or so," I said.

We stayed in the same location and waited to watch Billy Merlino drive past.

Bob Callen was on the air again. "SWAT teams are in position," he said.

Tony was rolling his head and wiping his sweaty face. "I need a Kleenex or something."

"Here, I've got a handkerchief. Use this," I said as I handed him my handkerchief. "Keep it."

"Yankee 4 to all units, subject is entering the parking lot and parking his car. He's out and walking toward the front door. He's wearing a blue jacket."

"We see him," Bob Callen reported.

Thirty seconds later, Bob reported, "Subject in custody."

"HOT DAMN!" I shouted. "This is like shooting fish in a barrel!"

I spoke too soon.

"Yankee 7 to all units, subject number three is on the move from his residence, driving a bronze Chevy Tahoe," surveillance agent Frank Brosnan announced.

"Excellent, here comes Turner," John remarked.

At about that same time, another surveillance agent came on the air. "Yankee 3 to all units, subject number four is in his car and heading out. He's driving a red Honda, license plate 705PZR."

"Okay, that's Rossetti, but I don't recognize the car. Do you, Tony?" I asked.

"No," Tony answered.

Approximately four minutes later, Frank Brosnan came on the air again. "The Tahoe just pulled into an apartment complex at 166 Quincy Shore Drive, city of Quincy. He's taken a parking spot in the open and staying inside the car. It appears he may be waiting for someone."

"Uhhh, roger that. This is Yankee 10 circling above, and I confirm he is just sitting in the Tahoe," said surveillance pilot John Gill.

"The plane spotted Turner also; he's keeping an eye on him from above. What's Turner waiting for?" I asked out loud.

Yankee 3, who was following Rossetti in the red Honda, called in. "All units. The red Honda appears to be heading toward Quincy. He is not making a direct run to the Dorchester location."

"What the hell is going on?" John asked.

"I'd guess Turner and Rossetti are meeting up before heading to TRC," Tony said.

Several minutes later, Yankee 3 reported, "The red Honda is turning into the apartment complex on Quincy Shore Drive."

"Yankee 10 to all units, I confirm the red Honda is parking directly next to the Tahoe. The driver of the Tahoe is out and entering the passenger side of the Honda."

Bill then called the circling plane. "Yankee 10, can you see the Honda?"

"Roger that. I've got a lock on that vehicle and will call it out," John Gill responded.

"Thanks," Bill replied.

"Yankee 10 to all units, the red Honda is proceeding onto Dorchester Avenue, appears to be heading for TRC," the plane called out.

"Man, I'll bet we see them drive past!" I said.

Sure enough, the red Honda passed the street we were on and continued toward TRC.

The SWAT team called out that they were ready.

"This is Yankee 10. The red Honda is approaching TRC. Hold on; he's slowing down but not turning into the driveway. The Honda is continuing past TRC!"

"What the hell?" I remarked.

"That's not good," Tony said nervously.

"This is Yankee 10. The Honda just drove two blocks past TRC and made a left turn. I can't tell what street that is, but there's a gas station on the corner. He's continuing down the street. He stopped, then turned right. He turned right again on the first street he came to. It appears he's heading back toward Dorchester Avenue."

After a half-minute pause, John Gill in the aircraft continued his narrative. "He's stopped at Dorchester Avenue and turning right. He's heading back toward TRC. He went right past TRC without stopping. He's continuing away from TRC. He may be heading back to the Tahoe."

Bill Chase called out on the air, "Yankee 3, go back to that Tahoe and maintain discreet surveillance."

"Yankee 3, roger."

"Yankee 10 to all units, it appears to me the Honda is heading back to Quincy."

"Ohhh, man, what now?" I asked out loud.

The next transmission was from the airplane, Yankee 10. "The Honda is definitely picking up speed and heading toward where the Tahoe is parked."

After several minutes, Yankee 10 was on the air again. "The Honda is entering the parking lot where the Tahoe is parked."

Yankee 3 came on the air. "I've got a visual on the Honda. It has pulled up next to the Tahoe. The passenger got out of the Honda and opened the trunk. He removed a black duffel bag and is carrying it over to the Tahoe. He opened the back of the Tahoe and put the bag inside. He closed the back of the Tahoe and got back into the passenger's side of the Honda. The Honda is heading out of the parking lot."

"Bill, that's the mother lode! All their stuff is in the black duffel! Looks to me like they want to make sure the coast is clear before bringing their gear in. We have to keep an agent on the Tahoe!" I said.

Bill Chase was on the air immediately. "Yankee 3, stay with that Tahoe and keep an eye on it."

"Will do, like glue," replied Yankee 3, a veteran agent who knew the significance of his mission.

The airplane had the primary eye on the Honda now.

"Yankee 10 to all units, the Honda appears to be heading back to TRC."

Once again those of us in the command car saw the Honda pass by heading toward TRC.

"The Honda drove right past TRC and turned right onto the first street. It stopped and is sitting next to the curb," Yankee 10 reported.

Bill Chase was on the air again. "SWAT teams, prepare to take that Honda!"

"Where is it exactly?" Bob Callen called out.

The airplane answered, "The Honda is on the move again; it appears to be heading toward Morrissey Boulevard. Head in that direction, SWAT."

Bill slammed his Mercury Marquis in reverse, did a fast turnaround on the city street, and peeled out toward Morrissey Boulevard located several blocks from our location. Tony was jumping up and down in the backseat, John was holding onto the dashboard, and I had my hands clasped onto John's front-seat headrest.

Three SWAT vehicles immediately started heading toward Morrissey Boulevard.

The airplane was on the air again. "The Honda just turned right onto Morrissey. He's putting the pedal to the metal!"

Bill got on the air. "SWAT teams, take that Honda!" he ordered.

"The Honda is really moving out!" Yankee 10 reported.

Bill did a squealing right onto Morrissey.

"There's the Honda!" I called out. It was just a few cars ahead of our vehicle and moving fast.

The Honda was approaching Devine Skating Rink on Morrissey Boulevard. He was definitely making a run for it. All of a sudden, we observed a blacked-out SUV pass us as if we were standing still.

"There's SWAT!" John Trahon called out.

Apparently, Stephen Rossetti, driving the Honda, observed the SWAT vehicle as well because he jumped the curb next to the skating rink and started driving down the sidewalk at breakneck speed!

Bill slammed on the brakes and lit up his blue lights. We blocked traffic on Morrissey Boulevard. I jumped out of the backseat just in time to witness the SWAT vehicle drive over the curb and block the Honda. Rossetti rammed the SWAT vehicle in the front right and came to a crumpled, smoking stop next to the parking lot of Devine Skating Rink!

All four doors of the SWAT vehicle flew open, and four black-clad figures flew from the vehicle and surrounded the Honda. One agent stood in front of the Honda and leveled his assault rifle at the windshield. The three other SWAT guys had steel batons, which they used to immediately destroy all four windows in the Honda, and they simultaneously grabbed and pulled Stephen Rossetti and David Turner out of the broken windows! Before they had a chance to think, Rossetti and Turner were prone on the ground, handcuffed, and searched. *WOW*, I thought, *what an incredible demonstration of professionalism by the SWAT guys. They look like they do this every day!*

At this time of the morning, the parking lot of Devine Skating Rink was crowded with kids and parents who were heading into the rink for a hockey game. I looked over at the stunned crowd who were transfixed and open mouthed. Suddenly an enormous roar erupted from the crowd of parents and kids. They were pumping their fists, howling, and some were slamming hockey sticks on the ground! They were really digging this scene.

I turned back to the car for Tony. I called out, "Look at this, we've got a fan club!" When I couldn't see him, I poked my head into the backseat of Bill's car. Tony was in a fetal position on the floor, moaning.

"What's wrong with you?" I shouted.

"This is too much; can we get out of here?" he asked.

"Sure, just keep cool. Everything is under control. It's all over now. Turner and Rossetti are packed up and on the way to the FBI office. I'll get you back to your car in no time," I said as I slid into the front passenger seat, where I grabbed the radio microphone.

"Yankee 3, do you still have an eye on the Tahoe?" I asked.

"Sure do" was the reply from Yankee 3.

"Okay, please stick with that car. You'll be relieved by a C-6 agent who will take over custody," I said.

"Copy that," Yankee 3 responded.

I walked back to the SWAT agents and shook their hands. "Thanks, guys; that was spectacular! Really smooth!" I said.

"Another day at the office!" Agent John Ennis laughingly responded as he took off his black "Ninja" hood.

"Looks like you'll need a wrecker for your vehicle," I said.

"I guess so, but the Honda is headed to a crusher," John laughed. "You know the crazy part? This Honda isn't registered to Rossetti; he probably stole it."

When I returned to Bill's car, it had been pulled over to the side of the road. John was arranging for a C-6 agent to take custody of the Tahoe. Tony was calming down by then.

I looked at Tony. "Okay, here's how this will play out today. I'm giving you the key to the hotel room I got for you. After we drop you at your car, you can grab some stuff from your apartment and move into the hotel. If Patricia wants to join you, that's fine. I'm going to be real tied up for a few days and can't get out to check on you, so I want you to have this," I said as I handed Tony a cell phone.

"Ever use a cell phone?" I asked.

"Once or twice," he said.

"The phone number is taped onto the phone. You should memorize that. I'm taking care of the bill so don't call Europe," I joked. "You should probably be moved in today. No telling how fast word will spread that you set this up. Merlino and the boys are going to figure that one out when they do a head count and come up short one criminal. You should be very proud of the job you did. You were fantastic throughout this whole case. Now decompress for a few days."

"Thanks" was all Tony managed to say.

We dropped Tony back at TRC so he could pick up his car. After that, Bill dropped me at my car.

I looked back at Bill and John and said, "So I'm getting a search warrant for the Tahoe. I'll call Rob Richardson; he's expecting me. We'll have to write it up and get it signed by a judge magistrate at his home. I'll let you know the minute that's done. First off, I'm meeting Neil Cronin back at the office. We want to interview Merlino, Rossetti, and Turner to see if they can shed any light on the Gardner. If they are involved in any way, now would be the time to talk."

"Don't promise anything," John warned.

"I understand. That won't happen," I said.

I arrived back at the office and found Neil at his desk. "You missed a fun time," I said.

"So I heard! You guys get all the glory!" he quipped. "I've asked for all four of the guys to be separated and put into individual conference rooms with a guard."

"Okay, let's start with the boss. Where's Mello?" I asked.

"Follow me," Neil said.

We walked down the corridor to the interview room where Carmello Merlino was sitting in handcuffs. He wasn't happy. I asked the agent guarding him to step out for a few minutes.

After closing the door, Neil and I sat in chairs opposite Merlino.

"So I assume you know what's going on here, right?" I asked.

"Yeah, you're making a big mistake, that's what. My lawyer will have me out of here in fifteen minutes," snarled Mello.

"Actually no," I said. "Your next stop is a holding cell until you appear before a judge for your initial appearance. Chances are that will be in a day or so. What you are looking at is a lot of time. We know what you were planning; we have it on tape. We know about the arsenal of weapons in the Tahoe; we're searching it. Turner, Rossetti, Romano, and Billy are all in the same predicament you are in. So you have one opportunity to talk to us and that's right now."

"Talk about what?" Mello asked.

"Let's start with the Gardner case," Neil responded.

"I don't know anything beyond what I told you guys already! I don't have the paintings; I don't know where they are!" Mello complained. "Is that what this is all about?"

"No. This is about the Loomis job. We just thought you might like an opportunity to talk about the Gardner case as well," I said.

Mello shook his head. "I got nothin'."

"Okay," I said as I rose up from my chair. "We'll see you in court."

Interviews with Rossetti, Turner, and Billy Merlino went the same way, which was fine with me. I wasn't particularly anxious to give these guys anything, but it was worth a shot.

Next, I returned to my desk and called Rob Richardson. "Ready for me to come over?" I asked.

"Yeah, how did things go?" he asked.

"Very smooth. Their heads are still spinning," I said.

"Okay, I'm preparing the affidavit and getting an appointment with Judge Woods at his home," Rob said.

"See you soon," I said as I signed off.

My next call was home. Linda picked up after one ring.

"Hi," I said. "We bagged everyone, and now I've got to get a search warrant for one of their cars."

"Everyone okay?" she asked cautiously.

"Sure, piece of cake," I responded.

"Really?" she asked.

"Yeah, really! There was a little drama at the end, but nobody got shot or hurt in any way. Not even the bad guys."

I told her about the arrest in front of all those kids and parents at the hockey rink, and it made her laugh.

"I've got to get over to the courthouse and pick up Rob. I'm going to be late because we have to collect evidence, then secure it back at the office. You know the drill," I said.

"Yeah, all too well. See you later, alligator."

"After a while, crocodile," I said as I hung up.

Rob and I met Judge Woods, who swore me to the affidavit and signed the search warrant for the Tahoe.

I drove directly from Judge Woods's house to the Everett garage, where I met Larry Travaglia, Dave Donahue, and Special Agent George DiMatteo. George was a certified bomb technician. For the next four hours, we searched David Turner's 1998 Tahoe. Inside we found the black duffel bag containing numerous items of evidence including a Ruger .223-caliber rifle with a round in the chamber; a Sig Sauer P226 9mm pistol with a loaded magazine and a round in the chamber; a Colt Combat Commander 9mm pistol; a Smith and Wesson Model 40F pistol with an obliterated serial number and a fully loaded magazine; and a Taurus 9mm pistol with a full magazine and a round in the chamber. The final weapon seized was a cardboard canister containing a live US military M67 fragmentation hand grenade, a lethal weapon of war designed to be thrown by soldiers at the enemy. The explosive material ignites four to five seconds after the grenade is thrown. The steel body of the grenade becomes steel fragments after detonation. The killing field extends out to a fifty-foot radius from point of detonation. Unfortunately for the participants of this attempted robbery, it qualified as a weapon of mass destruction, which would double their sentences upon conviction.

In addition to the weapons were four police-style bulletproof vests, masks, jumpsuits, plastic "flex cuffs," a police scanner, handheld radios, a cell phone, gloves, duct tape, and rope. All the evidence seized was transported to the FBI office except for the hand grenade, which was transferred to the Massachusetts State Police Bomb Squad storage bunker by bomb technician Trooper Timothy Murray.

These guys were in a lot of trouble.

The next day, Monday, February 8, SAC Barry Mawn scheduled a press conference at the FBI office. He wanted the evidence, except for the hand grenade, displayed on a table in the conference room. I set up the "show and tell" before the reporters arrived.

At 1:00 p.m., the reporters were allowed into the conference room and immediately started photographing the evidence display. Barry Mawn and US Attorney Don Stern made presentations detailing the undercover investigation and subsequent arrests. They talked about the arrested subjects, Carmello Merlino, David Turner, Stephen Rossetti, and William Merlino. Anthony Romano was credited for his huge contribution to the case. The story made a very large splash in the press and on all the Boston TV news stations.

Predictably my phone rang shortly after the press conference.

"Why did they mention my name?" Tony complained.

"Because you are the biggest part of this case and you're going to testify in open court. That's why you're staying where you're staying. By the way, don't tell anyone at the hotel your real name. Make something up," I said.

"Like Bird Dog?" Tony asked.

"It has a certain panache," I admitted.

"Can you do me a favor?" He asked.

"Sure, what?" I replied.

"Go see my brother and my dad."

"Why?" I asked.

"I want you to tell them you busted me and I had to work it off by doing this for you," he said.

"Are you serious?"

"Yeah! They'll believe it, and it'll look like I didn't have a choice in the matter," he said.

"I got a better idea. Why not tell the truth? You became aware of a violent crime in the making and agreed to bring it down before anyone was killed. I like the sound of that better. Remember: you are not a criminal; you're a drug addict," I said.

"I don't know," he said.

"Is Patricia going to join you?" I asked.

"Probably, but she hasn't committed yet, so I haven't told her where I'm at," Tony said.

"Good. I want to ask you something, and I don't want you to yell at me," I said.

"What?"

"Are you sure you can trust her? Somebody may offer her a bunch of money to divulge where you're located," I said.

"I'm not angry. I've actually thought about that myself, but I've decided to trust her. I've got to trust somebody besides you," Tony said.

"Okay. Who's going to play me in the movie?" I asked.

"The dork from *Honey, I Shrunk the Kids*," he laughed as he hung up.

EPILOGUE

Tony remained in the extended stay hotel for three months. During that time, I met once again with the parole board. Tony and Patricia asked to be allowed to relocate to Florida. Tony had a sister there and was familiar with that state. His skill as a veteran mechanic assured him ready employment in that field. Arrangements were made between the state of Massachusetts and the state of Florida to transfer the remainder of his parole to the east coast of Florida. His sister helped get him an apartment and, on May 7, he and Patricia loaded their furniture into a U-Haul truck and headed for their new life in the Sunshine State. The plan was for him to finish his parole commitment and eventually become our star witness in *United States v. Merlino et al.*, the mega federal case that was going to be held in Boston at a future date.

The story of the arrest soon became old news, and Rob and I began the tedious task of building our case against Carmello Merlino, Billy Merlino, David Turner, and Stephen Rossetti. Each of the defendants hired competent legal representation. This case wasn't going to be a walk in the park if they had anything to say about it, and they did. Bond was denied for all four defendants, who were incarcerated in the federal holding area of the Plymouth County Jail, located fifty miles south of Boston.

I kept in touch with Tony and started to sense that all was not well with him. His complaints were becoming more frequent; he was having problems with his parole officer and wasn't particularly motivated to find a mechanic job. Patricia called me directly and told me Tony was using drugs again. Despite my efforts to keep him on the straight and narrow, it wasn't going very well. The thrill of the case had worn off, he was depressed, and Patricia and he weren't getting along. Eventually he called me and said the state of Florida was going to revoke his parole if he didn't get the hell out of the state. I intervened with the Florida parole department, but they weren't interested. He was going back north or back to prison, so we brought him home.

I got him enrolled in three different drug rehab programs, which he walked away from. I had to keep him in some type of structured environment, but he solved that problem for me by getting caught buying drugs in the city of Lowell. When I found him in the police lockup, he looked really depressed. I knew we had a real problem. I met with the cops and explained his situation. He needed to stay away from other prisoners, so he went to the county jail in an isolation unit.

I decided to get Tony into the federal Witness Protection Program before he was killed. I met with the US Marshals Service in Boston, and with the help of Rob Richardson, we had Tony removed from state custody and incarcerated in a federal prison to serve his time for the drug arrest. He chose to remain in the general population but assured me he would go into solitary confinement if he felt threatened. Since he knew prisons a whole lot better than I did, I let him make that call.

After serving his sentence for drug possession, the Marshals Service officially enrolled Tony into the Witness Protection Program. He was deemed drug free and was moved to a midwestern state along with a new identity. Most importantly Tony was given a US marshal that kept close tabs on him.

By this time, Rob Richardson had left the US Attorney's office for a private-sector law firm. While I really missed Rob, the case was now being handled by two excellent and seasoned prosecutors, Jim Lang and Theo Chuang. I had worked with Jim on other cases including the John Quincy Adams theft, but Theo was new to Boston. Actually, he wasn't an employee of the US Attorney's office in Boston but was a temporary transfer from the Department of Justice (DOJ) in Washington, D.C. Prosecutors from the DOJ are routinely sent out to the various US Attorney's offices throughout the United States to help with the prosecution of certain violations. We were lucky enough to get him as a member of our team. This was going to be a two-prosecutor job.

Carmello Merlino, Stephen Rossetti, David Turner, and William Merlino were formally charged with conspiracy and attempt to affect interstate commerce by robbery, which is a violation of the Hobbs Act, plus two counts of possessing a firearm during a crime of violence—count one being the pistols and rifle and count two being possession of the explosive device (hand grenade). The grenade charge alone could have gotten them all life sentences.

The trial was held before Judge Richard Stearns in the Boston federal courthouse. It lasted five weeks. Each defendant was represented by an attorney, and AUSAs Jim Lang and Theo Chuang handled the prosecution. Tony was delivered to Boston by the US Marshals Service and placed in a secure location close to the courthouse. Jim Lang had put a hole in the defense balloon with his opening statement at the start of trial. He stood up and addressed the jury concerning Tony's criminal history. He admitted Tony Romano was a felon and had been in and out of prison most of his adult life. He admitted Tony's word would be suspect if that were the basis of the prosecution's case against the defendants. He pointed out, for the first time, that the jury would not have to rely on Tony's testimony, as they would be hearing numerous recorded conversations of Carmello Merlino, David Turner, Stephen Rossetti, and William Merlino discussing and planning this crime. Additionally, they would be shown all the evidence that was seized from the defendants on the day of their arrest, Sunday, February 7, 1999.

Dozens of witnesses were called during the trial. I was on the stand for four days, at the end of which I was totally wrung out after a relentless beating by four defense attorneys. Tony was on the witness stand for a week. He was incessantly grilled by the defense, who attacked his credibility and motivation. Unfortunately for them, they couldn't attack the words of the defendants themselves when they were played for the jury to hear. Tony was thoroughly exhausted at the end, but he held up and provided excellent testimony.

At the end of the trial, Judge Stearns instructed the jury and sent them into isolation. They deliberated for several days before announcing they had reached a verdict. The defendants had to be quickly transported from the Plymouth County Jail back to the Boston courthouse. Reporters were rushing to get seats. There was standing room only in the courtroom and outside in the hallway. It seemed the whole US Attorney's office had turned out to hear the verdict. I sought out AUSA Tim Feeley, chief of the Criminal Division and supervisor of Jim Lang and Theo Chuang. Tim was in the crowded hallway outside the courtroom. I took him aside and told him that no matter what the jury came back with, I wanted him to know that his guys, Jim and Theo, did a masterful job. Tim cracked a smile and thanked me.

Twenty minutes later, the jury was brought into the courtroom and order was called by the judge. The room was as silent as a tomb. Judge Stearns asked the foreman of the jury if they had reached a unanimous verdict on all counts. The foreman affirmed that a unanimous verdict had been reached. The judge requested and received the written verdict and read it himself. He then handed the slip of paper back to the jury foreman and instructed the bailiff to question the foreman.

The bailiff asked the foreman what verdict was reached on conspiracy and attempt to affect interstate commerce by robbery for defendant Carmello Merlino.

"Guilty," replied the foreman.

Regarding Stephen Rossetti? "Guilty," replied the foreman.

Regarding David Turner? "Guilty," replied the foreman.

Regarding William Merlino? "Guilty," replied the foreman.

The judge had to call the courtroom to order as the families of the defendants began to cry out.

The bailiff then asked the foreman what verdict was reached on possession of a firearm during a crime of violence and possession of a destructive device for defendant Carmello Merlino.

"Guilty," replied the foreman.

Now the wailing in the courtroom started again, louder this time, forcing the judge to rap his gavel and demand silence. The bailiff continued.

Regarding Stephen Rossetti? "Guilty," the foreman replied.

Regarding David Turner? "Guilty," the foreman replied.

Regarding William Merlino? "Guilty," the foreman replied.

The courtroom broke out into mayhem! The defendants sat back in their chairs and were quickly handcuffed and removed by numerous court officers. Billy Merlino's mother was screeching and wailing. Friends and relatives of David Turner and Stephen Rossetti were crying and slowly moving out of the courtroom.

I couldn't help myself; I had to bear-hug Jim and Theo. My heroes!

I wished Tony could have been in the courtroom to see this firsthand, but by this time he was back in the Midwest. I quickly called his US marshal and told him the good news. He assured me Tony would be notified immediately.

I went out with Jim and Theo to a local watering hole later that evening. We didn't draw much of a crowd from the US Attorney's office since tomorrow was another workday and they needed to be back at their desks early. We were completely gratified that the jury saw through everything and reached a just verdict in this case, but we were sorry we couldn't share our celebration with the star witness.

The defendants were returned to their cells at the Plymouth County Jail. The next, and last, court appearance was the sentencing on November 22, 2002.

Carmello Merlino was sentenced to forty-seven years in federal prison. He died three years later at age seventy-one.

William Merlino was sentenced to thirteen years in federal prison and was released in 2015.

David Turner and Stephen Rossetti were sentenced to thirty-eight years in federal prison, but in the fall of 2019, they once again appeared before Judge Stearns in Boston federal court. The federal sentencing guidelines had been revised, and it was good news for Rossetti and Turner. Judge Stearns was impressed with their prison record of good behavior and allowed them to leave prison after serving seventeen years of their sentence.

Anthony Romano left the Witness Protection Program and moved to Maryland. He met a new lady and actually settled into a peaceful and drug-free existence. I communicated with him regularly and was happy for him. Things were finally looking up for Bird Dog, but unfortunately, it didn't last. Tony suffered a massive cerebral hemorrhage on November 8, 2012, and died in the hospital two days later.

I was promoted to Supervisory Special Agent and retired from the FBI in February 2004.

INDEX

CPSIA information can be obtained
at www.ICGtesting.com
Printed in the USA
BVHW030245160222
629155BV00002B/15